C0-BXA-512

THE IMPACT OF NEW LABOUR

The Impact of
New Labour

Edited by

Gerald R. Taylor
Visiting Lecturer in Politics
Southampton Institute

First published in Great Britain 1999 by
MACMILLAN PRESS LTD
Houndmills, Basingstoke, Hampshire RG21 6XS and London
Companies and representatives throughout the world

A catalogue record for this book is available from the British Library.

ISBN 0–333–73991–4

First published in the United States of America 1999 by
ST. MARTIN'S PRESS, INC.,
Scholarly and Reference Division,
175 Fifth Avenue, New York, N.Y. 10010

ISBN 0–312–22048–0

Library of Congress Cataloging-in-Publication Data
The impact of New Labour / edited by Gerald R. Taylor.
p.   cm.
Includes bibliographical references and index.
ISBN 0–312–22048–0 (cloth)
1. Labour Party (Great Britain)   2. Great Britain—Politics and
government—1997–   I. Taylor, Gerald R.
JN1129.L32I48   1999
324.24107—dc21
98–49902
CIP

This book is printed on paper suitable for recycling and made from fully managed and
sustained forest sources.

10   9   8   7   6   5   4   3   2   1
08   07   06   05   04   03   02   01   00   99

Printed and bound in Great Britain by
Antony Rowe Ltd, Chippenham, Wiltshire

Contents

List of Tables and Figure

Preface

This book began life as a conference organized at the then LSU College of Higher Education in Southampton. During the process LSU sadly demised and became the University of Southampton New College and in the course of this change, and as a result of my own inadequacies as a conference organizer, the conference failed to materialize. However, by that time I had received a number of proposals for the Conference which were both exciting and stimulating. It seemed a shame to let this potential to examine a genuine 'phenomenon', as Sir Peter Temple-Morris would have it, of British politics come to naught. I discussed the possibility of reworking the proposals into book chapters with the contributors, invited further contributions from individuals working in the area and this collection is the final result.

I am grateful both to the original conference contributors for their sterling efforts and enthusiasm, and to those who succumbed to my pleadings to provide further chapters. I would like to thank them all for their forbearance and tolerance of my first efforts as an editor, and for their production of work quickly and promptly providing updates, corrections and amendments. I hope they feel the final product does each of them justice.

There are also a number of others who guided my deliberations about whom to include or who made important suggestions. These include Adrian Smith, Vicky Randall, Dominic Wring, Bob Franklin, Mark Evans, David Marsh and Joni Lovenduski. With regard to my contributions I am grateful for the comments and perspectives of Patrick Seyd, James Connelly and a research symposium at Southampton Institute where I tried the chapter out as a paper. The continuing inadequacies of my contributions are a result of my inability to correct the problems they observed while still saying what I wanted.

Thanks are also due to Library staff at the University of Southampton New College and Southampton Institute whose patience is appreciated. I would also like to record my gratitude to staff at Macmillan who helped to shape both this and my previous publication for them. Their professional assistance aided the presentation and the accuracy of my intentions.

I would also like to thank my wife, Sylvia, and our daughters, Sarah and Natasha, for trying to give me time and space. Finally I would like to thank anyone who has been involved in helping to prepare individual contributions to this text.

GERALD R. TAYLOR

List of Abbreviations

AMS	Additional Member System
AV	Alternative Vote
CBI	Confederation of British Industry
CCT	Compulsory Competitive Tendering
CLD	Commission for Local Democracy
CLPs	Constituency Labour Parties
COS	Charity Organization Society
CSM	Christian Socialist Movement
CSU	Christian Socialist Union
DETR	Department of the Environment, Transport and the Regions
DTI	Department of Trade and Industry
ECHR	European Convention on Human Rights
ECOFIN	Economic and Finance Ministers' Group
EMU	European Monetary Union
EOC	Equal Opportunities Commission
ERM	Exchange Rate Mechanism
F&HE	Further and Higher Education
FDA	First Division Association
FE	Further Education
FEFC	Further Education Funding Council
FoI	Freedom of Information
FPTP	First past the post
GCHQ	Government Communications Headquarters
GIS	Government Information Service
GLA	Greater London Authority
GLC	Greater London Council
GMB	General, Municipal and Boilermakers' Union
GNVQ	General National Vocational Qualification
HE	Higher Education
HMSO	Her Majesty's Stationery Office
INLA	Irish National Liberation Army
IRA	Irish Republican Army
LWAC	Labour Women Action Committee
LWT	London Weekend Television
MEPs	Members of the European Parliament
MPs	Members of Parliament

NATFHE	National Association of Teachers in Further and Higher Education
NEC	National Executive Committee
NHS	National Health Service
NIO	Northern Ireland Office
NVQ	National Vocational Qualification
OMOV	One member, one vote
ORF	Output-Related Funding
PLP	Parliamentary Labour Party
PM	Prime Minister
PUP	Progressive Unionist Party
QCA	Qualifications and Curriculum Authority
QNCA	Qualifications and National Curriculum Authority
RUC	Royal Ulster Constabulary
SCA	Shadow Communications Agency
SDA	Sex Discrimination Act
SDLP	Social Democratic and Labour Party
SV	Supplementary Vote
TECs	Training and Education Councils
TGWU	Transport and General Workers' Union
TUC	Trades Unions Congress
UCW	Union of Communication Workers
UDP	Ulster Democratic Party
UUP	Ulster Unionist Party

Notes on the Contributors

Patrick Ainley is Reader in Learning Policy at the University of Greenwich, School of Post-Compulsory Education and Training, and has published widely on all levels of education. His books include *The Business of Learning: Staff and Student Experiences of Further Education in the 1990s* (1997, with Bill Bailey), *Degrees of Difference: Higher Education in the 1990s* (1994), and *Class and Skill: Changing Divisions of Knowledge and Labour* (1993).

Hugh Atkinson is Principal Lecturer and Head of Politics at South Bank University. He lectures in comparative European politics on a range of undergraduate and postgraduate courses. His primary research interest is in British local government and he is co-author of *British Local Government since 1979: the End of an Era?* (1997). He is a former local councillor.

Peter Dorey is Lecturer in Politics at Cardiff University. His publications include: *The Conservatives: from Dominance to Decline* (1998) and *The Major Premiership* (editor, 1999). He is currently working on a monograph on incomes policies in postwar Britain.

Mark Evans is Lecturer in Politics at the University of York. His publications include: *Charter 88: a Successful Challenge to the British Political Tradition?* (1995), and *Constitution Making under New Labour* (1998), plus journal articles and book chapters on different aspects of constitutional doctrine and revisionism in Britain, the Irish Question, political participation, and the study of policy networks and policy transfer in British political science.

Colin Hay is Lecturer in the Department of Political Science and International Studies at the University of Birmingham and a Visiting Fellow at the Department of Political Science at MIT and Research Affiliate of the Centre for European Studies at Harvard University. His publications include: *Re-Stating Social and Political Change* (1996) and *Postwar British Politics in Perspective* (co-author, 1999); he is co-editor of numerous volumes, most recently *Demystifying Globalization* (1998) and *Theorizing Modernity* (1998). He is a winner of the Philip Abrams Memorial Prize, a member of the Editorial Board of *Sociology*, and, with David Marsh, editor of the series Globalization and Governance.

Mark Hayes is Senior Lecturer in Politics at Southampton Institute of Higher Education. His publications include: *The New Right in Britain* (1994) and various pieces on aspects of the conflict in Northern Ireland including the ideology of loyalism and the evolution of Republican strategy. He is currently researching anti-fascist activity in Britain.

Richard Heffernan is Research Associate in the Department of Government at the London School of Economics and a Visiting Associate Professor in the Department of Political Science at the University of California Los Angeles in 1998-99. He is co-author with Mike Marqusee of *Defeat from the Jaws of Victory* (1992), and the author of *New Labour and Thatcherism: Political Change in Britain* (forthcoming).

Russell Holden is Senior Lecturer in European Studies in the Business School at the University of Wales Institute Cardiff. Research interests include the relationship between British political parties and the European Union and the impact of theoretical issues in European political economy on the continuing integration process. He is completing his doctoral studies on the transformation and impact of Labour's European policy reversal on party modernization between 1983 and 1997, and is actively involved in the Policy Studies Association.

Peter John is Lecturer in Politics at the University of Southampton. Recent publications include *Analysing Public Policy* (1998) and articles in the *British Journal of Political Science* and *Policy and Politics*. His research interests include urban politics, rational choice, and research methods. He is completing a book on comparative French and British local politics and competitive bidding for urban funds.

Paul Norris is Senior Lecturer in Politics at Southampton Institute. His teaching and research interests are in British politics and political thought.

Sarah Perrigo is Lecturer in the Department of Peace Studies at the University of Bradford. She has written a number of articles on women, gender and on the Labour Party and is a Labour councillor in Leeds. She is writing a book on socialist ideas and the future.

Gerald R. Taylor is Visiting Lecturer at the Southampton Institute. He was formerly Lecturer in Politics at LSU College, Southampton (now University of Southampton New College) and Westminster University. His publications include *Labour's Renewal? The Policy*

Review and Beyond (1997); and, with Andrew Bradstock, *Essays in Political Thought* (1998). He is working on a political history of the Labour Party and, with Chris Sparks, on a book about historical influences in political thought.

Kevin Theakston is Reader in Government at the University of Leeds. His publications include *Junior Ministers in British Government* (1987), *The Labour Party and Whitehall* (1992), *The Civil Service since 1945* (1995), and *Leadership in Whitehall* (1998).

Matthew Watson teaches in the Department of Political Science and International Relations at the University of Birmingham. His research interests include the political effects of economic ideas; the political discourse and economic reality of globalization; the political economy of inward investment; and the macroeconomic policy of the new Labour government. His publications include: 'Re-thinking Capital Mobility, Re-regulating Financial Markets' and 'In the Dedicated Pursuit of Dedicated Capital: Restoring an Indigenous Investment Ethic to British Capitalism' with Colin Hay, both in *New Political Economy*; he is also co-author of *Postwar British Politics in Perspective* (1999).

Alan Wilkinson, Visiting Lecturer in Theology, Portsmouth University, is an Anglican priest, Diocesan theologian at Portsmouth Cathedral and a former tutor for the Open University. His research interests are in the church and society. His publications include *The Church of England and the First World War* (2nd edn, 1996), and *Christian Socialism: Scott Holland to Tony Blair* (1998).

1 Introduction
Gerald R. Taylor

The first anniversary of Labour's truly historic election victory of 1 May 1997 was marked by some interesting appraisals of their year in office. The left journal *Red Pepper* assessed the Government's performance on a range of issues according to measures of 'progress', signs of Thatcherism and hype. Interestingly, only on the constitutional issues of devolution and the adoption of the European Convention on Human Rights was progress seen as unalloyed. Overall hype and signs of Thatcherism clearly predominated (*Red Pepper*, May 1998, pp. 16–18).

From a very different perspective, in the *New Statesman*, Anthony Giddens saw the Labour Government as carving out a 'third way' between social democracy and neoliberalism (*New Statesman*, 1 May 1998, pp. 18–21), which itself reflects the positions set out by the Commission on Social Justice in their report on policy options for the Labour Party (1994). Giddens claims that Labour's 'third way' is distinct from social democracy in five ways. Firstly it replaces a class politics of the left with a modernizing movement of the centre; second, the 'old' mixed economy is replaced by a 'new' mixed economy; third, the imposition of corporatism is replaced by the new democratic state; fourth, internationalism makes way for the cosmopolitan state; and finally the strong welfare state is superseded by the social investment state. In each case Giddens sees these as to some extent compromise positions between social democracy and the market orientation of neoliberalism.

This is an interesting analysis because three of the 'social democratic' measures: the 'old' mixed economy, corporatism, and the welfare state, were, of course, compromises themselves. They were compromises between the then 'extreme' left position of communism and the market systems which had marked the interwar period in Europe. As for the other two, the extent to which Labour was ever committed to class politics of any description or internationalism, beyond the rhetorical, is an open question. Giddens seems to be suggesting that 'New' Labour is involved in a compromise of a compromise, presumably to be replaced another fifty years down the line by a further compromise, and so on.

Of course Giddens' position is more sophisticated than this thumb-nail sketch suggests, and commentators supporting the 'third way', stakeholder capitalism, communitarianism, cool Britannia, or any other of the variety of 'new' concepts New Labour is supposed to be embracing are right to observe that our society has changed since the 1940s and what worked, or maybe didn't, then definitely will not work now. Despite this, New Labour resonates with historical associations. Giddens' 'third way' brings to mind Harold Macmillan's 'middle way', the modernizing epithet bears comparison with Hugh Gaitskell, and Blair's leadership style and personal charisma parallels that of Ramsay MacDonald. None of these are very happy associations for the Labour Party, at least for 'old' Labour, which is perhaps why they are not made that often.

Another historical precedent is more recent. In the mid- to late-1980s trade unions were busily embracing New Realism in the face of a calculatedly hostile government strategy. At that time undergraduate examination papers on British politics often included questions along the lines of: 'Is New Realism either new or realistic?' It is tempting to ask similar questions about New Labour, but that task will not be attempted, at least not directly, here.

It is certainly the case that New Labour has earned its relatively recently acquired label in the first year of the Blair Government. Indeed it is hard to think of the Labour Party beyond this designation. This is not just the result of clever marketing, though that has undoubtedly played its part, but what it actually does signify is by no means clear. While we all seem convinced that New Labour is different, in some sense, quite what this means and whether it is a 'good thing' or not is a far more open question.

In some ways the Blair Government could hardly help being 'new'. It is, after all, the first Labour government for nearly two decades and as such is working in a remarkably changed context. No previous Labour government has had to deal with the legacy of Thatcherism, or, for that matter, of the breakdown of postwar consensus generally. No previous Labour government has faced the emergence of global-ization, at least not recently. No previous Labour government has had to cope with the 'taming' of trade union power, for what it was worth. All of these altered contexts would have made any Labour leadership appear different.

In addition, there have been the internal changes within the party. In the early 1980s Labour was subject to an activists' revolt which saw control of the party seemingly slip from the hands of the leadership. Labour's current leaders were forged in the battle to regain control of the party machinery. This provides an additional apparent difference from their immediate predecessors. Though whether they are that different from the leaderships of previous Labour governments, from MacDonald, Attlee, Wilson or Callaghan – that is, from the real 'old' Labour – is another matter. Whether these leaders would have reacted very differently in the context which Blair inherits is uncertain, but that is not our concern here.

What is at issue is what changes have New Labour wrought to their party, to British government, and to the policy options available, and whether these changes are fit for the context which we now have. In part, answers to these questions may require some examination of New Labour's inheritance and heritage, but it is not fundamentally about whether New Labour is new, or whether it is labour, whatever either of those terms might mean.

The collected essays here are intended to examine what New Labour has done, why and what results have been achieved. It is not intended to provide unequivocal answers. Such responses may, as yet, be impossible to provide. After all, what would have been the judgement of academics on Thatcherite conservatism in the autumn of 1980? Certainly not, I would suggest, what our judgement would be now. Similarly we must expect perceptions of and judgements on New Labour to develop and grow over the coming years, perhaps even, given the scale of their electoral success, decades, and to be shaped and reshaped perhaps well after their demise.

Tony Blair and his government have the opportunity to provide a new chapter in British political history, to become the first ever Labour government to win two full terms in office, and to shape British politics into the twenty-first century. For this reason alone they will be remembered and discussed well after they themselves have relinquished power. Here our efforts can be no more than an initial contribution. As such, the intention has been to provide coverage of the areas which currently seem to be the most significant for the future and a variety of interpretations of Labour's activities and politics. The contributors share generally left-leaning perspectives and a more or less critical approach to New Labour, some far more critical than others. We hope this will provide the reader with the basis to make their assessment of Labour 'in power'; we will leave history to judge our foresight in dealing with the areas we do in the way that we have.

STRUCTURE OF THE BOOK

The essays are gathered into three parts. The first of these covers New Labour's impact on the Labour Party itself in terms of ideology and belief, policy-making and organization, and presentation. The second deals with New Labour's governance, both in terms of its relationship with key organs of the British state and recent traditions of British politics, and its proposals to alter that state through constitutional reform. In many ways this seems the area where New Labour is most likely to provide a lasting legacy, of one kind or another – a prospect which deserves detailed examination. The third part considers Labour's various policy proposals in certain key areas.

Chapter 2 sets the scene not only for the discussions of changes to the Labour Party but also for the themes of the three parts. It argues that New Labour has reestablished and entrenched leadership control within the party through its dominance of policy outcomes, alterations to internal policy-making structures in the party, and the conscious stress of electoral ends to alter the character of Labour's 'ethos'. These are related to wider questions of the role of parties in British democracy.

In Chapter 3 Paul Norris examines the influence of stakeholder capitalism and argues that in abandoning stakeholder capitalism New Labour has missed an opportunity to put forward a radical agenda. Alan Wilkinson assesses New Labour's Christian Socialism in Chapter 4, in particular providing a historical context from Labour's heritage of Christian influence.

Rounding off Part I, in Chapter 5 Richard Heffernan examines the development of party relationships with the media and the extraordinary turnaround of media attitudes to Labour. This is assessed in the context of the impact that modern political communications has on the political process.

Part II begins with Mark Evans' overview of New Labour's constitutional reform in Chapter 6. He considers the development of New Labour's programme and assesses problems of implementation. In Chapter 7 Patrick Ainley uses education and training as the yardstick to measure New Labour's departure from the principles of the postwar welfare state and to examine what is being constructed in its place.

Kevin Theakston outlines Labour's relations in government with the Civil Service. Clearly, this is a crucial area after 18 years of opposition, and Chapter 8 delivers a full consideration of this developing relationship. In Chapter 9 Peter John develops Labour's attempts to decentralize power, particularly with respect to devolution. A positive appraisal of New Labour's tactics is given alongside an assessment of their overall aims and objectives. Hugh Atkinson concludes the second part by building on Peter John's work in his appraisal of Labour's attitude to local government. Chapter 10 considers the Thatcherite legacy for local government and the likely impact of New Labour in this area, examining the prospects for a change in the power relationships between central and local government.

Part III begins with Colin Hay and Matthew Watson's analysis of Labour's economic policy in Chapter 11. They assess the objectives behind Labour's approach and the strategies adopted in their first year in power. In Chapter 12 Sarah Perrigo considers New Labour's impact on the position of women, both as a result of the election of a greater number of women MPs than at any other time in history, and in terms of the various policy options and approaches proposed by New Labour. She rightly reminds us that New Labour has been successful in reaching out to constituencies who often felt themselves marginalised by Labour in the past.

In Chapter 13 Russell Holden critically examines New Labour's development of a more positive approach to European integration. He claims the lack of progress in revealing a clear set of policy commitments has been central to the changes in Labour politics and thus to the impact of New Labour. Chapter 14 sees Peter Dorey criticize New Labour's approach to the trade unions. He argues that trade unions have now become the new marginalized sector in the Labour Party and the repercussions of this may have severe implications for the future of New Labour and for Labour politics generally.

In the Chapter 15 Mark Hayes takes a critical look at New Labour's 'successes' in Northern Ireland. He argues that the Blair Government has continued the British political tradition of underestimating and ignoring the grievances of the nationalist community and that this represents a poor basis for a 'solution' to the problems of Northern Ireland. A conclusion then follows.

Taken as a whole the contributions represent coverage of the substantial areas of development and activity in New Labour's first year in government. We hope that they will help readers to achieve a clearer and more critical understanding of what may be a new age in British politics.

Part I
Party

2 Power in the Party
Gerald R. Taylor

This chapter focuses on the exercise of and attempts to utilize power in a very specific context: that of the Labour Party in the mid-1990s. Such a study does not necessitate an understanding of power in its totality, which is perhaps fortunate, and may not contribute greatly to a wider understanding of this much-debated concept (Lukes 1974, 1986; Russell, 1995; Dowding, 1996).

One of the most famous studies of power in relation to political parties is the classic analysis by Robert Michels of the German Social Democratic Party in the early years of the century (Michels, 1962). It was, of course, this work which was the basis of Michels' contribution to elitist theory and where he formulated his 'iron law of oligarchy', that is, the belief that all organizations necessarily manifest and produce some form of elite which effectively controls the organization itself. Michels also saw socialist parties as necessarily more concerned with democratic processes than other parties (Lipset, 1962, p. 15). Indeed for Michels,

> The life of political parties ... must, in theory, necessarily exhibit an even stronger tendency towards democracy than that which is manifested by the state. (Michels, 1962, p. 64)

The fact that German social democrats had created a party which was effectively controlled from above was enough, as far as Michels was concerned, to abandon the pretence of either democratic achievement or potential. In Britain a rather different spin was put on these ideas by Robert McKenzie (McKenzie, 1964). Far from seeing this as a problem McKenzie saw the elite dominance of British political parties as both a reflection of the British political system and a necessity if parties were to represent the wider constituency of their voters and supporters (Panitch and Leys, 1997, p. 11).

This raises interesting questions about the nature of democracy and the role of political parties within liberal democracies, but from the perspective of this book what is important is what it tells us about power within political parties, and influences upon that power. What it does suggest is that there is a connection between power within parties and the structures and requirements of the wider political systems within which they work. This, in itself, is hardly surprising given the desire of political parties to be elected and to wield power within those wider systems. As a consequence the possibility is raised that Michels' iron law of oligarchy is contingent with regard to political parties, at least in the form of its expression, on the political system within which those parties operate.

Electoral interests may provide some motive for the maintenance of elite structures, but the nature of such structures, the means of communication between elite and grass roots, and the potential for control of elite power may still be varied. How has this developed within the Labour Party, and particularly how has it been influenced by the arrival of the 'modernizers'? Further questions may also be asked regarding whether the nature of elite control is designed to reflect the interests of a wider constituency, but the point here is not to assess the nature of democracy, liberal or otherwise, any more than it is to discuss the general nature of power. Rather it is to consider specific changes and attempts at management and then assess what wider issues and questions that prompts in the context of the Labour Party generally and New Labour specifically.

Power within the Labour Party has itself been assessed from a number of perspectives. Studies have focused on the effectiveness of the elite in driving through their programmes within the Party, from varying perspectives (Hughes and Wintour, 1990; Heffernan and Marqusee, 1992); others have considered specific power battles within the party and the effectiveness of different contenders (Seyd, 1987), or particular longstanding relationships, notably with the trade unions (Minkin, 1992); occasional works have concentrated on aspects of Labour's internal machinery such as Annual Conference (Minkin, 1978) or disciplinary procedures (Shaw, 1988); and some have evaluated Labour's relationship with liberal democracy itself (Miliband, 1972). Such studies have added much to our understanding of the Labour Party in particular and the life of political parties in general, but the point here is to examine what has occurred under New Labour, and to what extent it has changed the party.

There are three areas which need to be considered if we are to reach an overall conclusion in this regard. Firstly we need to consider policy outcomes, to what extent they have reflected New Labour concerns, and to what extent they have taken root in the party as a whole. Not much time will be spent on policy, partly because a later section of this text is devoted to consideration of New Labour's impact in various policy areas, and partly because the very existence of the term New Labour and its connotations suggests a widespread acceptance that the Labour Party is now setting out a distinctive set of policy options largely driven by the 'modernizers' and their fellow-travellers.

The second area which requires attention is the internal policy-making structures of the party. Considerable and important changes have occurred in Labour's policy-making systems over the past few years and the question needs to be asked how this affects and will affect power relationships within the party. In short: whose positions have been strengthened by these changes and whose have been weakened? Finally, an area frequently neglected with regard to discussions of power within all parties is that of ideology, or what Drucker (1979) describes as ethos in respect of the Labour Party. This has been raised with regard to New Labour in particular because of the decision to amend Clause Four of the party's constitution which contained its main statement of ideological belief (Taylor, 1997, pp. 6–11).

These last two together represent a major departure in previous elite dominance within the party and change the background to and the character of future power contests. What will be addressed here is what this means in terms of biasing future power struggles in particular directions, either towards particular groups within the party or towards particular policy outcomes.

POLICY CONTROL

Over the past fifteen years the Labour Party has gone through a quite remarkable promenade of policy restatements and initiatives. Ironically they began with the publication of *Labour's Programme 1982* (Labour Party, 1982) which was intended as a codification of Labour's policies as agreed at the party's Annual Conference. The 280-page document was introduced by a foreword by Ron Hayward, then the party's General Secretary, which made no bones about the seat of policy-making power within the party:

> In the Labour Party, policy is made by the members. On all issues of principle, on all issues of fundamental policy, theirs is the final word. (Labour Party, 1982, p. 1)

It is rare to find such an unequivocal statement from any party of their reliance on their membership to provide policy, although even here qualifying words such as 'fundamental' are readily apparent. Of course, in practice Labour's parliamentary leadership has never seen itself as effectively bound by decisions made through the only avenue open to party members, Annual Conference, and, indeed, this statement is itself a reaction to the drafting of Labour's manifesto for the 1979 General Election which was undertaken by the party's parliamentary leadership ignoring Conference decisions (Shaw, 1996, pp. 162–3).

Statements such as *Labour's Programme*, and the much derided 1983 Labour manifesto, were seen as a major contributing factor, along with the policy they contained, to the disastrous 1983 defeat. However justified this view was, it provided a motive for policy reappraisal which has been an almost continuous factor in Labour's internal politics ever since. This has included a major, and well publicised, policy review between 1987 and 1992 (Labour Party, n.d.b), and the external Commission on Social Justice run by the Institute for Public Policy Research (1994). Tony Blair's election as Labour Leader came after a period of policy change which created a momentum capable of being channelled to the acceptance of a range of policies which might have proved less acceptable in other circumstances.

To what extent do the policies currently espoused by Labour reflect a departure from Labour's past associations, and do they reflect the true policy preferences of Labour's members and supporters? The first of these questions will be substantially addressed in Part 3, but it is worth noting two substantial points about the way in which policy is being approached by New Labour. Firstly, the 1997 General Election campaign demonstrated a distinct tendency to focus very narrowly on a small range of policies. This reached its summit with the pledge-cards produced by Labour, containing five promises by which Labour claimed it should be judged in office, each of which were very specific and highly focused on particular areas of unemployment, health service provision, law and order, education, and taxation. In Labour's manifesto these pledges were linked to ten slightly broader promises (Labour Party, 1997b). Secondly, these policy statements were closely linked to Tony Blair personally.

These were two elements of a campaigning strategy focusing on voters' 'trust' for Blair and his ability to carry through certain, tightly defined policy options. This is necessarily an incremental strategy which eschews radical statement or challenge to the basis of current provisions and policies. Nonetheless this strategy can be seen as reaping rewards in the sheer scale of Labour's staggering victory on 1 May 1997, and the way in which this has been seen as linked to Blair as party leader (Heath, 1997; Fielding, 1997, p. 33; Kavanagh, 1997, p. 32). Although Blair's influence can be exaggerated, part of the scale of Labour's victory was clearly the result of the pattern of voting and in spite of Britain's electoral system providing its traditional winning bonus to the victor, it still has implications within the party. Firstly the scale of Labour's victory alters power relationships within the parliamentary party itself, and secondly the fact and the scale of victory must be significant for party supporters, members and activists who have suffered 18 years of opposition.

Despite this, signs of dissent are beginning to emerge within the party. Policies such as changes to welfare benefits for single parents, and proposed changes in disability benefits, the charging of fees to students in higher education, and so on, have prompted opposition among some backbenchers, but this may be made more likely by Labour's sizeable majority. Interestingly the Lords have felt quite content to challenge the Blair Government despite threats of constitutional reform to change their composition and powers; perhaps this is a residue of Lords activism against the Thatcher governments in their prime and partly based on the apparent assumptions made then that government policy does not enjoy the full support of the wider public. Perhaps more significant, although also more difficult to predict and analyse, is the opposition some policies have engendered within the Labour Party itself. The scale of such opposition has yet to become fully apparent and has still to produce any unambiguous attacks on Government policy. Even though no clear splits are apparent in Labour's façade, internal discontent, maybe linked with a desire to be seen 'consulting' more widely, led the leadership to arrange a series of meetings to defend welfare reform. What was noticeable about these events was that a full range of Cabinet Ministers were expected to publicly defend the party's stance, and did in good old collective-responsibility fashion, thus tying themselves to the party's programme.

One final point needs to be made at this stage, regarding policy outcomes and power, and that is the influence of external sources of policy. In particular Blair's government has shown itself willing to adapt party policy and approaches to outside pressure. The decision to omit Formula 1 from a blanket-ban on tobacco advertising in sport, and the attempts to pacify supporters of the Countryside Alliance demonstration provide two early examples. Whatever the reasons for the Government's reaction to these particular events it suggests a different attitude to public pressure than was exhibited by recent Conservative governments. What this means in practice is as yet unclear, and the extent to which it is a departure from previous Labour government practice is also debatable. The question here is whether it has any implications for power and decision-making within the party. Such observations suggest the potential need for the leadership to dominate the party in order to obtain the policy preferences determined through contact with external pressures. Given McKenzie's view that this was necessary for the operation of 'democracy' in Britain this can be seen as a return to the style of government typical of the 1960s and 1970s. However, what would be a departure, if continued, is the visible influence of groups able to obtain enough publicity or public support and, on the other hand, of individuals with sufficient wealth and influence to make an impact. This brings into stark relief issues of the rationality of party membership, and in this case Labour Party membership. Under these circumstances what would be the motivation for individuals to remain within the Labour Party, to work and campaign for it when they were having clearly less effect on party policy than those organizing and participating in highly visible protest of various forms? In addition, the 'great and the good' may always have had privileged access to British government, but if this becomes as visible as it was during the decision on tobacco advertising and Formula 1 this may have adverse effects on the party leadership's authority both within the country as a whole and within their own party.

It would seem so far that New Labour's policy programme has been heavily focused on the personality of the leader as an individual, has courted external influence, and has not fully convinced all sections of the party, but how will elite control be exercised within the party? How has the machinery of internal decision-making changed and what does this suggest in terms of power over future policy outcomes?

POLICY STRUCTURES

Developments in Labour's internal policy structures have, naturally enough, been related to the perceived need for major policy reform over the period since 1983. However, even before then strains in the policy process and the power relations it reflected were apparent. After all, Labour's policy processes have always been faced with the task of bringing together disparate elements, and the main structure for achieving this was the party's Annual Conference.

The party's traditional structure has been confederal in nature, bringing together the parliamentary elite, constituency activists and representatives of affiliated organizations, the most prominent of which have, of course, been the trade unions. Of these Labour MPs have never had voting rights at Conference, though they have had the right to partake in debate, and of the three groups with voting rights, trade unions, constituency parties and other affiliated organizations, the trade unions have tended to monopolize Conference, wielding over 80 per cent of Conference votes (Minkin, 1978, p. 84). Of course such statistics need to be put into the context that Labour's parliamentary leadership has never seen its actions as effectively constrained by Conference decisions, trade unions have frequently tended to support leadership options, and Conference resolutions are characteristically ambiguous. All of these facts reinforce the belief that Conference is a less-than-perfect democratic decision-making body.

In consequence much of the detail, and often the general direction, of Labour policy was decided away from Conference in subcommittees of the party's National Executive Committee (NEC) and by the parliamentary elite. The NEC was itself responsible to Conference and responsible for implementing Conference decisions. As a result conflicts over Conference decisions and their application were frequently about the power relationship between the NEC and the parliamentary party.

In the 1970s the conflict between the NEC and Labour's parliamentary leadership developed when left-wingers on the NEC used their policy-making powers to challenge the policy paradigms on which the parliamentary party was operating in government. It was in this context that control of the 1979 manifesto was usurped by the parliamentary leadership, prompting the reaction of the early 1980s noted above. Under Neil Kinnock's leadership after 1983 the first steps were made to bring these two seats of power within the Labour Party together through the creation of joint NEC–Shadow Cabinet Committees for the creation of policy (Shaw, 1996, p. 169).

These were precursors of the seven policy-review committees set up during the policy-review period after the 1987 General Election. The policy-review committees contained a number of interesting features.

They were largely composed of representatives from the party's Shadow Cabinet and NEC, with the interesting addition of co-opted trade union General Secretaries; and the committee secretariats reinforced the NEC–Shadow Cabinet linkage by drawing on individuals working both within the party bureaucracy and for Shadow Cabinet members in Parliament (Labour Party, n.d.a).

Alongside these important structural changes, others were initiated with varying degrees of success. Attempts to introduce voting changes for the reselection of parliamentary candidates based around the adoption of one-member-one-vote (OMOV) were initially thwarted only to reemerge in other contexts (Shaw, 1996, pp. 171–2 and p. 190). In addition the first attempts were made to restructure Conference into what was perceived by the leadership as a more effective policy-making forum (Taylor, 1997, pp. 63–4). Two other developments are also important in the Kinnock era: the increasing use of opinion surveys to test and evaluate policy options (Hughes and Wintour, 1990, pp. 51ff); and the experience of organizing and assimilating consultations within and outside of the party (Taylor, 1997, pp. 51–9).

Before Blair's election, in the brief period of John Smith's leadership, change in party structures was continued. These included the extension of OMOV to selection of parliamentary candidates and selection of the party leader and a reduction in trade-union voting power at Conference to 70 per cent initially and later to 50 per cent (Shaw, 1996, pp. 193–4). While these provided some excitement at the 1993 Annual Conference, in contrast to the generally bland affairs leading up to the 1992 General Election, the most significant change was the creation of the National Policy Forum in 1993 (Taylor, 1997, p. 65).

These various initiatives and changes came together in 1997 in the publication of *Labour into Power: a Framework for Partnership* (Labour Party, 1997a). This document brought together various changes in the previous fifteen years and proposed a new policy-making structure within the party. It is interesting that the case for change is based on the need to create 'trust, mutual support and effective two-way communication' between the Labour Government and the wider party (Labour Party, 1997c, p. 2). This clearly is a departure from the perspective taken in 1983 that Conference was the decision-making body of the party whose decisions Labour governments should seek to implement.

The central proposals of these documents, particularly two-year policy-making cycles, rolling programmes of policy, and policy commissions, were initially proposed in the early 1990s (Taylor, 1997, pp. 59–65). The 1997 document integrated these with the National Policy Forum in a single policy-making system (see Fig. 2.1). Although Party Conference was to 'remain the sovereign policy-making body' (Labour Party, 1997c, p. 5), it would do so in the context of a very different policy machine. In the new policy-making system, Conference will no longer receive resolutions directly from the party's various sectors. Instead Conference will consider policy documents prepared over two years which have passed through discussion in no less than four internal forums: Joint Policy Committees, the successors of the NEC–Shadow Cabinet Committees, twice; the National Policy Forum twice; Policy Commissions appointed by the National Policy Forum; and the National Executive Committee. The Joint Policy Committees will 'have strategic overview of policy development' (Labour Party, 1997c, p. 5).

In addition the constitution of the National Policy Forum and the National Executive Committee will be reformulated to reflect a wider constituency within the party. Notably places on the NEC are awarded to the Government and parliamentary party, the European Parliamentary Party Leader and local government representatives (see Table 2.1). The National Policy Forum contains the whole of the NEC, sizeable representations from constituency parties, trade unions, regional parties, and places for the parliamentary party, Government, the European parliamentary party, the co-operative party, socialist societies, black socialist societies and local government (see Table 2.2).

This suggests that either of these committees will need to construct a considerable consensus within the party to challenge the preferences of the Joint Policy Committees. The role of the National Policy Forum so far has largely been one of policy testing, acting as a glorified panel within which potential policies could be floated for reactions. In the new system the Forum will have the responsibility of organizing the main consultation processes, including selecting the Policy Commissions which will receive submissions from both internal and external organizations. How will these changes affect power in the policy-making process?

The most obvious feature of the new system is the change in the role of Conference away from being a focus of debate controlled and directed by resolutions to one directed by a pre-existing policy process. The proposals argue that reports will be prepared in advance of the party conference for consultation and that consultation papers will include 'options, alternatives and minority proposals' (Labour

18

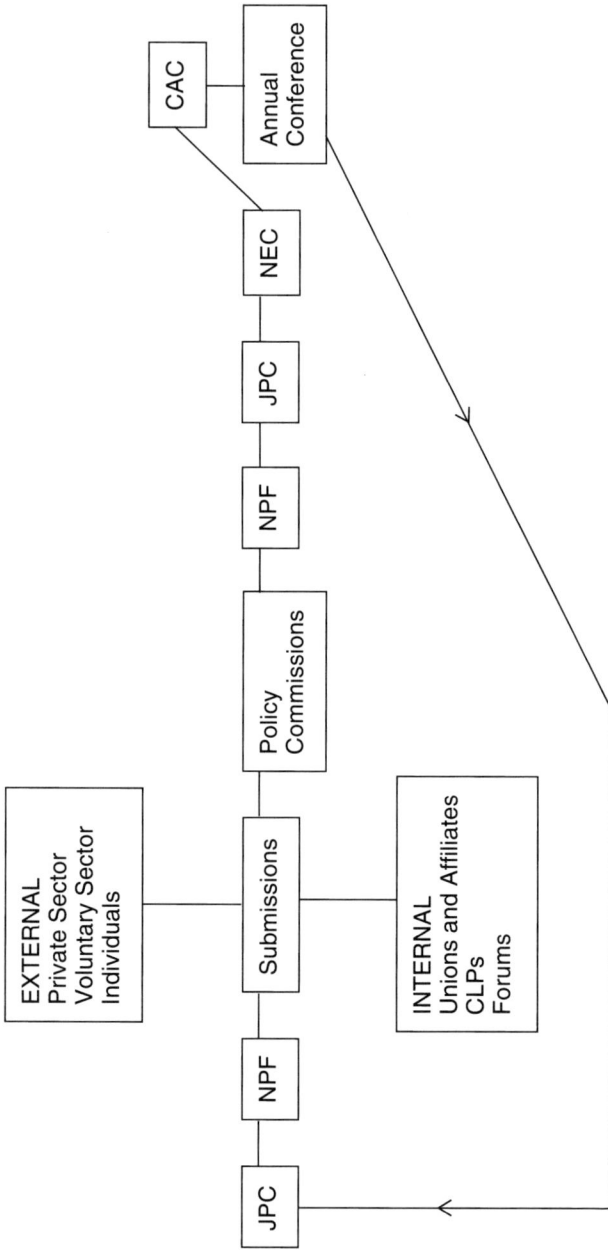

Source: Partnership in Power

Figure 2.1: Policy-Making System Proposed in *Partnership in Power*

Table 2.1:   National Executive Committee Membership

Before *Partnership in Power*	Amended by *Partnership in Power*
Leader (*ex-officio*)	Leader (*ex-officio*)
Deputy Leader (*ex-officio*)	Deputy Leader (*ex-officio*)
Treasurer (Annual Conference)	Treasurer (Annual Conference)
Trade Unions 12 (Annual Conference)	Trade Unions 12 (Annual Conference)
Constituency Labour Parties 7 (Annual Conference)	Constituency Labour Parties 6 (Annual Conference)
Socialist Societies 1 (Annual Conference)	Socialist Societies 1 (Annual Conference)
Women 5 (Annual Conference)	Young Labour 1 (Young Labour Conference)
Youth 1 (Young Labour Conference)	Government 3
Black Socialist Society 1 (BSS Conference)	Parliamentary Labour Party (inc. EPLP) 3 (MPs and MEPs)
	Leader European Parliamentary Labour Party
	Local Government 2 (Association of Labour Councils)
	Black Socialists Society 1* (Black Socialists Society Conference)
Total: 30	**Total: 32 (33)** * subject to minimum membership requirements.

Sources: *Labour Party Rule Book* (1995); *Partnership in Power*

Party, 1997c, p. 5). This suggests a considerable role for debate at party Conference, but debate which will be under the control, in particular, of the Joint Policy Committees and the NEC. The option to delay publication of sensitive reports will always be open and what is included within the reports as possible alternatives will be filtered by the Joint Policy Committees and the NEC. This will create a Conference which is more predictable for the party leadership, more open to direction from above, and less of a vehicle for the public airing of activist frustrations.

The Joint Policy Committees and the NEC, in turn, will include greater party elite representation, and the extent to which other voices are heard and the interpretation given to them will depend on these groups. One potential problem is that although the new system makes challenging the leadership more difficult, any such challenge which

Table 2.2:   National Policy Forum Membership Proposed in *Partnership in Power*

Constituency Labour Parties	54 (subject to minimum youth representation)
(Regional Groups of Constituency Delegates at Annual Conference)	
Regional Labour Parties	18
(Regional Conference or Policy Forum)	
Trade Unions	30
(Agreed Formula)	
Parliamentary Labour Party	9
(MPs)	
European Parliamentary Labour Party	6
(MEPs)	
Government	8
(not specified)	
Socialist Societies	3
(Socialist Societies Delegates at Annual Conference)	
Co-operative Party	2
(Co-operative Party NEC)	
Black Socialists Society	4
(Black Socialists Society Conference)	
Local Government	9
(4 Labour Group on LGA; 1 Labour Group on COSLA; 4 ALC)	
NEC	32
(*ex-officio*)	
Total: 175	

does emerge may gain considerable authority from the fact that it has had to be built on a wider consensus of views within the party.

One final aspect of policy control and power within the party has been that of background values and principles, the party's ethos. It is these changes and their effects which must now be considered.

PARTY ETHOS

In the Introduction to his text on Labour's political thought, H. M. Drucker claimed that

The [Labour] party is not simply an instrument for acquiring and using power – not simply a vote-gathering machine designed for policy-making and implementation. The party has a life of its own –

a fact which political scientists have acknowledged without taking sufficiently seriously. (Drucker, 1979, p. vii)

The argument here is that there has been a conscious and deliberate attempt by Labour's elite to focus on the party's 'vote-gathering' functions, thereby minimizing the party's 'life' with considerable impact on policy and politics within the party.

While there has always been a sector of Labour's elite who have wished to see the wider party concentrate on electoral achievement and leave the business of politics and worrying about principles to the elected politicians, there has also been a consistent streak of principled radicalism, however acquiescent, within the party. Labour's members have tended to join the party because they wanted to see change. Indeed, while Labour members tend to see themselves advancing socialism, helping the working class, ridding the country of Thatcherism or being politically active (Seyd and Whiteley, 1992, p. 74), Conservatives are more likely to see themselves infected with a general attachment to Conservative policies, principles or the party, interested in the social scene or at most opposing labourism (Whiteley, Seyd and Richardson, 1994, p. 96). In other words, Labour members, at least in the early 1990s, tended to be more strongly committed to a set of political values, even though sometimes this was expressed in terms of opposition to alternative values, than Conservative members, who saw themselves as more generally supporting a party seeking election. It is this spirit of political activism and principle which Labour leaders since 1983 have sought to undermine in favour of more electoral perspectives.

The most obvious challenge to Labour's intellectual traditions has, of course, been the reform of Clause Four of Labour's constitution, which used to contain Labour's famous commitment to common ownership. This, like so much of New Labour's immediate heritage, has its precursor in the period of the policy review under Neil Kinnock. In fact one of the most obvious historical echoes is with the attempts by Hugh Gaitskell to reform Clause Four in the 1950s (Jones, 1996). In fact the modernizers' concern for reform of Clause Four can be read more significantly as a response to the left challenge to the Labour Government's economic policy, based ironically on an analysis of what might today be termed 'globalization', in the late 1970s (Shaw, 1996, p. 112).

While no Labour leader had challenged Clause Four in the way that Gaitskell had since the 1950s, this reflected the fact that the clause had little impact on Labour policies (Thompson, 1995, p. 3). In the early 1980s the clause became a rallying-point for significant sectors of the party's left, even if approaches to 'common ownership' differed between these groups. It was partly for these reasons that Labour's ideological heritage once again became a matter of concern for the party's leaders. As a result the policy review was provided with its very own statement of *Aims and Values* (Labour Party, 1988) to provide an ideological underpinning. Essentially this document did little more than reiterate Labour's historical practice as a party of government while playing lip-service to the principles of Clause Four (Taylor, 1997, pp. 21–35). The serious challenge to Clause Four came with the arrival of Blair as party leader.

What does this tell us about Labour's internal power relationships? The first point to note is that Labour's leaders largely ignored the Clause; attempts at reform only became an issue during periods of strong left-wing influence, with the Bevanites in the 1950s and with the left-wing resurgence of the 1970s and early 1980s. The second is to note that Blair only advanced reform after he was elected as party leader in 1994. The third that the reform was not purely about Clause Four, but was equally about establishing the power and authority of Tony Blair as leader of the party, and through this process to establish the position of New Labour. Finally the aim was substantially electoral, presenting the Clause as being an electoral handicap and establishing the party leader as in charge of the party. The nature of the new Clause with which Labour's commitment to common ownership was replaced is not itself as significant as the fact that this was a top-down revolution, one in which the party machinery could be, and was, utilised by the supporters of change to push through reform (Shaw, 1996, p. 199).

The reform of Clause Four is part of a wider attempt to focus the party on electoral aspirations. This has eschewed a direct attack on the principles held by individual members within the party in favour of demands that the party remain united as a precondition to electoral success. This was expressed clearly by Neil Kinnock when he declared the beginning of the campaign for the next General Election the day after Labour's defeat in 1987. More recently this has been continued by Tony Blair through his emphasis on the importance of winning a second term in office. Those who might feel persuaded by matters of principle are reminded of the débâcle of 1983, or the fact of 18 years in opposition and informed that such dissent is damaging to the party.

Quiescence at the reform of Clause Four, alongside a number of other policy changes, might be regarded as one fruit of this emphasis on electoral considerations; another has been the decline of Conference as a centre of contention and challenge to the party leadership since 1989. This does not mean that Labour's individual membership is less principled than it once was, or that it is less concerned with realizing political change; rather it means that such members have been prepared to subdue their desire for change in order to achieve the unity they believe to be necessary to achieve electoral success.

CONCLUSION

It is tempting to read Labour's recent history as one of the re-establishment of the authority of the party leadership following the successful, and electorally damaging, challenges of the left in the 1970s and early 1980s. To a certain extent this is an accurate assessment. We must be careful, however, of some of the implications of this reading. Firstly, the reassertion of leadership power, its methods and context are based on the assumption that it was the left which caused the electoral defeats of the early 1980s, and 1983 in particular. This is a popular assumption, but by no means a proven one.

Secondly, the depth of Labour's electoral problems and the organizational capabilities and sense of mission of the modernizing elements within the party have taken elite power within the party further than it has ever gone before, notably in the reform of Clause Four and in control of the party ethos. As Dennis Kavanagh has put it: 'The effect of the changes [of the 1980s and 1990s] was a transformation in the structure and ethos of the Labour Party' (1997, p. 25). Should this transformation prove unsustainable or electorally unattractive in the longer term, Labour will find itself in uncharted waters.

Thirdly, the strength of potential opposition within the party has, as yet, been untested. It remains to be seen whether party members will accept admonitions to toe the party-line, keep the faith and not rock the boat should Labour fail to deliver on their expectations. Here, of course, the defining factor will not be what the party leadership has promised but rather what those who have supported them, worked for them and elected them expect them to provide.

Fourthly, while the party's leadership have managed to reform the party's policy-making structures and ethos to help maintain their grip on decision-making power within the party, this could be a two-edged sword. Should their authority become challenged, and should this challenge be successfully mounted through the new mechanisms which have been created, it may prove even more embarrassing for the leadership and potentially damaging to their control.

All this needs to be put in the context of political power in Britain as a whole. Here New Labour has seemed generally interested, for whatever reasons, in engaging with groups or individuals exhibiting particular forms of popular support or of influence. How this will develop remains an open question. Nonetheless there are interesting problems here regarding the nature of British democracy. On the one hand, Labour leaders have deemed it necessary to re-establish elite control in order to become 'electable'; on the other, their relationship with power-brokers outside the party appears to be becoming more open and public. Far from fostering the trust which was a keyword for Labour's 1997 election campaign, this may serve to reinforce jaundiced and cynical views of the party, its politicians and, more worryingly, of democracy in general.

This relates back to McKenzie's view of British democracy. The question of whom politicians should be accountable to is a very real one. The argument that they should be responsible to constituencies beyond their own political party is important and significant. Nonetheless if we are to accept this claim, particularly as one reinforcing the authority of party leaders over their own party, then politicians must demonstrate the mechanisms by which they are held accountable to these wider constituencies. Labour's traditional acceptance of the British state as a neutral, democratic and authoritative political system has prevented Labour's leadership from realizing that this is a declining view among a significant proportion of the British electorate.

The activities of the 'modernizers' of New Labour in this regard may be seen as a confirmation of Michels' iron law of oligarchy, the re-establishment and entrenchment of elite control within the Labour party after a period of membership influence. For Michels this would be no surprise; the question is whether the evidence suggests that this elite control is inevitable or contingent. McKenzie's focus on the structure of the British political system raises the possibility that the British political elite may be more accountable only with the adoption of constitutional reform. It may be that Labour's elite will reconstruct the British state in a way which will make elite power more open and accountable, but politicians are keen to perpetrate the myth of their accountability while identifying, and constructing, mechanisms which are inadequate for the purpose. Finally, if New Labour achieves an accountability beyond the party, it will have justified the politicians' claims to represent a constituency beyond their parties, but if this is the outcome, what are the implications for political parties themselves?

3 New Labour and the Rejection of Stakeholder Capitalism
Paul Norris

New Labour is the result of a continuous process of modernization begun by Neil Kinnock and continued by John Smith and Tony Blair. So in a sense, New Labour was 'born out of the ashes of the old' (Pimlott, 1997, p. 328). The most important aspect of New Labour is that it is not old Labour. As we entered the 1990s questions were being asked about what was the difference between the Labour Party and the Conservative Party. In the 1992 election campaign the Conservative Party succeeded in convincing the electorate that the main difference was taxation policy. Thus Labour were still seen as the high-taxation, high-spending, interventionist party. This was to have an influence on the modernizers in the Labour Party. A key element in transforming Labour into 'New' Labour was the abandonment of the old Clause Four of the Labour Party constitution. Although this meant little in terms of policy, it was a symbolic gesture which made it clear that New Labour was a party that believed in capitalism. It was this and Tony Blair's leadership which attracted business to New Labour. By the end of 1996 donations to the Labour Party amounted to £6 million. What we saw prior to the 1997 General Election was the repositioning of New Labour under the leadership of Tony Blair.

Despite this repositioning, there had been very little change in policy under Tony Blair. This was perhaps because Labour was already well down the road to outlining its policies for the next election when he became leader. What was significant was that everything was repackaged into New Labour soundbites and New Labour gloss. When the draft manifesto *New Labour, New Life for Britain* was published in July 1996, New Labour was portrayed as 'neither old left nor new right'. However, by the 1997 General Election it was clear that New Labour had accommodated 'the newly ascendant and seemingly unassailable neoliberal paradigm' (Hay, 1997b, p. 373). The 1997 election campaign was fought on the issue of competence. In this election New Labour was about tactics and organization, not about ideas and a vision for the future. It did, however, have a chance to project a new hegemonic project when it appeared to adopt the concept of 'stakeholder capitalism'. Since the election we have not heard much about stakeholding, but in truth this had been abandoned long before then.

There were times when Labour looked as though it would commit itself to an assault on the enthusiasm for market-led growth. In 1994 Labour's Industry Forum published its industrial manifesto, which generally emphasized financial reform and industrial strategy, thus issuing an implicit challenge to the ascendancy of macroeconomic conservatism and neoliberal economics. With the replacement of Robin Cook as industrial spokesperson, industrial policy was slowly deradicalized, and at the same time Gordon Brown firmly remained the Treasury's man. The Trade and Industry team was marginalized and the Treasury team reasserted its supremacy. The personnel on the present Labour front bench means that New Labour's ability to articulate a distinctive and progressive political economy has fallen foul of its prior determination to appease nervous and conservative financial markets. The commitment of Gordon Brown to the previous government's expenditure plans and his hostility to tax increases, meant that no matter which party won the election the Treasury were victorious.

A headline in *The Financial Times* summed up New Labour's overall position: 'Labour Sets Out to Make Similar Look Different' (21 May 1996). These shifts to the right and its acceptance of the assumptions of the Thatcherite revolution in political economy have deprived the Blairite project of the only sociopolitical content its intellectual backers had given it: stakeholder capitalism. One important source for the concept is provided by the French economist and businessman Michel Albert. His book *Capitalism against Capitalism* (1992) is to some extent a response to Francis Fukuyama (1992). Albert contends that Fukuyama is wrong because history will continue as the conflict is no longer between rival systems, but rather between different models of capitalism:

> With the collapse of communism, it is as if a veil has been suddenly lifted from our eyes. Capitalism, we can now see, has two faces, two personalities. The neo-American model is based on individual success and short-term financial gain; the Rhine model, of pedigree but with strong Japanese connections, emphasises collective success, consensus and long-term concerns. In the last decade or so,

it is this Rhine model – unheralded, unsung and lacking even nominal identity papers – that has shown itself to be the more efficient of the two, as well as the more equitable. (Albert, 1992, pp. 18–19)

This contrast of two capitalisms was taken up by Will Hutton (1995), David Marquand (1988, 1997a) and others. Will Hutton damns Conservative policies for reinforcing the long-term tendency of British capitalism, under the domination of the City, to pursue short-term speculative investment. Any reform of the British economy and the state must be in the direction of 'stakeholder social capitalism', taking as its model the possession by continental European and Japanese societies of 'strong institutions that allow their firms to enjoy some of the gains from cooperation as well as from competition' and which 'are created and legitimised by some broad notion of public or national purpose'.

The trade unions, shunned and excluded under the Conservatives, would find their place in these institutions as, like their German counterparts, 'social partners in the management of capitalism' (Hutton, 1995, pp. 316, 258, 297). Hutton's call for 'a less degenerate capitalism' was hardly a mobilizing slogan for the left (Hutton, 1995, p. 298). Nevertheless, here was an idea that would allow social democrats to claim they had a programme with some content, and indeed could offer an alternative to Conservative policies. What Gordon Brown called 'supply side socialism' could square the circle by building a form of capitalism which both achieved a greater degree of social justice and enhanced the competitiveness of the British economy.

It could be argued that 1996 was the year that marked Tony Blair's abandonment of stakeholder capitalism, because there are three major problems with the idea of stakeholder capitalism as envisaged by New Labour. Firstly, it seems to be a contradiction to the other ideological shift under Tony Blair, the rejection of any Keynesian strategy of using the power of the nation-state to manage the economy. The stakeholder capitalisms of Germany and Japan have relied heavily on a high level of state intervention in the economy. Yet Tony Blair in his 1995 Mais lecture committed Labour to 'the control of inflation through a tough macroeconomic framework' (*Financial Times*, 23 May 1995). In other words, he accepted the neoliberal arguments that the priority of government policy is to reduce inflation to a minimum, crucially by controlling public spending. The UBS chief economist Bill Martin commented that

Brown, Blair and his economic adviser have chewed, swallowed and digested the central-bankerly proposition that stability is the key to improved economic performance; so much that Labour's growth strategy comprises little else. (*New Statesman*, 19 July 1996)

Peter Mandleson and Roger Liddle suggested that a Labour government should seek to achieve a stable rate 'for growth value of gross domestic product at current prices – so called nominal GDP' (Mandleson and Liddle, 1996, p. 79). This policy, justified as a more realistic substitute for the narrow targets for growth in the money supply, which the Conservative governments failed to meet in the 1980s, has long been advocated by Samuel Brittan, one of the chief advocates of monetarism in Britain. What Brittan (1981) calls 'broad monetarism' does not sit well with the interventionism implied by the concept of stakeholder capitalism. Will Hutton criticised Tony Blair's Mais lecture for its 'underlying assumption that capitalism works best if left to its own devices' (*Guardian*, 28 May 1995). Hutton has also vigorously attacked the closely related 'myth of globalization', the idea, in other words, heavily relied on by Tony Blair and Gordon Brown, that the internationalization of capital makes national reform impossible (*Guardian*, 12 June 1995).

Secondly, as envisaged by Hutton and Marquand at least, the shift to stakeholder capitalism requires considerable institutional changes. These would be of two kinds. First of all, constitutional reform. Hutton argues that the 'semi-modern nature of the British state is a fundamental cause of Britain's economic and social problems' (Hutton, 1995, pp. xi–xii). Reforming British capitalism therefore requires reforming this 'semi-feudal state' (Hutton, 1995, p. 323) which presides over it, through the measures advocated by Charter 88. Thirdly, achieving stakeholder capitalism means overhauling British company law. David Marquand states that

> if the stakeholder concept means anything at all, it means a radical break with the traditions, institutions, and assumptions of Britain's shareholder capitalism. All the manifold varieties of the simple stakeholder model embody the simple proposition that property owners have, and must discharge, obligations to other interests, which also have obligations to them; that the decisions of a capitalist firm must reflect a subtle web of reciprocal obligations, involving its employees, its suppliers and the localities in which it operates, as well as its shareholders. That proposition provides the basis for the sharing of decision rights which are seen as the essence of Rheinish

capitalism. ... Either through law, or through the pressure of social convention, the power-sharing arrangements which lie at the heart of all stakeholder models are obligatory and enforceable. They have to be; otherwise there is no protection against free-riders. (*Guardian*, 24 June 1996)

Hutton also argues for 'initiatives in corporate governance', to

break the self perpetuating oligarchy of most British firms. . . . This could be negotiated initially as a voluntary code, but ultimately, it would have to be backed by legislation. (*Guardian*, 22 January 1996)

The Hutton–Marquand vision of stakeholding capitalism requires for its implementation a confrontation with entrenched capitalist interests in the shape of the City and its allies in the Treasury and company boardrooms. No sooner had Tony Blair pronounced the phrase 'stakeholder economy' in Singapore in January 1996 than he and his spin doctors sought to disavow any radical implications it might have. They were particularly eager to dissociate Blair's conception from the detailed proposals for institutional change which Hutton had spelt out in his book. Noel Thompson points out that

When [TUC general secretary] John Monks suggested trade unions as representative institutions through which working people could claim a stake in the management of enterprises and the national economy, the Labour leadership was quick to distance itself from his remarks. Similarly, when John Edmonds of the GMB saw stakeholderism as entailing new legal rights of job security, the response was equally cool. Those, like Will Hutton and David Marquand, who sought to give radical content to the idea . . . also received a Blairite brushoff. Thus Hutton was categorised dismissively as a 'well-liked, useful, freethinker, but not a great influence', while Blair himself was quick to rule out the kind of corporate legislation which might give substance to a new vision of corporate responsibilities and behaviour. (Thompson, 1996, p. 38)

In an interview with David Frost, Tony Blair stated that the 'stakeholder economy was a unifying theme or slogan' (quoted in Thompson, 1996). Mandleson and Liddle argued that it 'addresses the needs and inspirations of individuals, not interest groups acting for them' (Mandleson and Liddle, 1996, p. 25). But this is to deprive the concept of stakeholding of any substance, since its advocates are primarily concerned precisely to combat what they describe as the 'economic individualism' of the New Right by providing for the representation of interests wider than the shareholders and managers of the company in questioning economic decision-making.

The Financial Times of 26 June 1996, under the headline 'Labour Softens on Stakeholding', reported that a Labour draft manifesto industrial policy document 'fails to live up to the pre-publicity since it contained few specific reforms'. Alistair Darling told the paper:

> There is a limit to how many of Britain's corporate ills can be resolved by legislation. What you are trying to do is change people's behaviour and attitudes. (*Financial Times*, 26 June 1996)

The Financial Times, hardly a stronghold of old Labour thinking, seemed taken aback by the extent of the retreat:

> Perhaps most damning is the way Conservative Party officials admit to being surprised by Labour's decision to try to neutralize the stakeholder issue. They had been concerned that Labour would portray City fund managers as the 'union barons' of the 1990s and attack the government for failing to stop their excesses. . . . Labour insiders do not deny that it wants to neutralize the stakeholder debate rather than make a virtue of it. The decision stems from the Conservative Party's effective campaign representing stakeholding as a return to the corporatism of the 1970s. 'They are clearly scared rigid of the Tory line and as a result they have bottled what could have been an imaginative set of policies', one Labour official said. (*Financial Times*, 26 June 1996)

David Marquand also drew the same conclusion. Marquand wrote that if Britain is to become a stakeholder economy,

> the nettles of institutional design, change and resistance will have to be grasped. As yet, there is little evidence that New Labour is prepared to do this. It seems to be stuck in the traditional British rut of piecemeal voluntary incrementalism, buttressed by a traditional unwillingness to learn from continental Europe. (*Guardian*, 24 June 1996)

In July 1996 New Labour launched their most detailed policy document to date, *New Labour, New Life for Britain*. Its main economic commitment was the Thatcherite assertion that the 'priority must be stable, low-inflation conditions for long-term growth'. This gave Hutton and company the incentive to make a stand, calling for reform of both 'the way the stock market, ownership structures and corporate governance interlock' and 'the institutions of the British state' (*Guardian*, 7 July 1996). However in *The Times* of 23 April 1996 Peter Mandleson praised the East Asian variant of stakeholder capitalism, not those aspects stressed by Hutton. So, one year before the election, it appeared that New Labour had opted for the more or less unrestrained market capitalism of the Anglo-American model rather than the Rhine model championed by Hutton and Marquand. Even *The Observer* protested that New Labour had moved too far to the right. 'New Labour has swerved so sharply to the right that it is in danger of crashing through the central reservation' (30 June 1996).

There was some opposition within the Labour Party to these developments. Surprisingly some of the more publicized opposition came from Roy Hattersley. He dismissed Mandleson and Liddle's book *The Blair Revolution* as 'banal, pretentious and risibly inadequate' (*Guardian*, 27 February 1996). Hattersley's criticisms were an indication of how far New Labour had shifted, but they were also an indication of how muted other voices were. Hattersley commented that 'Large scale revolt has been avoided up to now because the Labour Party want to win' (*Guardian*, 2 July 1996). But protest was muted also because the socialist left had collapsed, and in a way that is what is new about New Labour and what makes it different from the Labour Party of the past – the absence of an organized socialist left with an alternative agenda and ideas. Not that New Labour is theoretical, because it is not. True, it has placed stress on the fashionable terms citizenship and community, but this has been mainly presentation rather than substance.

There are some contradictions within Labour policies that do not sit easily together. On the one hand there are, on paper at least, some radical commitments to constitutional reform, and on the other hand there is the acceptance of the neo-liberal agenda. This has led one commentator to observe that 'New Labour's agenda differs remarkably little from the previous regime's' (Marquand, 1997b, p. 336). Two key issues which helped the defeat of the Conservative government were health and education. These two areas require expenditure and therefore connected to this is the tax question. On this the Liberal Democrats have been more radical, but given the lead that Labour had in the opinion polls, perhaps they should have tackled this issue rather than evade it, because health and education need resourcing and the Government will be judged on this. Indeed, the Government's three main priorities became 'education, education, education' as opposed to its earlier strategy of economic institutional reform, international regulatory initiatives and education. The decision to stick to the tight spending limits of the Major government has not given the Labour government a great deal of room to manoeuvre and it has also highlighted a clash of philosophies within Labour, welfare to work versus raising benefits.

There is no reason to assume Labour will not fulfil commitments on issues such as devolution, a minimum wage and the windfall tax. Nonetheless, the radical edge has been removed. There is no clear annunciation of its aims and values and so far the response in trying to create a positive culture of active citizenship has been piecemeal. The problem is that New Labour had been stressing that it is not old Labour and has indulged in sloganizing rather than developing a new theoretical position. There does not seem to be a lot of substance about New Labour, and what substance there is, is in danger of being distorted by slogans. The New Labour government appears to believe, like its predecessor, that 'Britain's competitive advantage in the global market place lies in low non-wage labour costs, correspondingly low levels of social protection and deregulated labour markets' (Marquand, 1997b, p. 336). Because New Labour does not see any problems of power in its relations with capital, unlike old Labour which was well aware of them, 'it has no defences against the constant shift of that commodity towards the financial markets and the risk that their demands will become increasingly onerous' (Crouch, 1997, p. 359). Previous Labour governments were savaged by the opposition of organized capital and by accepting the neo-liberal agenda. New Labour is in a worse position to put forward a modernizing social reformist project.

The changes which have resulted in the transformation from old Labour to New Labour did not occur only under the leadership of Tony Blair. In fact the greatest changes in policy occurred under Neil Kinnock during the 1987 Policy Review. The crucial changes which occurred in the period between 1992 and 1997 were in motion before Tony Blair became leader in 1994. Under Neil Kinnock there was a transition from the left hegemony of the early 1980s to the reassertion of strong central leadership which was evident under Harold Wilson in the 1960s. The Policy Review of 1987–89 abandoned three long-standing commitments: renationalization of privatized industries, restoration of trade union immunities, and unilateral disarmament. By 1990 full employment had disappeared as an overriding aim, and Labour supported membership of the Exchange Rate Mechanism. The Plant Commission on electoral reform, set up by Neil Kinnock, reported in 1993 and recommended the Supplementary Vote. Tony Blair did manage to change Clause Four and did hold a party plebiscite on the 1996 draft manifesto.

Under the leadership of Tony Blair, New Labour has become more pro-business, more populist on morality and crime and has accepted that 'nothing can be done about markets (ever)' (Crouch, 1997, p. 358) thus accepting the powerlessness of the state in the face of such markets. They also appear to have, as Peter Riddell puts it, an 'obsession with presentation' (*The Times*, 8 December 1997). What New Labour has done under the leadership of Tony Blair is to reassure those in positions of power – the City, industry, the media – that a Labour government is not a threat. It could be argued that the general policy stance of Tony Blair and New Labour is simply the policy stance of Crosland, Gaitskell, Wilson and Callaghan, minus the civil libertarianism of Crosland, the egalitarianism of Keynesianism and the corporatism of the social contract. Jim Callaghan was very much a populist Home Secretary on law and order; Denis Healy was a conservative Chancellor imposing austerity measures in 1975; and there has been a retreat in defence and foreign policies to the policies which were dominant in the party from 1945 to the 1980s.

CONCLUSION

One could argue that New Labour was responding to the Thatcherized culture of privatization and individualism. New Labour felt that the 1997 election must be won at all costs, and this gave a different complexion to the evolution of Labour ideology and polices that had begun under Kinnock. There was also a different rhetoric, which was influenced by Bill Clinton's self-description that he was a New Democrat. New Labour prior to the 1997 election appeared to be obsessed by the electoral need to rid itself of the 'high tax' image which was thought to have lost it the 1992 election. It adopted policies which would 'make a difference at little or no cost', thus putting severe limitations on what it could deliver. As Iain Macwhirter pointed out:

> A decade and a half of free-market Thatcherism has reproduced levels of inequality unseen since Victorian times, and the social fabric is being destroyed by mass unemployment. New Labour has no particular remedy than to ask business people to be more responsible. Yet the reality of the market is that it lacks a social

conscience. The interests of the wider society always have to be imposed from without by democratic control. . . . Two Conservative parties is one too many. (*The Observer*, 19 November 1995)

This meant that New Labour was catering to existing ideas rather than seeking to build support for new ones. Thus, New Labour is not articulating a clearly different political vision, either ideologically or electorally. If it was, it would have to carry that vision into practice by forming a radical bloc of social forces behind its modernizing and reforming zeal. It would have to do something that no other Labour government has yet managed to do and sustain over any length of time. It would have to say to British business and banking leaders that private capital cannot and will not act as an adequate custodian of long-term interests of the British industrial base, or of the concerns and needs of those who work in, or depend on it. They need to shift initially into a partnership between private capital, the trade union movement and a democratized state and ultimately build a genuine industrial democracy. It is here, however, that there is a problem, because New Labour does not give such a radical meaning to the notion of stakeholder capitalism. Under New Labour 'stakeholding became little more than commending to employers the value of consulting their workforce' (Crouch, 1997, p. 358). New Labour does not think in terms of hegemonic domination and the consolidation of social blocs of support. It does not have the conception of putting together a new historical bloc in Gramscian terms. It does not think in class terms when charting either its immediate electoral prerequisites or its government allies. The Conservatives of course certainly do think and act in class ways, and always have.

New Labour has missed an opportunity in setting a new hegemonic agenda by abandoning the main principles of stakeholder capitalism as envisaged by Hutton and Marquand. Although not a left-wing socialist alternative, stakeholder capitalism did re-establish the social democratic tradition of Antony Crosland, and it did recognize that ethical socialism was born out of opposition to unfettered capitalism. New Labour however, has rejected the main tenets of Labour's progressive tradition – egalitarianism and solidarity – and, as Larry Elliott points out, merely acquiesces to the Tories (*Guardian*, 13 January 1997). Paul Foot makes the point that 'the more New Labour makes concessions to Tory barbarism, the more barbarous the Tories will become, and the more they will get away with it' (*Guardian*, 13 January

1997). New Labour has failed to learn that there is a need for a long-range political strategy. Also, rather than exorcizing its past in its pursuit of governmental power it may just serve to resurrect it, 'implicating the party in the disintegration of a deeply contradictory settlement' (Hay, 1997, p. 375). New Labour had an opportunity to shift the relations of forces away from the project that Thatcherism set in motion, so that the tendencies began to move the other way, to begin the debate about a new kind of society. As Ben Pimlott points out: 'New Labour can scarcely be characterised in any simple way as a recipe for transforming Britain' (Pimlott, 1997, p. 330).

4 New Labour and Christian Socialism
Alan Wilkinson

A photograph in the *Independent* on 30 September 1996 of the Blairs at the Labour Party Conference said it all. It showed the smiling couple walking from the rain towards a building with two men holding umbrellas over them. What the caption did not say was that they were going to the Conference service and that the two men with umbrellas (admittedly in mufti) were both priests, one Anglican (chairman of the Christian Socialist Movement [CSM]) the other Roman Catholic (the co-ordinator of the CSM). The omission by the newspaper of the religious context is characteristic of our society which ignores religious motivation, allegiance and institutions at both a popular and an academic level. So for example, Andrew Thorpe's recent *History of the British Labour Party* (1997) offers a wholly secular interpretation. Yet Christian influences on the Labour Party from the beginning have been considerable. In order to understand the current revival of Christian Socialism and the indebtedness of some of New Labour's leaders to its theology and moralism, we need to know something of its history since the mid-nineteenth century.

During the nineteenth century, the recurrent fear of revolution led to a policy of repression alongside church- and school-building in the early decades, and social reform and Christian Socialism later on. During the first half of the nineteenth century, Evangelicalism, the main religious tradition, supported Political Economy. Its morality was essentially personal. So compulsory charity through taxation was morally worthless (Hilton, 1988; Waterman, 1991). The Christian tradition taught that those with power should exercise it paternally. But what did this mean? For Evangelicals, life was a time of testing and it was foolish compassion to try to remove God-sent trials. Many believed that the chief cause of poverty was irreligion. The poor would prosper if they gave up drink, stopped relying on relief, sought education, worked hard, and thought of the Day of Judgement. J. B. Sumner (Archbishop of Canterbury 1848–62) a member of the Poor Law Commission, wrote: "'Turn not your face from any poor man'"; but inquire into the circumstances of his distress, and point out to him the mode in which the prudent regulations of society have directed that it should be relieved' (Atherton, 1994, p. 351). The churches, often unwittingly, were agents of social change, for example through education. The Church of England raised large sums of money for education, so by 1861 it was educating 76.2 per cent of the children in day schools, and by 1886 it was training 67.5 per cent of teachers (Kitson Clark, 1973, pp. 122–7).

Christian Socialism was one result of moral revulsion against the harsh concept of God implied by Political Economy. It looked for an inclusive theology with a God of universal compassion, not a Calvinist God for the elect only. It was also a version of that type of Victorian paternalism which wanted to enable, not repress, and which asked for moral citizenship in return for improved conditions and social inclusion. It owed something also to *noblesse oblige* and those Anglican Tories who disliked the New Poor Law and mounted piecemeal challenges to *laissez-faire* on moral grounds. So Bishop Samuel Wilberforce told the Lords in 1847 that he supported the Ten Hours Bill because 'it was wrong to create wealth by the sacrifice of the health and morals of a portion of the people' (Norman, 1976, p. 138). Christian Socialists strongly approved of paternalistic manufacturers from Robert Owen onwards, who behaved like Anglican Tory squires, and provided not only model physical conditions but also applied sanctions against immorality and laziness. Also, Christian Socialism resulted from the interaction between Romanticism and Catholicism (Anglican and Roman). Romantic writers from Blake to Morris rejected an atomistic view of society dominated by the market. Cobbett and Pugin looked back longingly to communal life in pre-industrial society. Anglican socialism owed much to the Anglo-Catholic revival which rejected erastianism, called on the church to stand against the state, recovered a sacramental view of life, was convinced that the church should be more classless and looked back nostalgically to the Middle Ages. Christian socialism also had roots in Nonconformity which provided many working people with responsibility as lay preachers and chapel officials. Though it was never so close to Labour as it had once been with the Liberals, many of the first Labour leaders were Nonconformists. The early life of Arthur Henderson, Foreign Secretary 1929–31, illustrated the regenerative power of the chapels. He was born in poverty, and a teenage conversion led him to become a Sunday School teacher, a lay preacher, a visitor to the sick and needy and to forswear drink, gambling and smoking. Dissent from the established church was as much a political as a religious act. Yet by the turn of the century, the

Free Churches (as they were now known) became so respectable that some Labour activists felt unwelcome. Some formed Labour Churches from 1891, but they became little more than political platforms and ceased to be an effective force by 1900.

Trade unions and Friendly Societies were characteristic working-class institutions. But they also exercised a strict discipline over their members – rights and responsibilities went together, as they do for New Labour. Their high moral tone owed much to the chapels which provided much of their leadership.

F. D. Maurice (1805–72) and his friends were the first Christian Socialists. Maurice was an Anglican priest and Professor of Theology at King's London. In 1848, alarmed by the revolution in Paris, he decided that socialism must be Christianized. Maurice and his group are important for four reasons. First, Maurice produced a theology which, because it was universalist and started with the goodness of the created order, was capable of being used to further socialism. For Maurice, the sacraments of baptism and eucharist showed that Christianity was a communal, not an individualistic faith. Second, by coining the term 'Christian Socialist', Maurice brought together two words which were widely thought incompatible. He said that his mission was to engage with 'the unsocial Christians and the unchristian Socialists'. Third, this was the first Christian group to present an alternative to *laissez-faire*, however sketchy. Maurice held many traditional views about society, but wrote that anyone who recognized that cooperation was a truer principle than competition had the right to be called socialist. He taught a positive view of the state just when its moral potential was about to be rediscovered. Fourth, the group had practical results, including the creation of the Working Men's College in 1854 with Maurice as principal, and the promotion of cooperative enterprise which Maurice believed would teach workers self-government and brotherhood and would incorporate them into national life. The group was too diverse to cohere and did not last beyond 1855 (Norman, 1987).

Cooperative schemes became increasingly attractive to Christians – they offered an alternative to the competitive spirit, did not threaten property and aimed to inculcate thrift and responsibility among the workers. They appealed to that minority of Christian Socialists who rejected collectivism and preferred self-help and mutual aid societies. When the movement transformed itself into a business enterprise like any other, E. V. Neale, one of Maurice's group who had devoted his life to it, was angry as were bishops from all over the world at the 1897 Lambeth Conference (Backstrom, 1974).

T. H. Green (1836–82), a philosophy don at Balliol, was a pivotal figure. He unwittingly produced a philosophical foundation for both New Liberalism and Anglican socialism. The purpose of the state was to promote the common good, but he hoped that this would be produced by voluntary not collectivist action. Only in community did the individual find true fulfilment. Green influenced a whole line of Anglican socialists – Henry Scott Holland, Charles Gore, R. H. Tawney and William Temple, all of whom had been at Balliol. Arnold Toynbee, another Balliol don, deeply impressed Samuel Barnett, the vicar of the slum parish of St Jude's Whitechapel which he had accepted, intending to regenerate the community. In 1884 Barnett founded Toynbee Hall in his memory in Whitechapel. Its role was to acquaint the future leaders of society with urban poverty and to aid local people to develop skills and leadership. Attlee, Beveridge and Tawney were among the many who worked there (Meacham, 1987). 'Toynbee Hall has as much claim to be counted among the ancestors of the Labour Party as Methodism, Taff Vale or William Morris' (Stedman Jones, 1980, p. 247). In recent years settlements have been derided as though it would have been better if the Oxford men had stayed in their colleges. Attlee was an Anglican agnostic, brought up in a well-to-do family with a strong social conscience. His life was changed by a visit to a boys' club in Limehouse run by his old public school. Fr Trevor Huddleston CR had a similar defining moment in Camberwell. At first, Barnett believed in the philosophy of the Charity Organization Society which was confident it could distinguish between the deserving and undeserving poor. Getting people off relief and into work was as central to the COS as it is to New Labour. George Lansbury, a devoted Anglican, was particularly critical of the assumption of Toynbee Hall and some East End clergy that the area needed imported leadership. Lansbury's work as a Poplar councillor proved this false (Holman, 1990).

In the 1880s there was an upsurge of socialism. The economy had become precarious. Evidence was mounting about the dire poverty in the cities. A committee of the 1888 Lambeth Conference of bishops reported there was no necessary contradiction between Christianity and socialism and urged the clergy to study socialism and to make contact with socialist groups. The Christian Social Union which Scott Holland founded in 1889 had an Anglican and eucharistic basis. It developed partly as a Fabian-type organization for detailed investigation of social problems, partly as a pressure group which exerted influence on social legislation through sympathetic MPs. It exercised a policy of preferential dealing, by blacklisting firms with

poor conditions and commending those with good records. Unwilling
to call itself 'socialist' (a term which still implied immorality and
atheism) it included socialists like the future Archbishop Temple,
New Liberals and one-nation Tories. Many members believed in an
extension of municipal and state action. B. F. Westcott, Bishop of
Durham and President 1889–1901, explained to the 1890 Church
Congress 'the essential idea' of socialism, as 'a theory of life and not
only a theory of economics':

> In this sense Socialism is the opposite of Individualism. . . .
> Individualism regards humanity as made up of disconnected or
> warring atoms; Socialism regards it as an organic whole. . . . The
> method of Socialism is co-operation, the method of Individualism is
> competition. . . . The aim of Socialism is the fulfilment of service,
> the aim of Individualism is the attainment of some personal
> advantage. (Westcott, 1890)

The CSU was by far the largest body of its kind in the churches,
with 6000 members. Between 1889 and 1913, 16 out of 53 new bishops
were members of the CSU. It also attracted some notable women into
its research work. But the CSU was too top-down to attract working-
class members (Jones, 1968, Chapter VI).

Charles Gore (1853–1932), successively Bishop of Worcester,
Birmingham and Oxford, was the most influential bishop of the
twentieth-century Church of England. He edited the most creative
theological symposium of the nineteenth century, *Lux Mundi* (1889),
the manifesto of Liberal Catholicism, which included a chapter on
politics with a high view of the state as the servant of the common good.
He founded the Community of the Resurrection, a monastic order, in
1892. Five of its six founding members were members of the CSU, of
which he was President, 1901–10. CR trained most of the black
Anglican clergy of South Africa, including Desmond Tutu. He and his
mentor, Fr Trevor Huddleston CR, a lifelong socialist, changed the
history of that country. Gore also inspired the creation of the Workers'
Educational Association in 1903 (Wilkinson, 1992). Unusually for a
church leader, Gore understood class conflict and the benefits won by
working-class militancy. But he rejected the left-wing image of Jesus as
a poor man betrayed by the upper classes. Did not his fellow carpenters
also desert him? He knew too much about sin to be a progressivist or
utopian like so many socialists of the time. Sticks as well as carrots were
needed. He advocated unemployment insurance, but also detention for
the workshy and redistributive taxation for the rich. R. H. Tawney, one

of the large number who owed so much to Gore, dedicated *Religion and the Rise of Capitalism* (1926) to him.

Of the churches, only Roman Catholicism had a substantial allegiance of working people, mostly Irish. Its social conscience was expressed mainly through ameliorative work. Cardinal Manning's concern for social reform aligned him more with the leaders of other churches rather than his own. Up to the 1970s English Roman Catholic leaders supported the *status quo*. During the two wars it gave much more uncritical support to the state than any other church. The Encyclical *Rerum Novarum* (1891) was a new beginning after previous negative attitudes to the modern world. It rejected both *laissez-faire* and socialism and upheld the right of workers to join (Roman Catholic) trade unions. Its message was ambiguous, but left-leaning Roman Catholics proclaimed it as the 'Workers' Charter'. John Wheatley, the first prominent Roman Catholic in the Labour party, was the most successful minister in the 1924 Labour Government. After the war, the Anglo-Irish Treaty and the decline of the Liberals opened the door for more Roman Catholics to support Labour. But Roman Catholic leaders were divided about Labour. When Wheatley as a young man campaigned for socialism around Glasgow, he was denounced from the pulpit and his effigy was burnt outside his house. But gradually he became acceptable to his fellow Roman Catholics and became an MP in 1922. Opposition to Labour's socialism continued among leading Roman Catholics until the 1960s.

For some, like Eric Gill and Conrad Noel, socialism was primarily a way of life. There were several small Christian Socialist societies. Many of their leading members were clergy who as Nonconformists or Anglo-Catholics were happiest as a perpetual opposition in church and state. That mentality helped to keep Labour out of power for most of this century.

State socialism seemed a natural development after the growth of state power during both wars. But a minority rejected state socialism. Fr Neville Figgis CR (1866–1919), an Anglican monk and a pioneer of pluralist thought, influenced Harold Laski, G. D. H. Cole and Ernest Barker. Figgis believed that freedom was the goal of politics and that power could corrupt and therefore should be dispersed in church and state. He rejected the concept of the general will and the monist state, insisting that the state should be a community of communities. In recent years, David Nicholls (1936–96) Anglican priest and political scientist, has powerfully restated Figgis's socialist pluralism (Nicholls, 1994).

The appointment of William Temple (1881–1944) as Bishop of Manchester in 1921 (Archbishop of York 1929–42, of Canterbury 1942–44) indicated a leftward shift in the leadership of the Church of England in the postwar period. R. H. Tawney, a CSU member, a close friend of Temple, Gore and Beveridge, made clear his Christian Socialist faith in *The Acquisitive Society* (1921) and *Religion and the Rise of Capitalism* (1926). The posthumous publication of his *Commonplace Book* (1972) was further evidence of that faith. Tawney, like Gore, Holland and Temple wanted to moralize economics. Capitalism was ungodly because it destroyed fellowship and idolatrous in its pursuit of wealth (Terrill, 1974) but the churches' work for a new eirenic spirit in industry was shattered by the General Strike. Partly by accident, the cautious Randall Davidson, Archbishop of Canterbury, emerged as 'the workers' friend' because the BBC refused to broadcast his proposals. Cardinal Bourne, anxious to demonstrate loyalty to the state, described the strike as 'a sin against the obedience we owe to God' (Mews, 1976; Oliver, 1968; Wilkinson, 1996).

In the 1930s, Christian Socialist pacifists still clung to the belief that there was a latent international harmony which could be actualized by negotiation. But theology was moving away from the goodness of creation and incarnation to the struggle and conflict of the cross, influenced by the American political theologian, Reinhold Niebuhr. He argued that Christianity's role was to deflate utopianism and unrealistic hopes which took no account of human sin and failure (Wilkinson, 1986, pp. 206–17). It looks as if Frank Field has been influenced by Niebuhr. Temple's phrase that 'the primary form of love in social organization is Justice' and his insistence that the politician must harness self-interest to the common good were both Niebuhrian. From 1940 Temple campaigned to persuade the churches and the nation to accept a very different type of society after the war, and Labour's victory owes something to these efforts. He had coined the term 'welfare state' in 1928. Pamphlets explaining his 1941 Malvern Conference on Christianity and Society sold over one million copies. His *Christianity and Social Order*, a Penguin Special, sold 139 000 copies (Temple, 1942). He took its message all over the country in a series of meetings, supported by Sir Stafford Cripps whose Anglican faith had revived under Temple's influence. Temple's political programme in his book had been vetted by Keynes and Tawney and was similar to that of the 1945 government, though more radical; for example, he proposed 'withering capital'. But he did not anticipate pluralism and assumed that after the war, Britain would accept Christianity as the basis of reconstruction (Suggate, 1987). Temple died before the Labour government was elected. But Cripps in an election broadcast asked Christian listeners to be 'selfless guardians of our neighbours' and servants of the community (Bryant, 1997, pp. 350–1). Like Attlee, he came from a family with a strong sense of social obligation. Frank Pakenham (now Lord Longford), as Minister for the British Zone of Germany 1947–48, memorably embodied Christian compassion and reconciliation. He had learned *noblesse oblige* as an Irish Anglican. He became a Roman Catholic but it was difficult being socialist as well. In the 1930s significant elements in English Roman Catholicism supported Franco. In 1945 the *Tablet* advised its readers to vote Conservative. Roman Catholic opinion was bitterly divided about the welfare state until the 1960s (Buchanan, 1996; Stanford, 1994).

In the postwar period, Christian Socialism rested on its laurels and looked back to Temple. Between 1945 and 1979 Anglican bishops criticized particular policies, but basically the churches trusted the intentions of the various governments. So when Margaret Thatcher's panzer divisions swept over the Maginot Line it was ill-defended with obsolete equipment. Several of Labour's leading figures were self-confessed rationalists. Labour had lost its Christian roots. Under Thatcherism, church leaders emerged to defend the wartime consensus, and suddenly appeared radical, when they were in fact appealing to the past. In their new role as leaders of the opposition, they were aided by three factors. First, Thatcher moved the debate on to a theological plane by presenting her policies in the language of nineteenth-century Christian Political Economy. (Clark, 1993) Second, the churches had learned a good deal about radical social theology from their world-wide networks. This was typified by *Bias to the Poor* (1983) by David Sheppard, Bishop of Liverpool. He played a leading role on Archbishop Runcie's Commission which produced *Faith in the City* (1985) an indictment of urban poverty. The Church Urban Fund, one result of the report, has raised enough from the dioceses to be able to award £29 million by 1998 to over 1300 inner city projects. The press conducted a programme of unprecedented ferocity against Runcie for his opposition to the policies and spirit of Thatcherism (Hastings, 1991). Third, the appointment of Basil Hume as Archbishop of Westminster in 1976 ended a long tradition of political conservatism by English Roman Catholic leaders. He tellingly voiced his distress, often in consort with other churches, about what he regarded as damaging government policies. As part of the theological response to Thatcherism, Roman Catholic social teaching emerged from the shadows. Despite its lofty tone and frequent ambiguities, it attracted Christian Socialists by its teaching on the common good and subsidiarity, by its condemnation of unrestrained capitalism, and its passion for social justice. Its themes were restated by the bishops in *The Common Good* published before the 1997 General Election.

After years of friction between Downing Street and Lambeth, it was a remarkable moment when on 9 September 1997 George Carey became the first Archbishop of Canterbury ever to address the TUC Congress. He was given a standing ovation. He claimed that the churches had been in the forefront of challenges to 'monetarism' and 'one-eyed individualism', quoted *The Common Good* on workers' rights and Tawney's celebration of the revolutionary character of the Magnificat. The congress applauded his references to Bishop Sheppard and welcomed the churches' report *Unemployment and the Future of Work* (1997) chaired by him.

It was a turning point in the revival of Christian Socialism when John Smith, as Labour leader, made clear the faith which motivated him in the 1993 Tawney Lecture. A Scottish Presbyterian and influenced by the Iona community, he paid tribute to Tawney's ethical socialism. Politics 'ought to be a moral activity and we should never feel inhibited in stressing the moral basis of our approach'. He celebrated Temple for recognizing the role of self-interest in society and yet rejecting the *homo economicus*. Though he only mentioned God once and made clear that he was not suggesting that all Christians should be socialists, the *Daily Telegraph* responded with 'Sanctimonious Smith' and *Tribune* warned 'Labour must not abandon secularism'. Smith had joined the Christian Socialist Movement, an ecumenical group founded in 1960. It affiliated to the Labour Party in 1986. By 1996 it claimed seven members of the shadow cabinet and 40 MPs among its 4000 members. After years when agnostics were in control of Labour, this growth of both Christian Socialism and the CSM is remarkable. It is also striking that in a party in which Anglicans have been rather few, three posts of particular moral responsibility have been filled by Anglicans – Tony Blair, Jack Straw and Frank Field. Both Blair and Straw were confirmed as adults – Straw as recently as 1989. All three have turned their backs on much of the ethical libertarianism of the 1960s. Field and Blair have written more than other Labour MPs about their faith, so we will conclude by examining their views.

Frank Field's life exemplifies those qualities of Christian citizenship, hard work and self-help he commends to the nation. He admires those like Thatcher, Tony Blair and Bishop George Bell who have stood alone for their beliefs – as he has had to do. But he is not partisan and gave the 1998 Keith Joseph Memorial Lecture.

First, in welfare Field proposes a new balance between the individual and the state. He complains that the Labour Party has been too concerned with changing structures without changing individuals. He often praises the Victorian Friendly Societies for combining self-help and mutual support with sanctions against the dishonest and rewards for good behaviour. He believes that it was in 'the replacement of those self-governing guilds and societies by top-down state provision that much of today's welfare ills are to be found' (Field, 1997, p. 27). Beveridge cut the link between welfare and self-improvement; it is the government's intention to restore it. Like Figgis, he distinguishes between the government which is only one body in the state, and the whole community, which includes many groups.

Second, Field represents that resurgence of the ethical tradition in the party associated with Tawney and more recently with Norman Dennis and A. H. Halsey whose *English Ethical Socialism* (1988) was a landmark. Dennis, in *The Invention of Permanent Poverty* (1997), scornfully rejects the 'no fault' theory of human behaviour. Halsey believes that 'the decline in the nuclear family is not merely at the root of many social evils but is the cancer in the lungs of the modern left'. Melanie Phillips praises Field for re-siting welfare within a 'framework of moral judgements' which had been swept away by a Marxist view of individuals as victims. Field himself believes that 'single parenthood is the major cause of family poverty' and advocates cutting 'the supply route' to it by changes in welfare and education and by cutting the routes to the creation of 'young unskilled unemployable males'. Welfare is not morally neutral and can teach 'idleness, fecklessness and dishonesty' (Field, 1996, pp. 24, 69, 97–8; Field, 1997, pp. 28, 29, 47–8). One of its roles is to teach values, 'To reward and to punish' by self-selection through willingness or unwillingness to accept conditions for benefit (Field, 1996, p. 111). Like Tawney, he believes that all human projects must take into account the Christian belief that human beings are fallen, but also are capable of being redeemed. He severely criticizes Richard Titmuss, whose views dominated postwar theories on social policy, for over-estimating human altruism and for underestimating human sin – a 'dangerous' and 'futile' legacy (Field, 1997, pp. 30–1). Instead, like Temple, Field advocates the use of self-interest to promote the common good (a crucial concept for Field), for example to persuade the better-off that it is in their interests to help the poor.

Adapting Prayer-Book language he explains 'the inward meaning of equality is given an outward expression in welfare's incorporation' (Field, 1996, p. 37).

Tony Blair has been called the most overtly Christian prime minister since Gladstone. Regular participation in the eucharist, whether Anglican or Roman Catholic, is central to his faith. It expresses for him the fact that 'the self is best realised through communion with others' (Bryant, 1993, p. 11). For the first time in its history, the Labour Party Conference service in 1997 was a eucharist, at Brighton parish church. Though Blair does not parade his faith, it gives a certain tone to his speeches. He exemplifies and promotes the recovery of ethical socialism: 'since the collapse of Communism, the ethical basis of socialism is the only one that has stood the test of time' (Bryant, 1996, p. 296). For some time he kept quiet about his faith but in 1991 joined the CSM. It was the Bulger crime in 1993 which led him as shadow Home Secretary to call for the country to be 'unafraid to start talking again about the values and principles we believe in. . . . We cannot exist in a moral vacuum' (Sopel, 1995, pp. 154–5). Christianity, he wrote, promotes change, but is not utopian and believes in the union of the individual and the community as in Holy Communion. Policies are time-bound, but when placed alongside Christianity, we discover timeless principles. It is

a very tough religion . . . judgemental. There is right and wrong. There is good and bad. We all know this, of course, but it has become fashionable to be uncomfortable about such language. (Bryant, 1993, pp. 9–12)

In his speech to the 1995 Party Conference he explored these themes in very biblical language:

I am my brother's keeper. I will not walk by on the other side. . . . [Your] child in distress is my child, your parent ill and in pain, is my parent: your friend unemployed or helpless, my friend: your neighbour my neighbour. (Blair, 1996, pp. 62, 71)

At Easter 1996 Blair took a great risk by writing an article for the *Sunday Telegraph* about his faith. He said he disliked politicians who 'wear God on their sleeves'; that he did not believe all Christians should vote Labour; that he only discussed his beliefs when asked. Christianity had led him to oppose the 'narrow view of self-interest' of modern Conservatism; Marxism suppressed the individual; but in Communion we start as individuals and are connected to the community. 'The Left got into trouble when its basic values became divorced from this ethical socialism, in which Christian socialism is included.' He presented himself as 'an ecumenical Christian', with a deep respect for other faiths. Christianity was both optimistic about human nature and knew our capacity for evil (Blair, 1996, pp. 57–61).

Blair's experience of community, apart from that of his family, has been of quasi-Benedictine institutions – Durham Choristers' School, Fettes, Oxford. At Fettes he helped with the chaplain's summer camps for slum children – as Attlee had once done. His references to community owe as much to the Bible and John Macmurray as to communitarians like Amitai Etzioni. Speaking at the celebrations of the tenth anniversary of *Faith in the City*, he called Temple 'perhaps Britain's greatest Christian Socialist', praised the report for exposing the consequences of economic individualism, called for a 'something for something' society and commended the vision of community in the writings of Chief Rabbi Jonathan Sacks (Blair, 1996, pp. 297–309).

Like Field, Blair admires Thatcher's readiness to stand for firm beliefs; unlike hers, his instincts are Anglican, inclusive and consensual. He seeks coalitions of interest:

> The ultimate objective is a new political consensus of the left-of-centre, based around the key values of democratic socialism and European social democracy. . . . To reach that consensus we must value the contribution of Lloyd George, Beveridge and Keynes and not just Attlee, Bevan and Crosland. We should start to explore our own history with fresh understanding and an absence of preconceptions. (Blair, 1996, p. 7)

When Blair redefines socialism, he sounds like Bishop Westcott quoted above. 'Socialism to me was never about nationalization or the power of the state; not just about economics or politics even. It is a moral purpose to life; a set of values; a belief in society, in cooperation, in achieving together what we are unable to achieve alone. It is how I try to live my life' (Blair, 1996, p. 62). He believes in devolving power, like Figgis and Temple. Sometimes he stands against consensus. We 'cannot be morally neutral about the family'. 'The breakup of family and community bonds is intimately linked to the breakdown in law and order' (Blair, 1996, pp. 68, 247, 249). He told the 1997 Labour Party conference: 'a decent society is not based on rights. It is based on duty. Our duty to each other.' Up to now, his references to Christianity have been ethically focused and thus acceptable to people of other faiths. But his Christian moralism has alarmed rationalists and libertarians.

These are very early days in the lifetime of this government. But certain interim questions arise. First, like many politicians (but unlike Field) Blair offers millennial visions but says little of the flaws in all human achievement. He is excited by modernity. This is better than the Merrie England of socialist nostalgia. But modernity can tyrannize. Second, both Field and Blair address their exhortations mainly towards the disadvantaged. New Labour is reluctant to challenge the wealthy about their moral responsibilities. A government which morally exhorts ought to have more austerity about its lifestyle. Third, there is an unresolved tension between Blair's libertarianism about gay rights and gender and his rejection of it over the family. What happens when pluralism threatens the common good? Fourth, Blair and Field are committed to remoralize society. But where is the ethical consensus to come from to make this possible? From the churches? From religious schools which probably they would like to multiply? What sanctions would society accept against those who reject conditions attached to welfare? Fifth, can the market be reconciled with the Christian critique of acquisitiveness?

A faith based on stories is more dynamic and flexible than an ideology. Wittingly or unwittingly, Blair has redefined Labour in ways which bring him closer to the minority tradition within Christian Socialism which was more biblical than ideological, favoured devolution more than statism, co-partnership more than nationalization, and which offered a paternalism which enabled but which asked for responsible citizenship in return. Tony Blair could discover precedents for his revisionism in a tradition which goes back to F. D. Maurice in 1848.

5 Media Management: Labour's Political Communications Strategy
Richard Heffernan

In an age when electors derive the majority of their political information from the news media, political parties are obliged to utilize television and the press to communicate with them. Parties have been using forms of mass communication to advance their partisan cause for the whole of the twentieth century. Political communications, the messages constructed through the mediated interaction of parties, mass media and electors are nothing new. Political campaigning is fought out in the news media because press and broadcast reportage are an integral part of elective politics. Parties attempt to turn this fact to their advantage by successfully projecting themselves through the media to the electorate-as-audience. This is now a significant feature of the political landscape, a widespread and increasingly sophisticated element not just of the modern professional election campaign but of daily political activity.

LABOUR AND THE NEWS MEDIA

The ability to secure favourable media coverage can help boost a party's popularity and public standing. Long-established features of the political scene such as the sound-bite and the photo-opportunity, the campaign consultant and the spin doctor are deemed even more important today (Franklin 1994; Kavanagh 1996; Scammell 1995; Rosenbaum 1997). In common with 'old' Labour, New Labour recognizes that political communications provide a set of strategies enabling the party to package itself as a product to be sold in the electoral marketplace. Since the mid-1980s, Labour has dramatically and systematically placed modern and professionalized media communications at the heart of its everyday appeal. Here, in the general elections of 1987, 1992 and 1997 (indeed throughout the permanent election campaigns of 1987–92 and 1992–97) political communications were in the forefront of its vote-gathering activities. Even when the party was electorally unsuccessful it praised itself, and was praised, for having won the campaign at the same time as it lost the election. Effectively presenting the case the party was making was considered as important as the case itself; indeed, because the communications strategy was unable to sell the policy product of 1987 or 1992, the product was deemed faulty and worthy of change. Effectively presenting Labour as a new, modernized 'saleable product' was part and parcel of efforts by Tony Blair and other Labour 'modernizers' to market and sell the attendant changes in policy and organization evidenced in the gradual emergence of New Labour after the benchmark of the 1983 General Election.

Labour's stance is an acknowledgement of the symbiotic association of political parties (as one set of actors) and the news media in the production of news. In common with other political actors, Labour has been actively engaged in attempting to produce the message it wishes to promote at the same time as controlling the manner in which it is presented by the media and ultimately consumed by the identified audience. Political news agendas are the outcome of the interaction of political actors, news media and citizens (Blumler and Gurevitch, 1995; McNair, 1996). Labour's political communication strategies are designed to influence its news media profile to favourably affect the way the electors perceive the party. Through judicious deployment of communications strategies, Labour's objective is to influence news-media outlets in order to influence their interpretation of events. It attempts to do this by either positively promoting itself or else negatively attacking its opponents (Heffernan and Stanyer, 1997, 1998).

In contrast to the news media's need to independently interrogate the activities of political parties, Labour's objective is to successfully 'sell' itself through favourable publicity. This is why it is so concerned to secure as positive a media profile as possible. Labour seeks any opportunity to command the news agenda. Its communications objective is to reduce the autonomy the news media has to report the party while simultaneously strengthening its own autonomy to project a favoured public identity. Despite the best endeavours of competing political organizations, the news media can and do serve as an autonomous forum for different interests and various points of view. The news media have to be managed; they cannot be commanded. Obviously, Labour does not control the 'media space' within which it operates; other actors, such as other party political opponents and the news media themselves, matter. Events also serve to drive the news agenda forward. Nonetheless, Labour devotes considerable time and resources to its attempts to shape public opinion by managing the information received by the public through the news media. Sometimes it succeeds (and succeeds spectacularly); at other times it fails.

The construction of political information produced by the interaction of political actors and the news media is subject to public consideration, analysis and interpretation. Autonomous and critical news media play an independent role in 'encoding' political messages that are 'decoded' by the electorate. Labour's principal objective is to limit the autonomy of the media and blunt their critical facilities in relation to their reportage of themselves. It does so by attempting to influence the 'encoding' process (Heffernan and Stanyer, 1997, 1998). Communicating is now an integral part of the construction of Labour's political message, not an add-on or an afterthought. In all its forms of public communications Labour consistently emphasizes the importance of a unified message, one developed through a series of common themes through which all party actors speak with one voice. This 'corporate image' is central to media management. Successful or unsuccessful media management becomes routine, almost standardized. Leadership speeches, policy launches, party conferences and rallies, party events, parliamentary interventions, by-election victories, even the domestic lives of leading party figures, all became 'public events' to be scripted and shaped by party media managers and deployed for news-media consumption in the effort to attract favourable public attention.

Thus, modern media management requires parties to dominate the campaign agenda by exploiting professional methods of publicity-gathering. Labour devotes considerable financial and physical resources to this activity. These are invariably developed by the party's 'strategic community' of media managers, typified by Alastair Campbell and Peter Mandelson, part of an interlocking network at the party's 'political centre' directed by the inner circle of Blair supporters. Labour's 'strategic community' is best symbolized by Millbank, which became the operational headquarters of Labour's 1994–97 'permanent election campaign'; it was set up in January 1996. The much-commented-on Millbank phenomenon draws its name from Millbank Tower where Labour's communications and research teams were housed in a 15 000-square-foot office space, a 'state of the art' campaign high-tech 'war room' based on the Little Rock headquarters of the 1992 Clinton campaign. Costing some £2 000 000, Millbank was the nerve centre of the Labour campaign. Headed by Peter Mandelson, appointed Labour's Chief Election Strategist by Blair in late 1995, Labour's 'media centre' employed some 250 party workers at the height of the 1997 campaign (Butler and Kavanagh, 1998).

In addition to traditional campaign methods emphasizing electronic news-gathering, steps were taken to enhance Labour's publicity profile by a number of 'attack and rebuttal' strategies. A Media Monitoring Unit allowed Labour to respond effectively to breaking news-stories by providing spokespersons with a 24-hour supply of the latest developments in the news. If information is power, Excalibur, a sophisticated storage and retrieval database costing some £300 000, also provided the campaign team with detailed information on the Conservatives and the Liberal Democrats (input from speeches, statements, policy documents, press and broadcast reports). In providing Labour with on-hand information about its own policy profile and press/broadcast reportage, Excalibur proved a very useful asset to Labour in its efforts to command the news agenda. 'Focus groups' organized by a team led by in-house PR consultant Philip Gould helped 'test out' Labour's 'product', exploring the best way to 'package' what the party was offering the electorate while ensuring there was as close a link as possible between Labour's aspirations and voter expectations.

As a result of Labour's staggering election victory in May 1997, Millbank was widely reported as a great success. Not one for hiding his light under a bushel, Mandelson echoed the observations of any number of commentators in describing Millbank ('my Millbank' he was reported as often saying (Jones, 1997)), as 'the finest, most professional campaigning machine that Labour has ever created' (*New Labour, New Life for Britain*, January 1997). Since May 1997, the Millbank model has been successfully taken into government. While Millbank is in many ways a shadow of its former self, its staff dramatically reduced with key personnel either recruited into government as ministerial aides or else, as with David Hill, formally Chief Press and Broadcasting Officer, employed by a lobbying/PR company, the highways and byways of Labour's Whitehall teem with would-be political communicators, all working to 'Millbank methods' to promote the Labour Government in its declared quest for the elusive second term. Essentially, Millbank has been mothballed for financial reasons, to be revived in its former glory when Labour replenishes its war-chest and the next general election draws nearer. Of course, Millbank did nothing new. It merely married existing campaign methods to new forms and did so more systematically and effectively than any party opponent.

THE MEDIA MANAGERS

In establishing a centralized election campaign, Labour's campaign managers placed great weight on the party being collectively 'on message'. Thus, the national, professionalized, centralized media operation superseded all local campaigns. Indeed, with regard to parliamentary elections, and increasingly other local elections as well, the locality is no longer an independent unit. While nominally accountable to the wider Labour Party in the form of the National Executive Committee (NEC) on which Blair enjoys strong support, Millbank is in reality under the direct control of the Blairite leadership. As with most contemporary political parties, the freedom of action of nominally autonomous Labour Party institutions such as the Parliamentary Party, the NEC and the Party Conference has been limited and power decanted from these bodies and invested in tightly knit formal and informal insider groups reporting to the collegial leadership. Labour's 'media managers' are in essence 'leadership insiders', an integral resource of the party leadership (Heffernan and Marqusee, 1992; Shaw, 1994, 1996; Anderson and Mann, 1997). Spin doctors, press officers, advertising agents, public relations advisers, pollsters and other technical experts all work to the party elite. Senior members of this media community form part of an interlocking network of formal institutions and *ad hoc* groupings which derive their power from their association with Tony Blair and his closest political associates.

The purchase that its strategic communications community has within Labour's ranks arises from the freedom of manoeuvre granted the party leadership after 1983. The control over Labour's campaigns and communications achieved by Neil Kinnock through first, Peter Mandelson in 1985–90 and, second, the Shadow Communications Agency of 1985–92 led by Philip Gould (and its informal post-1992 successors also organized by Gould) paved the way for Tony Blair to control communications first in opposition and then, with all the resources governmental office brings, from Downing Street. Building on Kinnock's internal reforms, Blair established a 'political centre' from which the leadership, in concert with other key players from the Shadow Cabinet and the

Cabinet, can exercise a 'command' over the party. While political communications strategies were previously only influenced by the leadership, they are now in practice controlled by the leadership. The emergence of modern forms of political communications goes hand in hand with the centralization of power and authority within political parties. Labour is far less pluralistic than it was, a feature of significant changes in the party's internal governance. Great efforts are made to characterize Blair's leadership as a 'personalised presidentialism'. This image is driven forward by organizational reform of the Labour party and by the natural prerogatives that accrue to any British prime minister able to demonstrate a commonality of purpose and strong electoral standing. Without doubt, it is certainly enhanced by the use of public relations political communications strategies.

Building on the practices of its predecessors, Labour has made Downing Street the focal point of all government communications. 'Spin' as much as 'strategy' has been an indispensable feature of Labour's approach to government since 1997. An over-reliance on spin doctors and public relations generally is a criticism levelled at Labour in office. The activities of senior government figures close to the prime-ministerial centre, like Alastair Campbell, Blair's Chief Press Secretary and a powerful unelected adviser, and Peter Mandelson, in the Cabinet, have drawn much publicity (McSmith, 1996). As part of Blair's 'political centre' its media messengers help 'control the message'. Labour's communications community can influence not only how Labour promotes its policy but what its actual policy is. On taking up his post as Labour's communication supremo back in 1985, Peter Mandelson defined his role as 'deciding what we say, how we say it, and which spokespersons and women we choose to say it' (*Guardian*, 25 November 1985). Of course, such professionals, while key politicians in their own right, do not do so as they would themselves wish. Their ability to influence Labour's agenda derives exclusively from the prerogatives of the party leadership. Their power is nonetheless significant; they remain 'functional deciders' and wield considerable influence within the quasi-medieval court which lies at the heart of Labour's political elite.

The close association between the exercise of political power and responsibility for the dissemination of Labour's message was tellingly illustrated in opposition by the so-called Gould Memorandum leaked to *Guardian* journalist Seamus Milne in September 1995. This private document, written by Blair's *ad hoc* communications adviser Philip Gould, called for a 'unitary command structure leading directly to the party leader' which would instal the leader as 'sole ultimate source of campaigning authority' heading up a 'cohesive, integrated political party sharing the same political ideology' (*Guardian*, September 1996). At the time Gould was in effect reporting what had already been agreed among those far closer to Blair. The term 'spin doctor' is therefore in many ways a misnomer. As part of the leader's inner circle the influence of senior news-media managers such as Peter Mandelson and Alastair Campbell cannot be overestimated. As opposed to functionary press officers, their ability to advise on policy and media strategy confers on them very real political power.

The centralization of government communications in Downing Street, and its outpost in the Cabinet Office, is overseen by Campbell and Mandelson. Despite an image as Labour's 'spin-doctor-in-chief', one he is forever keen to play down, Peter Mandelson is a politician and not a media professional. A brief stint as a television producer on LWT's *Weekend World* in the early 1980s called for a familiarity with Westminster Labour politics rather than media expertise. As illustrated by his appointment as Chief Election Strategist, in 1995–97, the equivalent of Chairman of the Conservative Party, Mandelson is no run-of-the-mill political communicator. Mandelson is one of Blair's Whitehall 'troubleshooters', a political actor with both power and influence arising from his proximity to Blair. Mandelson chairs the daily meeting of the Committee for the Communication and Presentation of Government Policy, an informal Official Committee with considerable powers comprising key Downing Street officials as well as representatives of other key governmental actors, most notably Gordon Brown.

While Mandelson is a key figure, the dominant figure influencing Labour's communication strategies is the Downing Street Press Secretary, Alastair Campbell. With his deputies Tim Allen (to May 1998) and Hilary Coffman he plays the significant role within the committee Mandelson chairs. A very close confidante of the Prime Minister, Campbell has had responsibility for the Labour leader's press relations since 1994. He is now the chief government spokesperson, able to command the attention of the parliamentary press lobby and help direct the work of Millbank Tower. As a 'special adviser' to the Prime Minister, Campbell is one of his key right-hand men, a senior counsel, and very much in the 'Downing Street loop'. The fact that he has authority over senior civil servants granted him through an Order in Council marks him out as anything other than a functional press secretary. Thanks to his position within the Blair centre he is a major player within the Labour government:

> Blair never moves from Downing Street without Campbell. He never appears on a platform without Campbell nearby. Never makes a speech that Campbell has not read or rewritten. Never walks into an important room without Campbell close behind. Never takes a decision that Campbell has not been consulted on. Never holds a significant meeting that Campbell does not attend or at least know about. Other Cabinet ministers slavishly repeat Campbell's latest line on the latest twist of governmental policy in their broadcast interviews. Not *vice versa*. With a salary of £87,936, he is even paid more than a Cabinet minister. (Kevin Toolis, 'The Enforcer', *Guardian*, 4 April 1998)

Campbell also attends meetings of the Cabinet and its Committees, albeit in a non-speaking role. Of course, as with powerful 'political' predecessors like Joe Haines and the ubiquitous Bernard Ingham, Press Secretaries to Harold Wilson and Margaret Thatcher respectively, Campbell is a singularly different Press Secretary to Gus O'Donnell, Christopher Meyer and Jonathan Haslam, 'non-political' civil servants who served John Major. Nonetheless, Campbell's power derives from the Prime Minister. He has no independent power base. Political correspondents listen to him because he is the 'voice of Blair'; ministers listen to him because he has the ear of the Prime Minister. Campbell is also responsible for the Government's Strategic Communications Unit, which is run from Downing Street. Its objective is to coordinate government initiatives and so ensure that announcements are made in a structured and coherent manner. Blair's ministerial handbook, a new version of *Questions of Procedures for Ministers* published in August 1997 entitled *Ministerial Conduct*, makes it clear that Downing Street must approve all speeches, press releases and new initiatives as well as decide upon their timing and presentation: 'all major interviews and media appearances, both print and broadcast, should be agreed with the No. 10 Press Office before any commitments are entered into' (Cabinet Office, *Ministerial Conduct*, London: HMSO, 1997). Departmental officials have also been instructed to keep a record of their ministers' media contacts. This grants significant theoretical powers to the prime-ministerial centre and to Downing Street insiders such as Alastair Campbell. Few ambitious but relatively powerless ministers would be willing to disregard such instructions should they consider their future preferment depends upon prime-ministerial largesse.

Acting for Blair, Campbell regularly advises (read: and can instruct) ministers on their media strategies. In March 1998, two faxes sent by Campbell under his name, not that of the Prime Minister, rebuking Social Security ministers Harriet Harman and Frank Field for unauthorized briefing of the press raised a great many eyebrows. Of course, significant actors within the Whitehall village with power bases of their own can effectively disregard any official Downing Street 'advice'. Others may leak and brief privately. Chancellor of the Exchequer Gordon Brown immediately springs to mind. With his own press operation headed by his spokesperson Charlie Whelan, a spin doctor outside the control of the Downing Street centre, Brown can successfully pitch his own messages to the news media. Other ministers may choose to do so more covertly. Blair's several entreaties to persuade Brown to dispense with Whelan's service have so far been unheeded by the Chancellor. Whelan is to Brown what Campbell is for Blair; however Campbell speaks with the authority of the Prime Minister on behalf of the whole government, while Whelan speaks only as a (usually) transparent 'Treasury source' for Brown. Overall, ministerial (and official) media leaking and briefing is part and parcel of the Whitehall village; the Blair centre can restrict it but cannot indefinitely prevent it. Nevertheless, Campbell and Blair are for the moment very keen to try, and have done so with considerable success.

MANAGING THE MEDIA

Two forms of political communication can be identified in Labour's approach to the news media. Political marketing involves the long-term promotion of the political party as a product, fashioning policy and appeal in light of certain designated goals, most usually successful office-seeking (Harrop, 1990; Scammell, 1995). It need not necessarily involve the day-to-day media strategy which links it to the outside world. This is where public relations forms of political communica-tions enable parties to communicate through the news media by managing its broadcast and print-journalist profile on a day-to-day basis (McNair, 1996; Heffernan and Stanyer, 1997). Here, the 'corporate identity' constructed through political marketing is 'sold' by the application of public relations methods. In turn, public relations strategies usually fall into one of two categories: proactive initiatives deployed by the party in an effort to seize the day-to-day agenda and so cumulatively build up a positive news-media profile and reactive initiatives where the party responds to news-events not of its own making which impact on that profile. New Labour places a high premium on both political marketing and public relations.

Of course, marketing the Labour Party did not begin with the invention of the red rose in 1986, nor with Tony Blair's accession to the leadership. Public relations communication methods are not new either. Nonetheless, Labour has systematically incorporated both approaches into its campaigning style. Labour wants to be seen as 'moderate', 'new', 'trustworthy', 'dynamic' and, most of all, of 'sufficient governing stature'. The best example of a recent marketing strategy is the invention of New Labour as a concept, one which distinguishes the reformed political party from an 'old-fashioned', 'out-dated', 'extremist', 'old' Labour predecessor. This was wholly played out through the news media. First mentioned in Blair's speech to the 1994 Labour Conference as part of the new leader's successful attempt to stamp his arrival upon party and public, the phrase 'New Labour' has well and truly stuck, a convenient shorthand for the modernized political organization fashioned since 1983. This unofficial rebranding is part of Labour's great efforts to establish a new corporate identity, a marketing strategy sold by means of public relations in order to attract electoral support to fulfil the party's office-seeking goal. To this end Labour is naturally keen to use the Parliamentary lobby as a public-relations communication resource; albeit one that is not as reliable (for Labour's purposes) as its media managers would like. Of course, there is nothing particularly new in this, either; all parties do likewise. Labour at present often does it better than most.

Millbank staffers assiduously bring their campaign techniques and tactics to bear on political correspondents. The daily exchange between journalists and Labour news-managers is one often fuelled by mutual dependence and antagonism. 'Millbank methods' set out to encourage reportage that casts the party in a favourable light, discouraging that which casts Labour in an unfavourable light. In accentuating the positive, media managers are as ruthless as they can be; hands-on and attempting to control the flow of information and restrict the autonomy of the media. Here, Labour attempts to 'construct' political news by deploying a series of proactive public-relations initiatives as well as attempting to respond successfully to news-events which affect the party but are not necessarily of its own making. Getting its message across involves Labour interacting with news and current-affairs journalists from a variety of media outlets (Jones, 1996).

As a former member of the parliamentary lobby, Alastair Campbell is a poacher turned gamekeeper, keen to influence journalist reportage by whatever means available. By cultivating some journalists and threatening others, Labour can offer incentives (inside information, initial coverage of Labour news events, personal access to senior Labour figures) and disincentives (exclusion from sources, intemperate criticism and dressing down, barring access to Labour figures) in equal measure. Campbell's abrasive style has elicited much comment. It is part of routine efforts to encourage reportage that casts Blair and his government in as good a light as possible. While television news provides much of the primary information consumed by the electorate, Labour's campaign strategists devote considerable attention to the broadsheets and highbrow radio. They all too often set the agenda broadcasters follow, although broadcast media can frequently alter news stories projected by the broadsheet press. With a Labour voting readership comprising both activists and supporters, *The Guardian* is considered a very important outlet, even though its reportage is much disliked by the Labour high command. *The Times*, with its large readership, is increasingly important, as are the quality Sunday newspapers. Other primary outlets include BBC Radio's *Today* programme, *The World at One*, *PM*, and *The World This Weekend*, widely considered 'primary definers' within the 'news producing community', as well as the nightly television news bulletins and news magazine programmes (Jones, 1997).

From 1994, at the urging of Alastair Campbell, greater emphasis was placed on the tabloid press, previously very hostile to Labour, with the exception of the Mirror group. Tabloids provide a mass readership numbering in their millions which Labour can address directly. While Blair succeeded in moderating the longstanding hostility of the Tory-supporting *Daily Mail* and *Daily Express*, his careful courting of the tabloids paid off in the decision of Murdoch's News International titles (specifically the *Sun* and the *News of the World*) to back Labour at the 1997 election. Relations between Labour and Murdoch newspapers were at rock-bottom in the 1980s and early 1990s. This changed dramatically following Blair's accession to the leadership in 1994. Following a series of private meetings, the Labour leader accepted Murdoch's invitation to address a News Corporation Conference in Australia in July 1995. Although strong denials were made that any private deal was struck, Labour did move closer to Murdoch and heavily qualified its past support for media regulation. For its part, News International swung heavily behind Blair-led Labour. An accommodation, if not a deal, was obviously reached.

Blair's relations with Murdoch's News International continue to generate interest. The decision of Campbell's deputy Tim Allen (a long-serving Blair staffer) to leave government service for an executive post with BSkyB and the Government's opposition to a Liberal Democrat Lords amendment outlawing predatory newspaper pricing (aimed at *The Times*) attracted attention in early 1998. The story of Blair's alleged attempt to lobby Italian Prime Minister Prodi on behalf of Murdoch's attempts to buy Berlusconi's media empire is another. While withholding details, the government, in the guise of Alastair Campbell, strongly denied that Blair was batting for Murdoch, claiming that Prodi had initiated the telephone conversation with Blair and that Blair was not doing anything for Murdoch that he would not do for other comparable British companies. While charges of improper use of prime-ministerial office do not stick, the relationship between Blair and Murdoch is significant. It is reported that they have regular face-to-face meetings at least every six months. It is interesting to note that News International titles always couched their support in terms of 'for Blair' the personality rather than Labour, the party. This is a significant departure from News International's relentless Kinnock-bashing (to say nothing of Michael Foot) of the 1980s and early 1990s.

MEDIA MANAGEMENT STRATEGIES

Labour takes the view that any initiative will be wasted if it is not widely and fully reported. Broadcast and broadsheet comment is carefully cultivated and coverage from the tabloid end of the newspaper market is encouraged. 'Public events' such as major speeches; policy announcements; government decisions and initiatives; media interviews; press releases and press conferences can help favourably influence the news media agenda and so benefit Labour. Timing announcements and targeting public events helps ensure maximum impact. While being an event in its own right, each initiative provides an opportunity to set up a series of favourable news stories.

Consistently warning itself against complacency, Labour in government often appears to prefer negotiating future obstacles rather than congratulating itself on straits already navigated. Blair himself is continually aware of the need for 'good publicity'. Back in May 1997, Labour made sure it hit the ground running. A plan for the activities of the 'first day' in office was carefully drawn up during the election itself followed by outlines for the 'first week' and, ultimately, the 'first month'. While Labour gave a great deal of attention to its first 'hundred days', the first anniversary was dramatically played down, the Government keen to avoid any possible backlash (although the G7 Summit held in Birmingham in May and the European Council in Cardiff in June were used as discreet showcases for Labour in government). Blair's tribute to Princess Diana following the announcement of her death in August 1997 is a masterful example of a public event. His remarks were delivered from a carefully constructed script drafted by Alastair Campbell and committed to memory by Blair. The deliberately crafted phrase 'the people's princess' caught the public mood. Showcasing the party and the government is the ultimate objective. To this end, great efforts are made to actively and continually promote a set of favourable messages. Constructing the message requires planning, planning and more planning.

Method is important. Labour prefers to deploy 'proactive' public relations strategies whenever possible; setting the news agenda rather than following it. Of course, the party is more often than not obliged to react to news agendas not of its own making. Warning the Government Information and Communications Service in October 1997 to 'raise its game and be at the heart of government', Alastair Campbell instructed press officers to be ahead of the game:

> We should always know how big stories will be playing in the next day's papers. If a story is going wrong, or if a policy should be defended, we must respond quickly, confidently and robustly. (*The Times*, 2 October 1997)

Obviously, Labour tries to 'prepackage' its proactive news agenda as effectively as it can. Campbell's memorandum, circulated to all Whitehall press officers, stated:

> My sense is that in many departments policy is discussed and developed on a completely separate track, and the media plan is then added on at a much later stage. We need to be in there at the start. (*The Times*, 2 October 1997).

Downing Street were extremely concerned that Whitehall focused on attempts at damage limitation at the expense of setting the agenda. Campbell complained that positive government announcements were not getting the attention they merited:

> The government must lay down big messages around every event . . . There are three parts to any story – the build-up, the event and the follow through. My sense is that the middle of these three gets all the attention. There is insufficient attention to advance publicity – the briefing of editors, feature writers and others both before and after. (*The Times*, 2 October 1997).

As a result, policy formation is itself a news event. Communicating that event forms part of a proactive strategy.

Of course, no government controls events; the Labour Government is no exception. More often than not it is obliged to respond to news stories outside its control, stories that if unchecked can significantly damage the government. The government is therefore obliged to respond to news events. Here, a reactive communications strategy has to be deployed. Numerous examples may be cited in Labour's first year in government. These range from the major incident to the minor: divisions between an 'off-message' Chancellor and Prime Minister over the Government's attitude to the UK joining EMU this Parliament; continuing press speculations regarding possible divisions within government centred on the relationship between Blair and Brown; the much-hyped question of 'sleaze' arising from Paymaster-General Geoffrey Robinson's offshore trust or Lord Simon's BP shareholding; stories concerning the drugs arrest of Jack Straw's son and Robin Cook's divorce; and the Lord Chancellor's supposedly 'exorbitant' refurbishment of his official residence. Labour's welfare reforms also elicited a great deal of critical commentary, particularly in light of the rebellion of 47 Labour MPs and the abstention of another 20 or so in the vote on benefit payments to single mothers in December 1997. The dangers of unfavourable media coverage were demonstrated in the furore over the exemption of Formula 1 racing from the ban on tobacco sponsorship in November 1997. The news that Blair had meetings with the head of Formula 1, Bernie Ecclestone, in the knowledge that Ecclestone had donated £1 million to Labour Party funds generated acres of critical news coverage. Stories of 'Labour sleaze' were only headed off by Blair's reactive decision to give a live interview on BBC TV to deny the accusations, apologize for his mishandling of the issue and successfully draw a line under the incident.

More interestingly, continuing media comment on the role of spin doctors within Labour government has generated negative publicity centred on Blair's governing style. Labour is often criticized not for what it does but for the way in which it makes policy. The significant influence Blair advisers exert from within Downing Street has attracted a great deal of attention and much criticism. The Commons Select Committee on Public Administration initiated an enquiry in May 1998 into the working of the Government Information and Communications Service and the role of spin doctors within Whitehall. Campbell and others have been called to give evidence. The Speaker, Betty Boothroyd, used a BBC interview in the spring of 1998 to make known her displeasure with Government attempts to use Parliament as a show-case for the Government by employing Government backbenchers to ask favourable questions of ministers. She also criticized ministers for persistently releasing information to the media before reporting them to Parliament, in breach of Commons protocol. Nonetheless, proactive and reactive public relations strategies are intended to limit the opportunities for journalists to interrogate what Labour is actually doing, so restricting news media autonomy. Journalists are encouraged to report rather than review events; to cover uncritically rather than comment unfavourably on Labour's activities.

SELF-REFERENTIAL IMPACTS OF POLITICAL COMMUNICATIONS

In either a proactive or a reactive form Labour's media strategy is to variously establish, influence, alter or reinforce the news agenda. The news media can be used to either promote Labour or attack the appeal and image of its opponents. In government as in opposition, political communications have provided a power-resource which enhances Tony Blair's authority and helps loosen the collegial con-straints that limit him. Within any nominally collegial executive there is no untrammelled leadership prerogative. Centralized control of political communications (showcasing the leader rather than the party; or, rather, the leader-as-party) provides one additional, and very important, resource which can make it less trammelled. Labour's political communication strategies help strengthen the party centre at the expense of the periphery. The Prime Minister's public utterances, or those delivered on his behalf by a favoured insider, can play a significant role in deciding the political direction of the government.

Examples abound of the efforts of the Blair leadership to use its near-monopoly of public relations and political marketing strategies to project its chosen profile. Where Blair speaks he is deemed to be speaking for his party. By utilizing the news media's preoccupation with political leaders, political communications strategies allow political leaders to lead from the front by establishing an identity the public and the party is obliged to note.

Thus, Tony Blair has been placed at the heart of the media projection of his party. It is a truism that modern media politics increasingly result in the marketing and packaging of the party leadership, not the wider political party; in the absence of wider political arguments, the leader is the personification of the party. Where John Major was portrayed as 'weak and indecisive', Blair is keen to be seen as 'strong and commanding'. Indeed, in opposition Blair made a virtue out of the fact that he commanded his party while Major was simply obliged to follow his. In contrast to Major, Blair is determined to be as proactive as possible, a Prime Minister in the Thatcher mould of 1983 or 1987, one eager to be seen to command events rather than simply react to them. That said, a political communications strategy will not necessarily make the weak leader strong. An army of spin doctors and campaign strategists would have made little or no difference, say, to the public persona and appeal of Michael Foot in 1983. No political marketer could successfully have sold the Conservatives to the electorate in 1997. Nonetheless, political communications can enhance the position of a powerful leader. The news media can be used to set the party's policy agenda just as much as critical news-coverage can undermine a party's national standing.

Of course, Labour may not always be collectively 'on-message'; indeed, its individual components may not have the same message. Parties do not necessarily speak with one voice, however much its leading lights wish that it did. Competing party actors can communicate to and about one another in a quest for personal or political advantage. Here, self-referential political communications involve Labour communicating with itself and the wider community of political commentators and not just the wider public. This is a significant feature of any political communications strategy. In 1996, evoking an image of figures drawn from a Stephen King novel, Labour MP Clare Short described Tony Blair's media advisers as 'people who live in the dark' (Heffernan and Stanyer, 1997), accusing these shadowy figures of exercising an undue influence, one above that of senior elected party figures. Unattributable briefings by a 'close supporter', 'senior aide' or 'spokesperson' of the party leader delivered on a lobby basis are the trade of the spin doctor, the source of information about the thinking and opinions of senior party figures.

Party figures often 'spin' against one another. Most usually, the party leadership uses the news media not only to communicate to its own party but to exercise its authority over the party. Leaks and briefings tell who is in, who is out, who is going up, who is going down, which policy is popular, which policy is unpopular. Clare Short herself fell foul of the spin doctors in opposition:

> When she publicly suggested [contrary to Shadow Cabinet policy] that under a fair tax system people like her 'would pay a bit more tax', Blair's office informed reporters that 'colleagues were questioning her competence and professionalism'. (Jones, 1997, p. 142)

TGWU General Secretary Bill Morris found himself publicly described by a unnamed leadership source in 1995 as 'confused, muddled and pusillanimous' for opposing the revisions of Clause Four (Jones, 1996a, p. xx). Other examples abound.

As significantly, covert disagreements among senior Labour figures all too often surface in the news media. A case in point are frictions between Tony Blair and Gordon Brown (and their various camp-followers) which surfaced in early 1998 following the publication of an 'unofficially authorized' biography of Brown (Routledge, 1998). The Chancellor and his closest aides had provided insider information for the book which emphasized continuing personal divisions between the two men arising from the inner-party tussle to succeed John Smith in May–June 1994. The book immediately became a media story. 'Sources' close to Blair eager to weaken Brown's standing as a covert rival to the Prime Minister publicly damned the book in unattributable briefings. A senior source inside Downing Street, widely assumed by the lobby to have been either Alastair Campbell or Peter Mandelson, claimed Brown had 'psychological flaws' and that his decision to sanction the book was a 'serious and silly move that weakens the Government' (*Observer*, 18 January 1998). These (and other) observations were later disowned by a Government desperate to play down divisions between Blair and Brown. Strategists all too often use the news media to publicly reprimand so-called dissident and would-be dissident Labour Party members, including members of the Cabinet and the Shadow Cabinet as well as backbench MPs. The object is to warn other members against stepping out of line (Heffernan and Marqusee, 1992; Heffernan and Stanyer, 1997;

N. Jones, 1996, 1997). Powerful players such as Brown also champion their cause through the news media. This and other examples of self-referential communication, the party speaking to itself (its centre, sub-centre and periphery sending messages to and about one another) forms part and parcel of any political communication process; it is a highly significant feature of Labour's media profile.

CONCLUSION

Claims by Peter Mandelson that political communications reflect the Labour Government's 'duty to explain' (Cabinet Office Press Release, 16 September 1997) should be taken lightly. In fact this Government, in common with all governments, has a 'mission to persuade'. Labour's political communications provide a means by which the party can successfully promote itself as a product within the electoral marketplace. Spin doctors 'explain, sell, justify, package' (*Guardian*, 6 October 1997). In addition, media reportage also encourages the presidentialization of politics common to all parties, because it enables political leaders to set the agenda within their own party. Thus, Labour's media strategies have consistently had the dual function of attracting attention to the party at the same time as they direct the attention of the party by advancing the particular agenda of the party leadership. In opposition and now in government, the Blair leadership routinely employs the news media to successfully sell itself in the electoral marketplace and also map out its preferred Labour strategy by agenda-setting within the party. To do these successfully the party has to employ communications strategies that blunt the critical edge of the news media whenever it is possible to do so. At this Labour has excelled.

Part II
State

6 The Constitution under New Labour
Mark Evans

INTRODUCTION

It remains a curious paradox in Britain's political history, that despite being the party which established the basis for a universal democratic way of life through the creation of the Welfare State and the National Health Service, Labour has until very recently remained unconcerned with constitutional and democratic matters. There have been some exceptions; for example, the Wilson governments of the 1960s and 1970s were responsible for both the creation of the Parliamentary Ombudsman and the introduction of legislation to confront racial and sexual discrimination, but it remains striking that agendas of constitutional reform have failed to gain the backing of the Labour leadership, at least when Labour has been in government. Indeed, the Labour Party has been characterized by what Anthony Wright (1990, p. 323) has termed a 'history of satisfaction' with Britain's constitutional arrangements (see Evans, 1994, for a detailed discussion).

Labour's constitutional revisionism has had two central strands: the leadership project, largely informed by pragmatism rather than principle; and alternative projects from within the Labour movement. Both of these strands are influenced to a varying degree by two dominant traditions: Fabianism and syndicalism. Both traditions have contributed to a long culture of revisionism which has existed throughout Labour Party history.

The Fabians, dominant within the Labour Party, have, by and large, bolstered Labour's preference for pursuing the favoured mode of governance of the British political tradition; strong, decisive and responsible government. A belief has prevailed that the existing institutions of the British state could be used as a socialist apparatus for social and political engineering; further, that these institutions have the ability to reform themselves and, above all, that a strong executive is crucial to this process of change. Hence the rejection of a written constitution and proportional representation rested on the ability of the former to undermine the notion of the sovereignty of Parliament and its trappings of legislative and executive power, forged through the dominance of party representation and discipline and the latter's threat to both Labour majority government and the direct relationship between the MP and his or her constituency. Instead the key constitutional revisionists emphasized the need to remove obstacles to the exercise of executive power (see Laski, 1925; Cripps, 1933; Jennings, 1934; and, Crosland, 1956).

Conversely, the syndicalist tradition has largely been informed by a dissatisfaction with both Labour's parliamentary leadership and the theory and practice of the centralized, sovereign state. In recent history, however, with the notable exceptions of Tony Benn, Dennis Skinner and Chris Mullin, the syndicalist tradition has neglected the question of political institutions. The motivation behind this has been the emphasis placed upon the extra-parliamentary struggle; the notion that capitalism can be overthrown from the 'bottom up' rather than the 'top down'.

As Table 6.1 illustrates, traditionally the Labour leadership has supported functional elite democracy: state collectivism forwarded

Table 6.1:   'Old' Labour and the Constitution

Source of constitutional satisfaction	State collectivism forwarded through an electoral majority. A constitution which allows for executive dominance.
Rejection of constitutional revisionism	The recasting of electoral representation on individual and proportional lines violates the class base of society. The recasting of the British Constitution on individual lines places the ultimate arbitration of the constitution into the hands of the Judiciary which violates the class basis of society. The rule of law is automatically based on property rights which entrench the structural inequalities of capitalist political economy.
Sources of disagreement with the Constitution	Obstacles to the ability of government to implement their programme (e.g. a politicized civil services, judicial review, the House of Lords)

through an electoral majority; a constitution which legitimizes executive dominance; and constitutional arrangements which are amenable to manipulation by the executive. The Fabians believed that for the Labour Party to be viewed as a plausible party of government it had to be seen as both 'strong' and 'decisive'. As Giles Radice (1989, p. 165) contends: 'The centralist tradition in the Labour party had always emphasized state ownership and central government initiative to promote greater equality and efficiency.' A shift in constitutional thinking in the late 1980s and 1990s, to a limited extent under the leadership of Neil Kinnock and John Smith and then more dramatically under Tony Blair, has posed a historic challenge to the Party's conventional wisdom.

THE RISE OF A NEW CONSTITUTIONALISM

The transformation of the Labour leadership's standpoint on constitutional matters may be viewed as a response to internal and external party dynamics.

Changes Exogenous to the Labour Party

The late 1980s and 1990s represented a critical moment for questions of democracy in the United Kingdom. Continued relative economic decline, the unresolved Irish and Scottish questions, the mounting pressures of European integration and public dissatisfaction with the way the UK was governed, all stretched Britain's unwritten constitution and increasingly demonstrated the lag between Britain's constitutional theory and political practice. Certain of these changes have emanated from broader structural changes in global forces and international governance, others from changes in the nature of domestic governance and statecraft.

The Global Economic Structure

There are two main sources of constitutional pressure which warrant some discussion here. The first relates to the erosion of the role of the state as a general regulator of the national economy due to the internationalization of finance, political integration and geopolitics. The resultant interdependency has led to the internationalization of domestic economic policy-making in the sense that economic policy-making is increasingly constrained by what goes on elsewhere (see Cerny, 1996).

The second source of constitutional pressure provides the crucial context for understanding the nature of constitutionalism in the UK throughout the postwar period: the weak position of Britain within the global economy. For example, since the mid-1970s the Conservatives have identified economic crisis as the key context for taking strategic electoral and political decisions. Will Hutton (1995) argues that the weakness of the British economy stems from the semi-modern nature of the British state. As markets are embedded in a country's social system and values, it largely falls on the state to govern both the economy and society. Hence the character of a state's political institutions shapes the democratic character and efficiency of governance. For Hutton, as the constitution defines the responsibilities and institutions of government, it is a central determinant of how the country is governed and the economy is run.

Supra-ideological Structures

Following the breakup of the Soviet Empire and the disintegration of the Eastern bloc, the discourse of liberal democracy has assumed global dominance as the organizing principle of the capitalist state. As a consequence there has emerged a renewed interest in the nature of legitimate statecraft, with the notion of democracy as the central organizing principle for its creation (see Beetham, ed., 1994). In Britain the liberal democratic discourse has provided the political space for the emergence of constitutional reform groups campaigning for a modern constitutional settlement (e.g. Charter 88).

Domestic Ideological Structures

Domestically the Thatcher and Major years provided an object lesson in the impact of ideology on the policy agenda. The Conservative project owed something to New Right ideology which has unsuccessfully attempted to redraw the basic relationship between government and the people and reassert the right of government to govern. The limits of Britain's unwritten constitution have been reflected in its inability to provide effective checks and balances to control the pursuit of Conservative statecraft. It is thus an era which has demonstrated the fragilities of Britain's constitutional arrangements.

The Impact of Supra-institutional Structures

This set of pressures emerges from the conflict which arises between Britain's constitutional sovereignty and the drift towards 'global interconnectedness'. For example, developments from within the European Community and latterly the European Union have meant that since the Heath government signed the Treaty of Accession in 1973 many of the traditional functions of the British state have gradually withered away as a consequence of the erosion of the legislative sovereignty of Parliament. Furthermore, Britain's various treaty obligations have had a significant impact on the autonomy of the British state. The UK is now legally bound by a whole host of international treaties and obligations, relating to such matters as defence, the environment, human rights, social rights, aviation and taxation (see Oliver, 1992, p. 21).

New Governance

A state's constitutional settlement is largely determined by its institutional and territorial design. However, processes of internationalization also impact on institutions and processes internal to the nation-state. This 'hollowing-out' of Britain's conventional institutional form thus reveals a further source of pressure on Britain's unwritten constitution. The term clearly infers that the political powers of the British state are being eroded in particular ways. Rhodes (1994, pp. 138–9) has argued that there are four key interrelated trends which illustrate the reach of this process: privatization and limiting the scope and forms of public intervention; the loss of functions by central government departments to alternative service delivery systems (such as agencies) and through market testing; the loss of functions from the British government to European Community institutions; and the emergence of limits to the discretion of public servants through the new public management, with its emphasis on managerial accountability, and clearer political control created by a sharp distinction between politics and administration.

Public-sector change under the Conservatives has had three interrelated effects on the unwritten constitution. First, the Europeanization of public administration has led to the erosion of parliamentary sovereignty. Second, the sectoralization of policy-making and its accompanying institutional complexities have obscured the accountability routes and powers of British government. Third, the introduction of new institutions has placed limits on the influence of elected representatives and exposes the absence of elective control over non-elected state personnel.

A further constitutional pressure at the heart of government is worthy of comment here: the erosion of the 'Westminster model' of parliamentary government. The 'Westminster model' has formed the basis of the British political tradition and provided the political orthodoxy of British government. This model generated the ordering principles to the British political scientist's account of British politics. Hence, notions such as continuity, gradualness, flexibility and stability became the buzz-words of Britain's unwritten constitution. However, the legitimacy of the 'Westminster model' rests on the ability of its conventional constraints to effectively control the executive and hold it to account. Both Labour and Conservative statecraft has provided ample evidence of the limits of convention as a constitutional check. The Nolan Reports on standards of conduct in the House of Commons and the Scott Enquiry into ministerial conduct during the 'arms-to-Iraq' scandal have both demonstrated the habitual infringement of constitutional conventions.

Territorial Management

The efficacy of Britain's unwritten constitution has posed a further challenge through the strained union with Scotland, Wales and Northern Ireland. Historically, the Scottish and Welsh demands for independent assemblies will be viewed as the most developed expression of the will for 'continental pluralism' in Britain. In sum, the notion of the unitary state which lay at the heart of Britain's unwritten constitution no longer fitted the territorial map it sought to govern. Nowhere else is this better exemplified than in the North of Ireland where a civil war over the constitutional future of the North has been waged.

Crisis Management and the Civil Liberties Gap

This political pressure has both an economic and a strategic dimension. The former emphasizes the importance of government providing the market conditions for economic recovery. For New Conservatives this required the removal of obstacles to market volition, such as the postwar consensus, the regulation of industrial relations, the abrogation of the powers of local government and the reduction of social welfare commitments. The strategic dimension was derived from the need to establish an image of governing competence in order to achieve electoral success. Thus the 1980s heralded a return to 'strong, decisive, responsible government' as a response to the 'ungovernability' crises of the 1970s, in particular, the demise of the Heath and Callaghan governments at the hands of organized labour. Civil liberties are one of the first casualties of crisis management, and the emergence of a 'civil liberties gap' has been a direct corollary of the absence of effective constitutional checks and balances.

The New Politics

The character of political participation in Britain is changing. Although working-class protest remains very much alive, new types of political action involving civil disobedience, and new groups of actors have emerged. Social protest is no longer centred purely on the 'have-nots' at the bottom of the class hierarchy but also those of economic and political standing. This new class is better educated, ideologically sophisticated and more willing to experiment with new forms of political action. Social protest has grown in the UK, moving upward in the class hierarchy, building on a new generation, the growth in higher education, the change in women's roles, and springing from a post-materialist value system. Moreover, the criminalization of direct action and the clamp-down on the pursuit of alternative lifestyles appears to have succeeded in bringing more and more young people together and uniting them in a common struggle. The changing nature of group activity has had much to do with the absence of receptive and responsive political institutions. Indeed, the rise in direct action among single-issue groups may be attributed both to the absence of political opportunities afforded by a 'strong state' and to the inability of Britain's unwritten constitution to act as a focus for social and political change.

These changes only go so far in explaining why New Labour adopted a wide-ranging constitutional reform programme; for a more complete assessment, we must now look at changes internal to the Labour Party.

Internal Party Revisionism

The revisionism of Neil Kinnock, which developed after 1983, dealt with the modernization of internal party machinery and the removal of obstacles within the party to policy innovation. This included a consolidation of the defeat of the Bennite left and the strengthening of the power-base of the Parliamentary Labour Party to make policy through the National Executive Committee. Arguably, these changes permitted the emergence of a new policy agenda crystallized around pro-Europeanization, pro-nuclear defence, the rejection of a general commitment to nationalization and a commitment to a market-oriented mixed economy. The view of the Labour leadership on constitutional reform had been in flux since the drafting of *Democratic Socialist Aims and Values* in 1988, which aimed at providing an ethical framework for the Labour Party Policy Review. This document revised the party's position on constitutional matters in general and laid the foundations for the launch of a piecemeal constitutional reform programme in January 1991. Although the programme entitled *Charter of Rights: Guaranteeing Individual Liberty in a Free Society* did represent a shift in Labour thinking on constitutional matters, it was still temperate in its radicalism.

Through the establishment of the principle of 'one member, one vote' and thus the limiting of the political power of the trade unions within the Party, John Smith took Kinnock's revisionism one step further. Moreover, partly as a response to the increased tartanization of the Labour Party (Geekie and Levy, 1989) and partly due to a further electoral defeat in 1992, Smith had also been convinced of the need for constitutional reform.

However, it was not until the untimely death of John Smith in May 1994 and the election of Tony Blair to the Labour leadership in July of that year that Labour's constitutional revisionism took on an almost evangelical zeal.

THE REFORM PROGRAMME

For Tony Blair the constitutional reform project represents a means for achieving stakeholder politics through constitutional methods:

> These reforms would contribute to the health of our democracy. They would tackle the culture of secrecy, enshrine in British law people's legal rights, give us a reformed Parliament which could operate more effectively as a modern legislature, and allow the people to decide how the Commons was elected. (Blair, 1996, p. 86)

The idea of stakeholder politics is thus about creating a new relationship between the government and the people based on trust, freedom, choice and responsibility.

Delivering Constitutional Reform

The reform of Britain's semi-modern constitution will be an immense task for even the most radical and prepossessed administration, never mind a Labour Party with a historical penchant for playing 'policy on the hoof'. It is thus timely that a project has emerged that deals in specifics rather than declamatory statements which merely extol the virtues of constitutional reform. The Constitution Unit provides a much-needed way forward from the visionary monographs written by David Marquand (1988), Ferdinand Mount (1992), Anthony Wright (1994) and Will Hutton (1995), which all succeeded in exciting but failed to furnish a *modus operandi* for delivering constitutional reform. The Constitution Unit was set up in April 1995 to conduct 'an independent inquiry into the implementation of constitutional reform' in the UK. The Unit aims to 'analyze current proposals for constitutional reform; explore the connections between them; and to identify the practical steps involved in putting constitutional reforms in place'. Their recommendations are contrasted with New Labour's actions below, in an attempt to provide a reasoned appraisal of the design of the constitutional reform programme.

Institutional Machinery

Delivering Constitutional Reform emphasizes the interlinking nature of constitutional reform measures. To deal with this, the Unit proposed the creation of a minister in charge of constitutional reform to provide 'central strategic leadership from a senior Cabinet Minister' (1996, p. 5). The minister would receive administrative and strategic support through a Strategic Policy Committee. New Labour has crafted a machinery for constitutional reform within the cabinet committee system of the core executive with Blair's close friend and ally Lord Irvine as overall coordinator of a system of cabinet committees devoted to different aspects of constitutional reform. However, perhaps the most interesting innovation in this regard has been the forging of a Lib–Lab joint consultative committee on constitutional reform by Tony Blair and the leader of the Liberal Democrats, Paddy Ashdown, which lies at the centre of this web of committees. The committee is bound by the Official Secrets Act but not by cabinet collective responsibility and its members have access to civil service papers.

This decision was taken without consulting the Liberal Democrat membership and has been viewed by several members of the Liberal Democrat Federal Policy Centre as a further erosion of the Liberal Democrats' distinctiveness as a political force in Britain. For Blair, however, it was clearly an attempt to embark on a constitutional reform programme with as much consensus as possible.

The details of the arrangements for the new committee were completed by Peter Mandelson, the Prime Minister's Chief of Staff Jonathan Powell, and Lord Holme, one of Ashdown's closest political allies, former Chair of the Liberal Party. The committee is comprised of six ministers (Gordon Brown, the Chancellor; Robin Cook, the Foreign Secretary; Jack Straw, the Home Secretary; Ann Taylor, Leader of the Commons; John Prescott, Secretary of State for the Environment, Transport and the Regions; and Peter Mandelson, Minister without Portfolio) and five Liberal Democrat members (Paddy Ashdown, Robert McLennan, Lord Holme, Menzies Campbell and Alan Beith), with the Prime Minister in the chair and the Cabinet Secretary at his side.

Procedural and Legislative Issues

In Chapter 2 of their report, the Constitution Unit review the forces which, they argue, will drive and shape the reform process, highlighting the historical and constitutional framework for reform. Chapter 3 moves on to consider whether Whitehall is equipped to deal with wide-ranging constitutional innovation and assesses what changes might be needed to enable the system to deal more effectively with such a programme. First the problem of procedural time is considered. Historically constitutional bills have been reviewed by 'Committee of the Whole House'. On average, past bills have taken between 100 and 200 hours of floor-time out of the 400 hours allocated to each session. This would mean that under existing procedure only two constitutional bills could be reviewed per session. It is unlikely therefore that a wide-ranging programme of constitutional reform could be introduced in the lifetime of one government. The Unit thus identifies procedural reform as a prerequisite for further constitutional innovation and proposes three measures: the partial referral of bills for full debate to a standing committee which would minimize time spent on the floor; the advance timetabling of bills to ensure that all parts are subject to scrutiny and debate and thus minimizing incentives for filibustering; and thirdly, the selective use of carry-over to maximize procedural time. New Labour has not chosen to reform the Commons and may live to regret it as their parliamentary majority narrows.

The Unit then presented New Labour with a choice of three different legislative strategies for delivering constitutional reform. The 'Big Bang' approach associated with the Liberal Democrats, the 'Paving Motion' approach associated with Charter 88 and a 'gradualist' or 'incremental' approach akin to Ferdinand Mount's (1995) evolutionary perspective on constitutional reform (see Table 6.2). The Unit uses the problem of procedural time to bolster its support for the third approach. Logical but ahistorical advice. The momentum behind even a great reforming administration is always short-lived and rarely survives into a second administration. Nevertheless New Labour has chosen the path of incrementalism with all its pitfalls.

The final chapter of the Constitution Unit's report considers the mechanisms that might be used to build consensus and ensure consultation around constitutional reform drawing on UK and international experience. It is here that both the Constitution Unit and New Labour are at their weakest. In the penultimate section on 'Consultation, Consensus and Inquiry' the Unit falls into the trap of advocating the same 'top-down' implementation processes which have failed conspicuously in recent British political history (as the Community Charge and Child Support Agency débâcles illustrate). The reform process should not purely be the preserve of political elites. Mechanisms for opening up the process to public debate, of extending the boundaries of the political, must be sought for beyond the formulaic treatments deployed through referenda.

Devolution

On 27 June 1996 George Robertson, the Shadow Scottish Secretary of State and Ron Davies, the then Shadow Welsh Secretary of State, announced Labour's intention to hold pre-legislative referendums on devolution (George Robertson MP, House of Commons 1997a, pp. 5–6; Ron Davies MP, House of Commons 1997a, pp. 6–7). In a report published on 5 March 1997, the new Joint Lib–Lab Consultative Committee on Constitutional Reform, led by Robin Cook and Robert MacLennan, set out a policy to introduce a Scottish Parliament with legislative competence over matters pertaining to the Scottish Office including health, housing, education, local government and law and

Table 6.2: Proposals for the Legislative Form of Constitutional Change

Form	Proponent	Features	Perceived weaknesses
'Big Bang'	Liberal Democrats	A Great Reform Bill incorporating the key features of their programme – reform of the House of Commons and Lords, devolution to Wales and Scotland, establishment of regional assemblies, reform of quango appointments, incorporation of ECHR and a Bill of Rights.	Unrealistic and impractical – problems of detail, difficulty of ensuring consensus across reforms with the strong expectation of party discipline on all issues. It would also require parliamentary reform to be effective.
'Paving motion'	Charter 88	The passing of a paving motion at the beginning of the reforming Parliament outlining principles to inform the framework of reform; the nature of the legislation to be passed and the intention to establish a Constitutional Grand Committee to oversee the legislation.	It would be time-consuming and undermine parliamentary sovereignty through binding parliament to future action.
'Incrementalism'	Labour	'The ambition and the extent of the programme I have set out will not be achieved in one bill, but over a period of (life) time' (Tony Blair).	It runs the danger of a boredom factor with constitutional reform emerging, reflects a pragmatic approach and doesn't learn from history.

order, to be elected by the additional member electoral system (AMS). With regard to Wales it recommended the establishment of a directly elected assembly providing democratic control over the functions currently devolved to the Welsh Office 'empowered to reform the quango state and providing a democratic forum for the development of policy' also to be elected by AMS (House of Commons, 1997a, pp. 11–13). Labour's election manifesto affirmed these commitments (Labour Party, 1997, pp. 33–4) promising the decentralization of power to Scotland and Wales once given popular legitimacy through referendum. The Referendum (Scotland and Wales) Bill thus formally recognized New Labour's argument that a constitutional settlement which was organized around 'English questions' could no longer be tolerated.

The verdict of the referendum in Scotland was 3:1 in favour of a parliament in Edinburgh and not far short of 2:1 in favour of a parliament with tax-varying powers. The Campaign for a Welsh Assembly failed to inspire the same passion. Labour dissidents were more numerous in Wales. Five Labour MPs rebelled against the government's plans, and the results demonstrated greater antagonism for a Welsh Assembly where English culture predominated, particularly in border regions, and where the Welsh language had been anglicized historically. Despite being in disagreement with the Labour Party over the future government of Wales, there can be little doubt that Plaid Cymru played a key role in the Campaign for a Welsh Assembly and helped to tip the result in favour of an assembly. Indeed without the referendum coming close on the heels of the 'Yes–Yes' vote in Scotland and the role of nationalist activism it is difficult to see how New Labour could have won.

Next Steps

The Scotland Bill (Bill 104 of 1997/98) went through its second reading on 13 January 1998. The Bill introduces a new system of election (AMS) to the Scottish Parliament and provides for the Scottish Parliament to have legislative powers over all matters not reserved to Westminster. The Bill also creates a Scottish Executive to be headed by a First Minister. Hence the Scottish Executive and the Scottish Parliament will inherit the current powers of the Westminster Parliament and the Secretary of State for Scotland over local government. Thus the new Parliament will have the power to make primary legislation affecting local government (including the power to alter the existing arrangements for local taxes) and the Scottish Executive would inherit the Secretary of State's powers, including the power to make secondary legislation. In addition, the Bill also removed the statutory requirement of 71 Westminster seats for Scotland, but does not contain any other arrangements to modify the role of Scottish MPs at Westminster. The Government of Wales Bill is moving faster through the legislative process than its Scottish counterpart. It completed its House of Commons committee stages on 2 March 1998. Indeed the Welsh Assembly is expected to be in full operation before the Scottish Parliament. Elections to the Welsh Assembly by AMS are planned for May 1999 after which the functions currently exercised by the Welsh Office and its ministers will be transferred to the assembly. Although the Scottish Parliament will be elected at the same time, it will only assume the powers of the Scottish Office and its ministers in the autumn of 1999, with a grand Opening of Parliament scheduled for January 2000.

'Rights Brought Home': the Human Rights Bill

The view of the Labour leadership on individual rights has been in flux since Roy Hattersley and Neil Kinnock drew up the document *Democratic Socialist Aims and Values* (Labour Party, 1988), which laid the foundations for the launch of a piecemeal constitutional reform programme in January 1990. The Charter of Rights provided a state-centred approach to the realization of the 'new' socialist goal of individual liberty, to be attained through parliamentary means. While Labour agreed that 'True liberty requires action from the Government', they disagreed with organizations such as Charter 88 that the best way to achieve this was through the creation of a written constitution and a bill of a rights.

Hattersley argued that democracy could be achieved through good government rather than a written constitution and a bill of rights. The Charter of Rights set down specific legally enforceable rights which would be introduced through separate acts of parliament rather than through a general bill of rights. For Hattersley, a bill of rights is no more than a declamatory statement with 'public relations value': 'it avoids a statement of rights so general that they have to be interpreted by the courts – institutions which may not define rights in the positive way which we regard as necessary' (Charter 88, 1991, pp. 6–8).

While the Charter of Rights represented a challenge to the British political tradition, its ordering principles were informed by the same model of satisfaction which had dominated the development of

Labour's response to the constitutional reform debate throughout the twentieth century. In sum, the Charter of Rights would not provide a significant constitutional check on executive dominance and reorder the relationship between government and people.

The 1992 General Election campaign manifesto reaffirmed the Labour party leadership's partial conversion to constitutional reform promising the abolition of the House of Lords, the introduction of a Freedom of Information Act and a 'Charter of Rights'. A further election defeat radicalized the constitutional reform agenda and created the space for significant movement on the rights issue. Before the 1997 General Election the Labour Party published a consultation document, *Rights Brought Home*, which set out in some detail the case for incorporation of the European Convention on Human Rights into British law. It argued that individual rights protection under common law in the UK didn't and couldn't work and thus proposed that British people should be given easier access to their convention rights. A white paper was introduced in the autumn of 1997 building on this work.

The Human Rights Bill maps out the Government's proposals for enforcing Convention rights. The bill first sets out the obligations of public authorities under the ECHR:

> it is unlawful for public authorities (executive agencies, local government, the police, immigration officers, prisons, courts and tribunals and companies responsible for areas of activity previously in the public sector such as the privatised utilities) to act in a way which is incompatible with the Convention rights. (2.2)

Notably Parliament is excluded from the new requirement which reflects the continued role of the sovereignty of parliament at the heart of the British constitution. However, the bill does expose public authorities to wide-ranging scrutiny:

> people or organizations should be able to argue that their Convention rights have been infringed by a public authority in our courts at any level. (2.4)

A public authority which is found to have acted unlawfully by failing to comply with the Convention will not be subjected to criminal penalties, but the court or tribunal will be able to grant the injured person any remedy which is within its normal powers to grant (2.6). The Bill also provides for legislation (both Acts of Parliament and secondary legislation) to be interpreted so far as possible so as to be compatible with the Convention. If the courts decide in any case that it is impossible to interpret an Act of Parliament in a way which is compatible with the Convention, the Bill enables a formal declaration to be made that its provisions are incompatible with the Convention. Crucially, however,

> A declaration that legislation is incompatible with the convention rights will not of itself have the effect of changing the law, which will continue to apply. But it will almost certainly prompt the Government and Parliament to change the law. (2.10)

Moreover, the government has reached the conclusion that courts should not have the power to set aside primary legislation, past or future, on the grounds of incompatibility with the convention. Once again this conclusion arises from the importance which the government attaches to Parliamentary sovereignty (2.13).

The Bill is equally as hollow with regard to questions of enforcement and the amendment of legislation:

> On one view, human rights legislation is so important that it should be given added protection from subsequent amendment or repeal. ... We do not believe that it is necessary or would be desirable to attempt to devise such a special arrangement for this Bill. (2.16)

It is interesting to note that the position will be different with regard to Scotland and Wales. The government has decided that the Scottish Parliament will have no power to legislate in a way which is incompatible with the convention; and similarly that the Scottish Executive will have no power to make subordinate legislation or to take executive action which is incompatible with the Convention. The same provision will apply to the Welsh Assembly.

Bringing Rights Home argued that Parliament itself should play a leading role in protecting Convention rights. In order to achieve this goal, the Government proposes the creation of a Parliamentary Committee on Human Rights which would have the remit of 'conducting enquiries on a range of human rights issues relating to the convention, and produce reports so as to assist the government and Parliament in deciding what action to take' (3.6.). The nature and composition of the Committee has yet to be decided, but three options have been considered: either a Joint Committee of both Houses of Parliament; a separate Committee for each house; or a Committee which meets jointly for some purposes and separately for others. *Bringing Rights Home* also devoted some attention to the idea of creating a Human Rights Commission with the task of enforcing convention rights. The bill, however, remains uncommitted on this issue (3.11).

In sum, incorporation of the ECHR is not likely to provide a significant constitutional check on executive dominance and fundamentally reorder the relationship between government and people. Majority governments will still remain largely a law unto themselves. However, it may provide a moral impediment to excesses of executive despotism and facilitate an era of judicial activism and assertiveness. At the very least it may encourage individuals and organizations to exercise their rights of citizenship more often and use the courts to hold public authorities to account for their actions.

Electoral Reform

The basis of the Labour Party's traditional defence of the first-past-the-post electoral system is that it allows for 'decisive reform' and thus 'strong', 'decisive' government. Indeed this elitist conception of democracy has underpinned the leadership view for much of this century. However, it is possible to identify a weakening in the Labour leadership's position following the vote at the 1990 Party Conference which took the decision to consider alternatives to the first-past-the-post voting system. Although the National Executive Committee rejected the initiative, it was agreed to set up a Working Party on Electoral Systems to be chaired by Professor Raymond Plant. The committee served a dual purpose both as a practical companion to Labour's 'Charter of Rights' and as a response to the growing electoral reform lobby within the Labour Party. Moreover, in the aftermath of his resignation Labour leader Neil Kinnock joined the Labour Campaign for Electoral Reform which suggests that there had been a conflict of opinion between Hattersley and Kinnock on the issue.

After a two-and-a-half-year-study of electoral systems, the Plant Commission concluded that first-past-the-post (FPTP) was inappropriate to the modern British political system. Its 16 members deemed the following electoral systems suitable for Britain's electoral arrangements: regional lists for the second chamber and the European Parliament; AMS for Scotland; and Supplementary Vote (SV) for the House of Commons. Ten members supported the move away from FPTP and the other six the *status quo*. The then Labour leader John Smith supported their proposals for a reformed Second Chamber and the European Parliament but remained unconvinced of the need to change the electoral system for the House of Commons. Under a New Labour government Tony Blair also remains 'unpersuaded' on the need to reform the electoral system for the House of Commons. However, the creation of a Commission on Electoral Reform and a referendum on the issue has opened a window of opportunity for change.

The Jenkins Independent Commission on the Voting System

Lord Jenkins of Hillhead (former Labour minister and co-founder of the SDP and the Liberal Democrats) was appointed by Tony Blair to chair the Independent Commission. The Commission's terms of reference are:

> The Commission shall be free to consider and recommend any appropriate system or combination of systems in recommending an alternative to the present system for Parliamentary elections to be put before the people in the Government's referendum. The Commission shall observe the requirement for broad proportionality, the need for stable government, an extension of voter choice and the maintenance of a link between MPs and geographical constituencies. (Home Office Press Release on Electoral Reform, 1 December 1997)

The commission will report in the autumn of 1998.

While its remit is to recommend an alternative to FPTP it also needs to suggest an electoral system which both Tony Blair as a sceptic and the Liberal Democrats as enthusiasts can live with. On Tony Blair's part this would clearly indicate an electoral system which retained the single-member-constituency link, allowed for majority government and granted some concessions to both the growing lobby in support of proportional representation inside the Labour Party and the Liberal Democrats. If this criteria is operated then there are only three likely contenders: AMS, AV or SV electoral systems.

Of course the Labour government has already introduced electoral reform for European Parliamentary elections. Under the new system the UK electorate will vote for 87 MEPs of whom:

- 71 shall be elected for 9 electoral regions in England
- 8 shall be elected for 1 electoral region in Scotland
- 5 shall be elected for 1 electoral region in Wales
- 3 shall be elected for 1 electoral region in Northern Ireland

The system of election in England, Scotland and Wales will now be a regional list electoral system. The number of seats allocated to a party will be filled by the persons named on the party's list of candidates in the order in which they appear on that list. In Northern Ireland, however, as a consequence of the troubles and the distinctive nature of the Northern Irish multiparty system, the single transferable vote system will be used. The new electoral system is intended to be in place for the next elections to the European Parliament in June 1999.

Freedom of Information

Traditionally the central reason for successive British governments rejecting a Freedom of Information Act has been the perception that it would undermine the Westminster model's principle of ministerial accountability to Parliament. Thus in Britain, the release and content of information has been controlled by ministerial discretion and the British polity has been characterized by closed rather than open government.

Throughout the 1970s, partly as a response to the growing campaign for open government and partly as a result of the influence of the revised American Freedom of Information Act, the nature of official secrecy reached a position of some political salience. However, as Marsh observes: 'parties have advocated open government in opposition and talked about it when in government but failed to take any action' (Marsh and Tant 1989, p. 19).

Unlike its predecessors, New Labour appears committed to an open system of government which allows the citizen to observe how government works, and not simply to see the information base of governmental decisions. Tony Blair appointed Dr David Clark MP to the Cabinet position of Chancellor of the Duchy of Lancaster and gave him the task of realizing Labour's election manifesto pledge to introduce a Freedom of Information Act and establish 'open and transparent government' (Queen's Speech to Parliament, 14 May 1997). On the same day Clark announced the establishment of a Freedom of Information Unit in the Cabinet Office (Office of Public Service) to carry through these commitments.

'Your Right to Know' – the Labour Government's Proposals for a Freedom of Information Act

We are still awaiting the publication of New Labour's Freedom of Information Bill but we have already been given some general clues as to what it will and will not contain through the publication of a White Paper entitled *Your Right to Know* on 12 December 1997. The government intends to give every individual a statutory right to know about the information and records which government keeps. Six key features of the government's freedom of information legislation may be identified (see Hansard, 12 December 1997):

(1) *Inclusiveness*
   It is intended that the FoI Act will apply right across the public sector encompassing: government departments and agencies; local councils; quangos; nationalized industries; the National Health Service; courts and tribunals; schools and colleges; police authorities; the armed forces; public service broadcasters; privatized utilities; and, private sector organizations carrying out duties on behalf of government.

(2) *Access to Documents and Information*
   The right of access would be extended to official records and information held by the bodies covered by the Act.

(3) *Limited Exemptions*
   It is proposed that the system for safeguarding information should be based on seven 'specified' interests. In most cases information could only be withheld if its disclosure would cause 'substantial' harm.

(4) *A Duty to Publish*
   It is intended that public authorities will take a positive approach to openness and publish information as a matter of course.

(5) *Strong Enforcement Procedures*
   In order to ensure compliance with the act, an Independent Information Commissioner with wide-ranging powers (including the power to order disclosure) will be appointed to oversee the implementation of the legislation.

(6) *An Integrated Approach*
   Rights of access to current and historic information will be brought together through the integration of the relevant sections of the Public Records Office into freedom of information legislation to ensure a single legislative approach to the release of both past and present records.

These features add up to a radical package of reforms. Long-term freedom-of-information campaigner Maurice Frankel has declared that it 'will lead to an outstanding Freedom of Information Act that is in many respects better than overseas laws', and it will 'for the first time give the British public a genuine right to know what its government is doing' (*Observer*, 14 December 1997).

Indeed if the Bill is as radical as the White Paper it will certainly represent a decisive challenge to the culture of secrecy which has dominated the Westminster model of parliamentary government.

Reform of the House of Lords

None of the members of the House of Lords, the second chamber of the British Parliament, is democratically elected. The chamber is composed of hereditary peers, a number of senior judges and bishops of the Church of England and 'life' peers appointed by the government. The 763 peers of succession (those who have inherited peerages) who have a right to sit and vote in the House of Lords constitute a substantial majority of its 1185 members. There are very few hereditary peerages to which women can succeed. These factors mean that women and ethnic minorities will inevitably always be under-represented in the House.

The story of the reform of the House of Lords is also an incomplete one as the large Conservative majority in the House of Lords has meant that the pace of reform has been dependent on the ability of government to develop an all-party approach to reform. It is thus a further plank of the government's programme where reform will be reached through negotiation rather than imposition.

Lord Irvine of Lairg, the Lord Chancellor, was given the job of chairing the Cabinet committees dealing with the issue. Initially Labour planned a two-stage reform process. It was first intended to abolish hereditary peerages and then to proceed to a comprehensive reform after the next election. In opposition the Prime Minister defended this position on the grounds that by first developing a meritocratic body the mechanism would be created through which the future role of the second chamber could be discussed and debated within a more progressive setting (Blair, 1996, p. 85).

The first stage was scheduled for autumn 1998 and announced in the Queen's Speech. This was of course unacceptable to the Conservative Party who feared that once hereditary peers were stripped of their voting rights, the Lords would become dominated by life peers appointed by the Prime Minister, thus creating 'the biggest quango in history'. Moreover, once a potential obstacle to New Labour legislation had been removed the push factor for reform of the House of Lords would wither away.

In order to allay fears that this strategy would create an unworkable second chamber, Lord Irvine invited the Conservative leadership to attend discussions. This was an attempt by Lord Irvine to proceed on the issue by cross-party consensus. The approach was welcomed by the Conservative Party; indeed it was hoped that a consensual approach will pave the way for a 'Big Bang' reform of the Lords: the removal of hereditary peers at the same time as the creation of a new independent second chamber is put in its place. This strategy has been severely affected by the Lords' trenchant opposition to 'closed' regional lists for European elections. The eventual resolution to these interlinked constitutional reforms is, as yet, unclear.

CONCLUSION

The political will of those pushing for reform and their ability to resist defenders of the British political tradition is thus an imperative for successful constitutional reform, but political will on its own will not be sufficient. Constitutional reform touches on every element of economic, social and political life and thus requires a sophisticated process of implementation if it is to be successful.

Despite these obstacles there is enough evidence to suggest that constitutional reformers should be optimistic about the long-term prospects of radical constitutional change in Britain. Even if Tony Blair's programme doesn't perfectly fit the radicalism of some group agendas (e.g. Liberty or Charter 88), it is likely that existing reforms will spill over and spill around and thus increase the radicalism of reform and the scope and intensity of change in the future.

Political spill-over consists of a convergence of the expectations and interests of national elites as a response to constitutional change. This may result in a transfer of loyalties (authority-legitimacy transfers from Westminster to Edinburgh) or, at minimum, in a transformation in the activities of political elites. Technical spill-over refers to a situation in which the attempt to achieve a goal agreed upon at the outset (e.g. freedom of information) becomes possible only if other (unanticipated) cooperative activities are also carried out, for example its harmonization with rights legislation. In this way cooperation in one sector can spill over into cooperation in another, previously unrelated sector. Moreover, once introduced, constitutional reform creates the possibility for further reform because it inspires political parties and groups to press for change.

7 New Labour and the End of the Welfare State? The Case of Lifelong Learning
Patrick Ainley

INTRODUCTION

The final abandonment of the repeatedly postponed White Paper on Lifelong Learning in February 1998 indicated that post-compulsory education would remain in the state bequeathed by the 1992 Further and Higher Education Act. Similarly, the pattern of compulsory schooling is fixed by the 1988 Education Act. As the architect of that Act, Kenneth Baker, interviewed on its tenth anniversary, said: 'the changes of ten years ago . . . have been accepted. . . . The core curriculum, tests, league tables, grant-maintained schools, CTCs – they are all there and being built upon' (*The Times Education Supplement*, 23 January 1998). This chapter argues that these two Acts, taken together with Lord Dearing's minor adjustments to them, frame a new settlement for education comparable to that of 1944. The notion of a Learning Society that the new settlement is supposed to create is questioned, in particular with regard to whether the changes in this area that New Labour have made since coming to power indicate an end to the welfare state. It argues that a new type of post-welfare, contracting state was introduced during the Thatcher period and evidence is presented from the field of learning policy to show that New Labour in government is further developing this new state. Finally the historical precedent for this in the way that Old Labour introduced the original welfare state after the war but in 1951 handed it over to be run by Conservative governments for the next 13 years is noted.

TOWARDS A LEARNING SOCIETY?

The New Labour government has picked up and run with the previous (Conservative) government's proposal to turn Britain into a 'learning society' by the year 2000. For both parties, as well as the employers' Confederation of British Industry (CBI) which first revived the term, a 'learning society' is one which systematically increases the skills and knowledge of all its members to exploit technological innovation and so gain a competitive edge in fast-changing global markets. This is supposed to be necessary because the industrial competitiveness of UK plc is widely accepted as being dependent upon a highly skilled workforce, able to innovate and to produce goods and services of high marketable value. At the same time, the incremental pace of technical change demands workers who are flexibly able to adapt to new technology throughout their working lives.

To be as flexibly employable as possible, education and training (conceptually united as learning) should no longer be 'front-loaded' upon the young, but lifelong. Individuals are thus encouraged continually to invest in their own human capital. Through Lifelong Learning they can 'transfer' portfolios of updated knowledge and skills from one project to the next in varied and flexible careers (for example, CBI, 1994, which advocates that graduates should abandon any notion of 'a job for life'). 'Lifelong Learning' therefore follows the 'Foundation Learning' of a basic National Curriculum of supposedly necessary knowledge in schools, as for example in the separate 'Foundation' and 'Lifetime' National Training and Education Targets, three times revised but intended to measure progress towards the Learning Society goal.

What Avis *et al.* (1996) call the 'new consensus' on the Learning Society goal is broader than just learning policy. More importantly, it includes also a new neo-liberal orthodoxy on economic policy (Lee and Harley, 1997). An important component of the new orthodoxy is to conceive of learning policy as integral to economic policy, as in the absorption of the former Department of Employment by the Department for Education and Employment. This tendency carries so far that the new Chancellor of the Exchequer, Gordon Brown, could declare in his first Budget speech on 2 July 1997 that even 'childcare is now an integral part of economic development' – although Brown was referring primarily to parents.

The new economic orthodoxy has been described by the magazine *Working Brief* as having 'three principle tenets'. These are:

(1) Inflation should be controlled by interest rates, preferably by an independent central bank.
(2) Budgets should be balanced and not used to influence demand – or at any rate not to stimulate it.

(3) Unemployment is solely a problem of the labour market. (August/September, 1997)

These are also the principles underlying the Maastricht Treaty and the convergence criteria for EU member countries to enter the common currency. They 'boil down', as *Working Brief* says: 'to the use of strict demand policies to keep unemployment at a level high enough to restrain inflation' so that 'when unemployment falls to six per cent, financial policy is tightened for fear of "overheating"'. Government economic policy thus sustains a reserve army of the permanently unemployed 'underclass' alongside perpetual insecurity among a periphery of part-time and short-term contract employees.

Contradictorily, the new government's social policies aim at the same time to overcome this social exclusion which its economic policy sustains and generates; for instance, through the Social Exclusion Unit, announced in summer 1997 and modelled on Margaret Thatcher's 1987 Action for the Cities programme. The New Deal for unemployed youth, however, is designed to increase the supply of labour, whereas, as *Working Brief* points out:

> It is only in the context of a stronger overall demand for labour that measures to help particular categories of unemployed people (i.e. the young and long-term unemployed or lone mothers) are likely to have any significant effect on total unemployment.

Unlike previous and counter-cyclical training interventions, New Deal has been launched at a time of falling unemployment. It is, moreover, a one-off event funded by the £3 billion windfall tax on privatized utilities. However, the emphasis upon compulsion expressed by Ministers at its launch is likely to prove counterproductive (Bender, 1997) and is symptomatic.

The new consensus on combining economic and learning policy embraces also a major ideological shift among mainstream politicians and policy-makers in favour of measures to 'reform the welfare state' and end 'welfare dependency'. Thus, former Conservative government Employment Secretary, Peter Lilley introducing the Jobseekers Act could define 'the real issue ... [as] how to reduce benefit dependency' (HMSO, 1995b, para 40). Meanwhile, Frank Field, who was Chair of the House of Commons Social Security Select Committee during the same period and who has now become a Minister of State for Social Security, describes the 'passive benefit system' introduced in the 1940s as 'broken-backed' and seeks to 'transform' the social security system.

THE END OF THE WELFARE STATE?

What Lowe (1993) called the classic welfare state is generally agreed to have been established in the UK after 1945. With its founding moments in the cross-party cooperation of national government during the war, the classic welfare state remains, as Blackwell and Seabrook recorded, 'the most enduring creation of British Labourism' and 'the English working class's great existential protest against the way they were told life had to be' (1985, p. 37). Since its foundation, the welfare state has clearly been changing but lately has been described as in crisis, under threat, in transition, restructured, reconstructed, rolled back, transformed or dismantled, its end dated variously in 1973, 1975, 1979, 1981, 1987 and 1989 and a 'new' or 'post-welfare state' announced (Hewitt and Powell, 1997). While most commentators hesitate to pronounce the end of the welfare state, there is a general consensus among social policy analysts that, as Clarke *et al.* put it, 'something happened' to the welfare state from the 1970s (1994, p. 1).

Lowe defined a welfare state of the classic type as:

> a society in which government is expected to provide, and does provide, for all its citizens, not only social security but also a range of other services, at a standard well above the barest minimum. (1993, p. 14)

The implicit social contract between state and citizen was linked to the commitment by government, made for the first time in the 1944 White Paper on Employment Policy, 'as one of their primary aims and responsibilities the maintenance of a high and stable level of employment' (HMSO, 1944). This commitment was abandoned surreptitiously at first by the Labour Chancellor Denis Healey in 1976 as a condition of International Monetary Fund loans and then openly by Thatcher, who also abandoned the then-existing Keynesian economic orthodoxy that unemployment was cyclical and temporary, and accepted instead that mass unemployment had become permanent and structural (Ainley and Corney, 1990, p. 122). New Labour talks instead about 'full employability', for example, in Gordon Brown's address to the first Labour Party Conference after the Party's return to power, but this is not the same as full employment.

It can also be argued that there has been a crucial change in the administration of the state if the classic, postwar welfare state is compared with the state today. This change is neatly encapsulated by

Harden's 1992 notion of 'the contracting state'. This apt formulation captures the dual sense in which the new type of state is contracting, both as to its mode of operation by contracting or franchising out responsibility to private or semi-private providers and by its contracted and concentrated power which is vested by a presidential style of government in an increasingly powerful Treasury subservient to the Central Bank. These new administrative arrangements were institutionalized in the Public Service Agreements, or Contracts, the Treasury made with individual Departments following the July 1998 Comprehensive Spending Review.

Whether these changes taken together amount to introducing a new form of post-welfare state, the transformation has been described by Jones (1996a) and Jones and Peck (1995) in terms of a transition from welfare to workfare, refining Jessop's 1993 new 'Schumpeterian workfare state'. More broadly, the transition which has occurred in recent years is conceived by the regulationist school of economists as from a Fordist to a post-Fordist development paradigm (for example, Lipietz, 1992). More colloquially, the change is seen as one from a social democratic system of representative politics to a more presidential style of media-manipulated 'post-politics'. Thus, Blair and Clinton succeeded to the transition from the corporatism of the old welfare state in the UK and its equivalent in the USA accomplished by Thatcher and Reagan and followed by an attempted but failed Republican and Conservative consolidation under Bush and Major.

In whatever way it is conceptualized, what is argued here as the transition from corporate welfare to contracting post-welfare or workfare state can be seen as signifying a shift in the balance of forces embodied in the postwar (classic) welfare settlement between capital and labour. This shift has gone furthest within Anglo-Saxon-dominated countries. It was pioneered particularly by New Zealand – the first country to introduce a welfare state at the beginning of the century and the first to dismantle it in the 1980s under a structural adjustment programme imposed by a Labour government (Kelsey, 1996). Former British Labour MP and now Vice-Chancellor of the University of Waikako, Bryan Gould, writing in *The New Zealand Political Review* claimed that the first act of the new Chancellor, Gordon Brown, in contracting out monetary policy to the Governor of the Bank of England was modelled specifically on New Zealand (quoted in *Jobsletter Online*, 1997). Australia is, however, presented by New Labour ideologues as an alternative, third, or middle way between the extremes of the USA and the Europeans, excoriated as incorrigibly corporatist by Blair.

The change from corporate welfare to post-welfare contracting state not only changes the social contract within states between what the Germans still call 'the social partners', whom government previously brought together through tripartite measures, but also represents a shift in the former balance within capitalist economies between private and state monopoly capital. In place of the old mixed economy of private and state sectors, this has resulted in a 'new mixed economy' in which the power of government to intervene in the economy is much reduced by de-, or rather, re-regulation (Standing, 1997). In the new mixed economy, the semi-privatization of the state sector is complemented by the state-subsidization of the private sector, especially of multinational capital attracted to invest by massive state subsidies and allowances. This new mixed economy is well illustrated by UK Conservative education policy which semi-privatized schools, colleges and polytechnics through opting-out and incorporation, while the private schools were subsidized by the state through the Assisted Places Scheme of state-supported places in private schools. This last is now being phased out, although what Caroline Benn (1984) called 'the charity scam' of tax exemption through the charitable status accorded to private schools still continues under New Labour government. In other areas, New Labour has extended full, not just semi-, privatization; for example, by inviting private companies into Local Education Authorities to run Education Action Zones.

Changes in the form of administration of the state and the balance of forces within it have been accompanied by a wider class-recomposition in society. As noted by many commentators during the 1980s, while the restructuring of class and gender relations increased material inequalities, it also reduced the level of subjective awareness of them. These illusions have been sustained by the more or less deliberate political and ideological construction by Conservative governments during 1979–97 of a new division within the working population, separating a regionally and racially stereotyped so-called 'underclass', stigmatized by the poverty that disenfranchises its members from equal participation in society (Jordan, 1985, p. 8). In this sense, the dismantling of the welfare state and the construction of a penal state in the unprecedented growth of the prison population under the Conservatives were two sides of the same coin. Education and training at all levels are heavily implicated in the social exclusion of this marginalized 'underclass' through credentialism (or rather through the lack of any worthwhile credentials). As well as by lack of worthwhile qualifications, this new 'rough' is divided from the new 'respectable' working-middle of society by housing, immigration, social security and policing policies with the results so graphically described by Davies (1997). Meanwhile within the new working-middle class, the manual–mental division of labour between traditional 'working' and 'middle' classes has been eroded by the use of new technology and the growth of services, as well as by the extension of post-compulsory education.

A permanently unemployed reserve army of the old, traditional working class represents the collapse of the full-employment ideal underpinning the postwar consensus. The classic welfare state has been effectively undermined by the removal of the fundamental guarantee of unemployment benefit as social insurance. Entitlements to benefits for many claimants and for many items for which they were previously entitled to claim were replaced following the 1988 Social Security Review by discretion and are no longer grants but loans. In place of entitlement, alongside a heightened role for institutionalized charities and the voluntary sector, an 'active benefits regime' of workfare has replaced welfare. In fact, from October 1996 with the introduction of the Job Seeker's Allowance, the unemployed officially ceased to exist, redefined as 'job-seekers'. Under the 1995 Job Seekers Act, the powers of compulsion given to Employment Service Agency staff, who now manage the jobcentres, make most government training schemes compulsory. This amounts to a US-style work-for-benefits system and ends any notion of entitlement to benefits as social insurance. As powers of direction now include education courses, this could be said to constitute also a 'learningfare' regime.

One can even imagine a 'learning society' in which the unemployed are redefined out of existence. Their numbers have already been obscured by the 33 changes made to the way unemployment figures have been calculated since 1979 but at any one time average around two million, though some definitions of those wanting work range as high as five million – depending on whether part-time workers and those on schemes and in education are included. In a similar way, compulsory Youth Training for 16–18 year-olds ended youth unemployment at a stroke of the pen in 1986 (Ainley and Corney, 1990). In such a learning society, like actors resting, no one would ever be unemployed but only 'learning'. To such a bizarre prospect, the New Labour notion of employability gives a further twist, for if anyone was unemployed in a 'learning society' they would only have themselves to blame through not having made themselves employable enough!

LIFETIME LEARNING IN A POST-WELFARE STATE

Vouchers and Individual Learning Accounts guaranteeing a basic 'learning entitlement' with loans (or private resources) to top-up on particular courses at more prestigious institutions, have for some time been touted as a solution to the funding of all post-compulsory (life-long) learning. Indeed, the funding of Welfare to Work combines aspects of the method by which the Further Education Funding Council (FEFC) funds its colleges with the output-related funding (ORF) for Training and Enterprise Councils. To anyone who knows anything of the Byzantine complexities of the FEFC methodology, as well as the distortions that have been produced by ORF, this is a recipe for disastrous confusion (Jones, 1996b; Gravatt, 1998).

The new policy of 'learning for full employability' is not only one of 'Education without Jobs' (Ainley 1992), replacing what Finn (1987) called 'Training without Jobs' in the 1980s, but also one of 'Education with McJobs', as students and trainees work their way through college while employed part-time in a pattern that is extending up the age range (Ainley and Bailey, 1997). For students – like social security claimants – the former classic welfare entitlement to free higher education has been replaced by loans. Since the publication of Dearing's third report on higher education in July 1997, the addition of fees and the removal of grants saddles students with total debts and loans estimated by the Campaign for Free Education to vary by course and institution from between ten and twenty thousand pounds.

For the mass of five million-plus full- and part-time Further and Higher Education (F&HE) students and trainees, this new 'learning policy' represents a proletarianization of the professions for which Higher Education (HE) in particular previously prepared its students, rather than the professionalization of the proletariat that is officially presented by the expansion of F&HE. Included in this proletarianization, as part of the accompanying dismantling of welfare bureaucracies, are professional teachers at all levels.

Moreover, the rapid succession of policy changes under the Conservatives in the vocational education and training area did not lead to the vaunted revolution in training, as admitted in the

'Competitiveness' White Paper (HMSO, 1995a), let alone create a 'learning society'. Nor is the continuation of similar policies likely to do so under New Labour, as higher education illustrates (Ainley, 1994). The market mechanisms which have been accepted by HE management typically devolve funding for teaching and research down the established hierarchy from the government's Treasury to funding councils to institutions and cost centres within them. As in the other areas of the contracting state, this centralizes control in the hands of the funder of the contract while making the fund-holder, to whom funding is given, accountable for fulfilling the conditions of the contract. Fund-holders may then subsequently subcontract to subordinate agencies for specific tasks regulated in a like manner. At the same time, if the clients of services (in this case students) can be constituted as a market through empowerment by loans or vouchers that they can spend according to the courses on offer, then determination of funding is opened to the market and the wider, social purposes of education, which might formerly have been open to democratic control and accountability, are lost. The piecemeal process by which these new contracting arrangements were introduced as well as their consequences is well illustrated in further education where arguably they have gone furthest (see Ainley and Bailey, 1997).

The new forms of devolved funding were introduced in schools and colleges at the same time as the Conservative Government switched in 1987 from the policy of 'Training without Jobs' that had been pursued since 1976 based upon the German model. During this phase of policy, as Jones and Wallace record:

Employment, training and education policies, backed by social security policy, moved towards constructing just two groups of young people: trainees or students. (1992, p. 149)

The proportions of these two groups was then reversed in pursuit of a North American version of lifelong learning. Dearing's (1997) proposal to concentrate research in 'centres of excellence' – predictably in an Ivy League of elite universities – relegates the rest of HE to teaching-only and combines the worst of both worlds: elite HE for the few with mass HE for the many; while his attempt to transfer the 13 per cent of HE teaching that currently goes on in FE into HE draws a third line against polytechnic further education, relegated like US community colleges to feeding local students to their associated state universities. It also contradicts Dearing's basic brief of reversing the Tories' previous go-stop policy on higher education expansion by using

FE as access to mass HE to meet Blair's target of half a million more F&HE students by 2002. Of course, this is also contradicted by introducing fees and removing grants for HE students.

Such policies reintroduce tripartite distinctions associated with former divisions of labour and class and previous phases of education policy, a tertiary tripartism of the most traditional type. This is very clearly seen in Dearing's successive reviews of, first in 1993, the National Curriculum and then in 1996, of 16–19 qualifications. By providing the possibility of introducing General National Vocational Qualifications into schools at 14 in his first review, Dearing signalled an alternative vocational route for those who fail the academic National Curriculum. This was confirmed by the suggestion in his second review of a work-based route linked to FE for non-academic 14-year-olds. Now the National Curriculum will be 'disapplied' for schools and students in the Education Action Zones.

Moreover, Dearing's review of 16–19 qualifications also suggested amalgamating the Schools Curriculum and Assessment Authority, which oversaw the testing of the National Curriculum in schools, with the National Council for Vocational Qualifications, the body previously responsible for vocational qualifications, to make a new Qualifications and National Curriculum Authority (the QNCA, now QCA). A process of academic drift of GNVQs as 'alternative A-levels' could effectively leave NVQs with employers and the TECs managing training locally. The differences between academic and vocational courses would then be entrenched and attempts to bridge the divide between them not succeed, especially while the New Labour government retains a commitment to the 'gold standard' of academic A-level just as enthusiastically as the previous Conservatives. So here again Dearing expressed a clear intention to re-establish a traditional three pathway pattern – gold, bronze and iron; A-level, GNVQ and NVQ to be undertaken in sixth forms, FE and in work or on training schemes respectively and leading on to Ivy League or State HE supported by community colleges on the US model.

Yet, despite chronic qualification inflation and diploma devaluation, the new Americanized system of F&HE at present includes one-third of the age range in some form of HE (half of 17–20 year-olds in Scotland), while two-thirds now remain in school or college to 18. Even though this is still only what Spours (1995) called a 'medium participation system' as opposed to a 'mass' one (Scott 1995), it has afforded opportunities for students not previously in any form of institutionalized learning to 'drift up' the system as well as to be 'cooled out' of it at a later stage. If just the one-third of the age range now expected to progress to HE, together with many more adults, can be helped to think creatively and generally by their extended education experiences, this represents a major cultural change. On the other hand, if this third of labour market entrants and others are bamboozled, not only by post-modern approaches which deny any possible coherence to their learning but also by a narrow and instrumental focus upon outcomes or competences for non-existent future occupations, then the new Americanized F&HE will only preserve archaic social distinctions through academic certification, while creating new divisions between an uncertified 'underclass' and the rest.

TOWARDS A CERTIFIED SOCIETY?

The new post-welfare, contracting state may have 'disorganized dissent' by displacing responsibility for policy failure (Ainley and Vickerstaff, 1993) but the Conservatives could not avoid ultimate responsibility in the 1997 election. Yet the New Labour government too – or rather, its Treasury, as the ultimate fund-holder – while it may hold all the purse-strings and write and rewrite the conditions of the contracts, is left managing a system dedicated to the logic of the market. Politicians can then only present themselves as well-meaning and full of good intentions in face of the exigencies of the global economy.

Major's governments attempted to sustain a period of market-based consolidation in the hope that the new state mechanisms Margaret Thatcher had put in place would attritionally wear away resistance to the new contract culture. Meanwhile, under its new leader, Tony Blair, the New Labour Party had embraced the new market paradigm, signalling the abandonment of its traditional adherence to the old paradigm by replacing Clause Four of the Party's constitution that pledged common ownership of industry as the totem of old Labour corporatism and the classic welfare state. Blair's reiterated determination to reform the welfare state at the expense initially of single parents and disabled people can thus be taken seriously, while his pre-election pledge to abolish the quango state cannot.

Instead, a 'pinking of the quangos' can be anticipated, as Conservative placepersons are replaced by retired headteachers and sympathetic academics, similar to those who have already been drawn into advisory roles to central government in order to coopt potential critics. Despite some extensions to representative democracy and concessions to national and regional feelings through devolution and promised regional assemblies, what could be called the new regionalism (shadowing that of the EU and existing Government Offices), leaves the changes to and prunings of the local state made under Thatcher firmly in place.

Local management of schools, and the effective extension of opting-out to all State schools, for example, preserves the contracting arrangements characteristic of the new state, allowing some schools to accumulate surpluses while others go to the wall. Equally, wasteful competition between school sixth forms and colleges, as well as among colleges, also continues to be spurred on by unaltered funding methods, as does similar competition for students between FE and HE and between HE institutions, all leading to impending closures and mergers of colleges and universities. In Further Education, the FEFC mechanism set up under the Conservatives appears set for auto-destruction, leading to closures, mergers and semi-privatizations through franchising and other manifestations of what has been called 'the virtual college' (Reeves, 1995). As John Akker warned when he was Secretary General of the lecturers' union NATFHE, 'This could end in the destruction [of FE], or at the very least lasting damage to the education and training infrastructure' (quoted in Ainley and Bailey, 1997, p. 122).

The commitment of the New Labour government to education and training therefore appears questionable, despite its repeated protestations. Especially as: 'Over the long run,' as Robinson argues, 'the most powerful "educational" policy is arguably one which tackles child poverty' (1997, p. 3). Instead, the government's emphasis upon standards is, as Halsey, Heath and Ridge said: 'a plea that certain kinds of traditional knowledge ought to be valued' (1980, p. 111; q.v. Hall *et al.*, 1981). What Graff calls a 'literacy crisis' is associated in the USA with concern about the changing demographic composition of the young adult population. While Gee records how:

> The proclaiming of 'literacy crises' is a historically recurrent feature of Western 'developed' capitalist societies.. [and] is often a displacement of deeper social fears, an evasion of more significant social problems. (1996, p. 2)

From this perspective, the learning-society goal, despite its vocational rhetoric of relevance to employers' needs, can be seen as a social policy of selectivity (Offe, 1974) aimed at gaining legitimacy for heightened social control (Broadfoot, 1996).

Yet the result of reconstructing the state along the lines of a holding company has been to produce an inherently highly unstable system. Holding companies suffer particular organizational dysfunctions, managing at arms' length a complex range of diverse organizations to which self-management has been devolved. Subcontracting typically involves loss of detailed control, although financial control is increased. Another effect is fragmentation, for it is difficult to maintain and enforce national standards or public goods without considerable interference in the activities of the subcontractor. The new public management, borrowing from the new managerialism pioneered in the private sector, is also potentiated by new technology (management by e-mail) using quality indicators as performance targets of outputs (management by objectives). A contracting core of management no longer in direct contact with the work being undertaken comes to rely upon indirect indicators of performance. This leads to the well-known 'All Pigs Flying' scenario (Ainley, 1997). As well as new divisions between core management and a periphery of contract workers, this makes it difficult to determine which are real indicators and which are virtual ones. The contracting state may therefore also become the virtual state.

It was ironic that the Conservative Government was so deeply riven by internal divisions, exacerbated by an identity crisis over Europe, that it could no longer sustain the new type of state it had introduced. A more united New Labour government, more remote from the same national crisis of identity, may therefore be able to maintain the new settlement for some time longer than the Conservatives could any more hope to do. As their successors, the New Labour Party would then indeed be the 'true heir to radical Thatcherism', as its leader told Rupert Murdoch it was in July 1995. With the Tories relegating themselves by their choice of leader to the position of the anti-European party, this restores the Labour Party to the position of 'natural party of government' to which it aspired under the old welfare settlement. There is a precedent for this possibility in the way that old Labour established its proudest creation, the classic welfare state, in the original postwar settlement, only to lose power to the Conservatives in 1951 who then maintained the new settlement for the next 13 years. Whether this will happen again remains to be seen.

8 Labour and the Civil Service
Kevin Theakston

This chapter assesses the impact of New Labour on Whitehall. Previous Labour governments have, on the whole, done little to disturb the civil service's established order (Theakston, 1992). Back in 1945, the Attlee government was content to operate the system it inherited and did not believe that there was anything fundamentally wrong with the civil service. The Wilson government in the 1960s appointed the Fulton Committee but failed to deliver many of the modernizing reforms demanded by Whitehall's more radical critics. The 1974–79 Labour government plainly had no stomach for administrative reform and reneged on a manifesto commitment to scrap the Official Secrets Act. Will the Blair government be different? What does New Labour think about the massive changes made by the Conservatives to the civil service and the Whitehall machine since the party was last in office, and what are its own plans for the mandarinate?

MINISTERS AND MANDARINS

Whitehall had prepared for Labour's victory with great care and the 'handover' in May 1997 was well-organized. After 18 years of one-party rule, civil servants were anxious to demonstrate that they had not been 'politicized' and were ready and willing to serve the incoming Labour administration. Some were actually glad to see the back of the Tories; others welcomed the professional challenge of 'trying to make the [new] government work and make it successful', as one permanent secretary put it. Claims of 'a buzz of excitement in Whitehall' were not exaggerated – 'we're moving again, we're afloat' gushed one official (*The Times Higher Education Supplement*, 3 October 1997). The feeling was that a transfusion of energy and new ideas was overdue, but of course the relatively narrow ideological gap between 'Majorism' and 'Blairism' also facilitated the switch of loyalty from one government to another.

New ministers, on the whole, were impressed with their civil servants and established good working relations with their departments. 'It was a revelation to discover [officials] were engaged with, rather than resistant to, their new masters', reported one minister. Another said he was 'struck by the extent to which the civil service had been diminished and downsized though still as committed and ingenious as ever' (*Fabian Review*, September 1997, pp. 18–19). Used to working with their small staffs in Opposition, some ministers were, however, surprised by the size and complexities of the government machine – 'huge vehicles are hard to turn around', admitted one.

Blair and his advisers had no truck with the idea that the civil service had been 'politicized' by the Tories in a crude partisan sense. There was thus no 'hit list' of senior civil servants they wanted to remove (Mandelson and Liddle, 1996, pp. 247–8). All the same, the decision to press quickly ahead with the merger of the Environment and Transport departments to form John Prescott's 'super-ministry' involved the early departure of Sir Patrick Brown, permanent secretary at Transport, and a man closely associated with Conservative privatization policies. There were also claims that some senior DTI officials were moved because Labour ministers were finding it hard to work with them. On the other hand, Gus O'Donnell, close to John Major as the former PM's press secretary, was picked by Gordon Brown to become the Treasury's top economist and head of the government economic service. A spate of senior vacancies is giving Blair the chance to stamp his personal style on the mandarinate. The highly rated Sir Richard Wilson, chosen by him as the new Cabinet Secretary and Head of the Civil Service, is likely to be a reformer and a centralizer, in tune with Blair's own approach and thinking.

The Labour leadership claimed to be more concerned by the way in which the civil service policy-advice role had been downgraded by the Tories: after years of being ignored or keeping their heads down, officials would have to relearn how to 'speak truth unto power' (Mandelson and Liddle, 1996, pp. 248–9). At the Home Office, Jack Straw felt that the civil-service policy input was too weak; he had to say to his officials that 'they are not punching hard enough and that he wants their ideas. They were so cowed under Thatcher that it has taken them a while to understand' (*New Statesman*, 1 August 1997, p. 27). There were fears that, if anything, the civil service was being 'over-eager to please the new government' (Draper, 1997, p. 119).

While, in general, there is less mistrust between new ministers and the permanent civil servants than in, say, 1964 or 1979, there have been 'some frictional problems', as the outgoing Cabinet Secretary (Lord) Robin Butler acknowledged (*The Sunday Times*, 4 January 1998). Heavy-hitters such as Jack Straw and John Prescott have won the respect of officials as forceful and decisive ministers who know how to use the Whitehall machine effectively. But some other ministers – notably Gordon Brown and Harriet Harman (Social Security) – seem to want to keep officials at arm's-length, as if afraid of 'being sucked in to some pernicious system', as one insider put it. There were also reports that some senior Foreign Office officials, disliking Robin Cook and viewing his 'ethical' foreign policy with cynicism, were privately gleeful to see him damaged by the political storm over his ousting of the diary secretary in his private office and claims that he had considered appointing his mistress to the job. The Sierra Leone affair further strained relations between ministers and their diplomats, and raised questions about the running of the Foreign Office, as Cook appeared to distance himself from alleged staff failures.

The appointment of an increased number of political/special advisers – up from 38 under Major to over 70 now, with a big increase in Downing Street (including Jonathan Powell as 'chief of staff', Alastair Campbell as press secretary, and an expanded prime minister's policy unit) – is not in itself a problem. Whitehall's old pros are used to dealing with these ministerial aides and advisers and Labour is right to argue that, used properly, they can reinforce, not subvert, the political neutrality and integrity of the civil service. But some officials say that there are more separate meetings between ministers and advisers, with no officials present, than under the previous government, and worry about a possible communication problem. There is growing disquiet in the Treasury in particular about the centralization of power in the hands of the tightly knit group of advisers around Gordon Brown through whom everything has to be filtered (the key figures being economic adviser Ed Balls and chief 'spin doctor' Charlie Whelan), and the Chancellor's apparent reluctance to listen to civil service advice. Indeed, the long-serving Treasury permanent secretary, Sir Terry Burns, retired early after failing to mesh properly with Brown's team.

Labour ministers and their key aides have been very critical of the Whitehall media operation. A number of departmental press officers were sacked or resigned after clashing with ministers, and Alastair Campbell warned the official government PR machine to 'raise its game'. The feeling was that Whitehall had a lot to learn from the Labour Party's slick Millbank machine in terms of a tough and pro-active approach to the media, 'spin' and instant rebuttal. Some of the claims made about Orwellian-style 'Ministry of Truth' news management were undoubtedly exaggerated. Given the confrontational style of modern journalism, and the advent of 24-hour news media, innovations like Whitehall's new media monitoring unit and the central 'strategic communications unit', set up in Downing Street, seem sensible. The move to put the twice-daily briefings by the Prime Minister's press secretary on the record was also a long overdue step. An official working party was set up to review the work of the Government Information Service (GIS), with Labour sources claiming that their aim was to professionalize, not politicize, the GIS while making media-handling more of an integral part of the policy-making process. However, establishing and maintaining clear boundaries between civil service and party-political roles in this area could well give rise to difficulties and controversy in the years ahead.

STRENGTHENING THE CENTRE

Blair and his closest advisers were clear in advance about the quasi-presidential – 'Napoleonic' (Hennessy, 1998) – style of premiership that they wanted to introduce. Thatcher, not Major, would be the role-model. 'Strong leadership at the centre is the making of any government', insisted Peter Mandelson and Roger Liddle (now a member of the Downing Street Policy Unit) in their book-cum-blueprint *The Blair Revolution* (1996, p. 237). 'The machinery will happily function in neutral if left to itself, but will not move forward without strong prime-ministerial direction.'

Unlike Wilson in 1964 and Heath in 1970, Blair did not come into office wanting to make a mark by radical and large-scale restructuring of the departmental architecture (though the Overseas Development wing of the Foreign Office became a freestanding Ministry of International Development, and the new Department of Environment, Transport and the Regions was an overdue measure of bureaucratic rationalization). Sir Richard Wilson is also known to be sceptical about the benefits of tinkering with the machine. Over the longer term, important structural changes cannot be ruled out, however, as one way of dealing with 'turf wars' (involving the Home Office and the Lord Chancellor's Department) over control of justice policy and questions about the future of the embattled Ministry of Agriculture.

Blair's team were most anxious to strengthen the central machinery of government by reinforcing the critical Number 10–Cabinet Office axis and improving central coordination of policy-making and presentation. The aim was to drive through the Prime Minister's strategy, counter tendencies towards 'departmentalitis', and avoid being trapped by bureaucratic inertia. Significantly, whereas Kinnock had planned to recreate a 'think-tank' (along the lines of the old Central Policy Review Staff) for the Cabinet as a whole, Blair wanted a beefed-up Policy Unit for the prime minister alone. (In practice this is not only bigger but also more 'political' than under previous PMs – its 12-strong staff includes just one seconded civil servant.) Downing Street 'chief of staff' Jonathan Powell and press secretary Alastair Campbell established themselves as powerful 'inner circle' advisers. Peter Mandelson, formally a non-Cabinet Minister without Portfolio, occupied a unique position as a prime-ministerial 'enforcer', power-behind-the-throne and 'presentation' supremo during the government's first 15 months, with unrivalled access to civil service papers and a place on key Cabinet committees (Draper, 1997, pp. 22, 35, 108). In the July 1998 reshuffle, Jack Cunningham took over this coordinating and troubleshooting role as minister for the revamped Cabinet Office.

With the eclipse of Cabinet as a decision-taking body, the atrophying of the Cabinet committee system (outside the interlocked group of committees on constitutional reform policy), and Blair's informal style of conducting business, the classic Cabinet Secretariat functions have been downgraded (Hennessy, 1998). Apart from its brokerage role, knocking heads together in Whitehall and acting as a compromise-creating machine, Mandelson and Liddle (1996, p. 242) envisaged the Cabinet Office taking on a more 'proactive' role, providing policy innovation and pushing forward the government's programme. Blair ordered that the famous door linking Number 10 and the Cabinet Office should be 'more permanently ajar', and the Prime Minister's advisers and his Policy Unit now work more closely with the Cabinet Office. Sir Richard Wilson is likely to be a tough, 'hands-on' Cabinet Secretary, getting a strong grip on the machine on behalf of the PM. Peter Mandelson (1997, p. 9) has spoken of the new regime's 'strong central hub'. There was some talk in Opposition of a full-blown Prime Minister's Department, but it was ruled out. Arguably Blair has *de facto* built up something akin to this already, ordering Sir Richard Wilson to work on plans made public in July 1998 to reshape and bolster the Cabinet Office, aiming to strengthen the centre's strategic-planning, management and implementation capabilities. Given the crisis management, improvization and drift which characterized the central machine under John Major, criticized even by insiders as 'the system with a hole in the middle' (*The Economist*, 20 March 1993, pp. 25–6), the return to firm leadership is welcomed in Whitehall. In the long run, however, top officials and Cabinet ministers could increasingly question, resent and perhaps resist the strong central control over their fiefdoms. Discipline and coordination are one thing; attempts to usurp great departments of state quite another (*The Times*, 22 May 1997).

The pre-election talk about the so-called 'wicked issues' – persistent and intractable, mainly social, problems which cut across departmental boundaries and the established structures of government – has spawned a host of task forces, advisory groups and reviews: over 40 being set up in the government's first 100 days (*New Statesman*, 1 August, 1997, pp. 27–31). At the centre, starting work in December 1997, and hailed by Peter Mandelson as 'the most important innovation in government we have made since coming to office', is the new Social Exclusion Unit. Set up for an initial period of two years, and formally part of the Cabinet Office's Economic and Domestic Affairs Secretariat, though reporting directly to the Prime Minister, it is perhaps the most recent example of the tendency in British government to mobilize extremely small groups of people to deal with extremely big problems. Its 12-strong staff come from five Whitehall departments and Number 10, and also – unusually – from business, local government, the police and the voluntary sector. It is a ginger group-*cum*-think-tank, with a remit to plan, advise and coordinate, and not itself spend money. Blair says that it is a demonstration of the government's new approach to policy-making. Past attempts to overcome departmental rivalries and develop coordinated and comprehensive social policy strategies were usually not wildly successful (*New Statesman*, 22 August 1997, p. 11). One of the great tests for the Blair government is whether it can really make a difference here.

As always, the Treasury is a powerful and ubiquitous force in Whitehall. In the past, Labour governments have often sought – always unsuccessfully – to create counterweights to the Treasury and its economic orthodoxy (such as the ill-fated Department of Economic Affairs in the sixties). In Opposition, Gordon Brown talked, controversially, of making the Treasury a 'catalyst for change' and a 'force for innovation', provoking John Prescott to hit back publicly with warnings against a 'super-Treasury' with an enlarged role. But Blair's circle were clear about the need for a strong Treasury to resist the clamour of special interests, lobby groups and their allies in the spending departments (HC Debs, 27 October 1994, col. 1109).

Brown's influence inside the government was underlined by his appointment as chairman of the Cabinet's economic affairs committee (Blair being the first PM for over 30 years not to chair this committee), and by his (and the Treasury's) leading role in the 'welfare to work' review exercise. The Comprehensive Spending Review also gave the Treasury a finger in every pie across the government as a whole, and the new system in which Departments agree 'contracts' with the Treasury, setting out detailed objectives and targets, with progress being monitored by a public-spending Cabinet committee chaired by the Chancellor, confirms its role as the powerhouse of government. At the same time, there is concern that the Treasury's traditional departmental outlook is ill-suited for the tasks of positive governance and handling the 'wicked issues'. The relationship between the Treasury and Number 10 has been marked by tensions over the sharing of information, the activities of rival 'spin doctors' and the handling of some key policy issues (including the single-currency issue and the row over lone-parent benefits). Both the new Performance and Innovation Unit in the Cabinet Office, which may be intended to provide a prime-ministerial counterweight to the Treasury, and the selection of a Treasury 'high-flyer', Jeremy Heywood, as the Prime Minister's next principal private secretary, have been interpreted as a sign that Blair wants to get more control over Brown and make the vital Number 10–Treasury nexus work more smoothly (*The Times*, 16 February 1998). This could be crucial for the stability and success of the government.

FREEDOM OF INFORMATION REFORM

Blair promised a decisive break with the traditions of 'closed government' accepted by previous Labour administrations. 'No Government can be successful which cannot keep its secrets', Attlee had insisted in 1945 (Theakston, 1992, p. 178). 'Openness is essential for good government' was the line now (Select Committee on Public Administration, 1997a, q. 1). Freedom of Information (FoI) reform can be seen as a key test for New Labour partly because old Labour had failed, in the 1970s, to deliver it.

Six successive Labour manifestos promised an FoI Act, but when there was no immediate legislation in the new government's first Queen's Speech, open government campaigners became alarmed about possible ministerial backtracking or fudging of the commitment.

The promised White Paper was delayed; rumours circulated that David Clark, the Public Service Minister responsible for the measure, would be sacked; there were reports about supposed civil-service foot-dragging; key ministers (including Peter Mandelson) were said to be sceptical or opposed; and there were protracted arguments over the details in the relevant Cabinet committee, chaired by Lord Irvine, the Lord Chancellor. Ministers rejected the 'off-the-shelf' solution of putting the *Code of Practice on Access to Government Information*, introduced by the Conservatives in 1994, into legislative form. Cabinet Office insiders were worried that the White Paper might have more expectations than it could realistically deliver, but in the event the government's reform blueprint was welcomed by commentators and FoI campaigners as a surprisingly radical document which could herald a revolution in Whitehall and give Britain one of the world's most liberal information regimes (HMSO, 1997b).

The government claimed – with some justification – that its pro-posals struck the right balance between extending people's access to official information and preserving confidentiality where it is still necessary and important. They go significantly further than the existing *Code of Practice* and the FoI laws of most other countries. First of all, in terms of scope, there will be very wide institutional coverage, extending well beyond central government departments and agencies to cover thousands of bodies across the whole public sector (including local government, the health service, quangos, and so on.) as well as the privatized utilities and private-sector suppliers of contracted-out functions. (The blanket exclusion for the security and intelligence services has been criticized, however. Second, whereas the 1994 Code only provided access to 'information' (opening up the possibility of 'doctoring' material), there will instead be rights of access to a wide range of official documents and other records. Third, there will be fewer exemptions than allowed under existing provisions – covering, as expected, information relating to national security, defence and international relations, law enforcement, and personal privacy; though there are likely to be arguments about where the lines should be drawn in the areas of commercial confidentiality, 'the safety of the individual, the public and the environment', and information supplied in confidence. However, the proposal is that information in these categories can only be kept secret if disclosure would cause 'substantial harm' – a tough test.

One of the most crucial exemptions relates to what the White Paper calls 'the integrity of the decision-making and policy advice processes in government.' Even in Opposition, Blair's advisers were adamant that full disclosure of official policy advice to ministers risked undermining civil service impartiality and could stifle the free and frank exchange of views inside government and the Cabinet system (Mandelson and Liddle, 1996, p. 205). Here the lower test of simple 'harm' is proposed, to give government what the White Paper describes as the 'space and time in which to assess arguments and conduct its own debates with a degree of privacy'. In return, the government pledges to make as much of the factual and background information contributing to the policy-making process as possible publicly available (symbolically, it published on the Internet an 83-page document of background papers for the FoI White Paper). All the same, doubters wonder whether civil servants will try to 'get round' the new law: will there be more unminuted 'conversations' or sensitive information written on the ubiquitous yellow sticky labels which could be removed before files were handed over (Select Committee on Public Administration, 1997b, qs. 77, 95)?

The rules in this area are, of course, intended not only to provide constitutional cover for civil servants but also political protection for ministers. The First Division Association, the top civil servants' union, commented: 'public confidence in truly open government depends on ministers realising that "substantial harm" to the public interest is not always the same thing as substantial harm to their own political fortunes' (*FDA News*, January 1998). For this reason a strong appeals and enforcement mechanism is vital, and the White Paper proposed the appointment of a new independent information commissioner with full powers to order disclosure (at present, the ombudsman who polices the 1994 *Code of Practice* can only recommend disclosure). It will be a key, and powerful, post and while Whitehall may want to instal a 'safe' figure (perhaps a retired Sir Humphrey), MPs, the media and outside groups will want a tough and independent-minded arbiter.

Truly open government will depend on FoI legislation acting as a catalyst for wider change in the whole approach of government to secrecy and openness: making openness 'part of the official culture rather than an irksome imposition', as the White Paper puts it. The government says that it wants public authorities to take a positive approach, publishing much more information as a matter of course. Progress here may be slow and uneven. Ingrained bureaucratic mind-sets are one problem – political will is another. David Clark insisted that 'the emphasis under this Government will be on releasing, not withholding, information' (HC Debs, 4 June 1997, col. 384). But how this commitment can be reconciled with the Blair government's obsession with control, 'spinning' and presentation of information remains to be seen.

The fierce Cabinet committee arguments in the summer of 1998, about the timing and the details of the promised draft FoI bill, suggest a developing defensiveness and executive government focus. There were reports of a rearguard action against the extensive powers of the information commissioner and the White Paper's proposal that ministers would have no veto or 'override' power on the release of information. The Treasury tried to argue down legislation on cost grounds, and FoI campaigners were dismayed when responsibility for the measure was transferred to the Home Office, where Jack Straw had emerged as a leading opponent of greater openness in government. The shelving of plans to introduce a draft FoI bill in the autumn raised fears that the issue might be slipping down the government's agenda and key provisions watered down. Perhaps it is only to be expected that ministers become less keen on openness as they settle into office and the pressures and problems mount up, but delivering a strong FoI measure remains crucial for New Labour's reforming credibility – as critics will not fail to point out.

BETTER GOVERNMENT

'Be radical' – underlined three times – Tony Blair urged David Clark, Chancellor of the Duchy of Lancaster, in a memorandum about government plans to modernize public services (*The Times*, 6 October 1997). Putting the clock back on the Conservatives' far-reaching managerial and organizational changes across the public sector had been explicitly rejected by the Labour leader: 'We seek to build sensibly on what is in place. We keep what is good and working. We change what isn't' (*The Times*, 30 June 1995). Thus Next Steps agencies, the Citizen's Charter, market-testing, contracting-out and even possible privatization of civil service functions are here to stay – despite being criticized or opposed by Labour in Opposition.

Now covering 77 per cent of all civil servants, the agency programme (launched in 1988) is virtually complete. Where agencies (an old Fabian idea, which can be traced back to the Labour-appointed Fulton Report of 1968) are working well, Labour does not plan to change the structure. It has also accepted the major shift of management responsibilities (for pay, grading, recruitment, etc.) from the centre to individual departments and agencies which has occurred over recent years The emphasis now is to be put on improving agency performance (HMSO, 1998c). Jack Straw moved swiftly to 'assert and reinforce ministerial responsibility' for the much-criticized Prison Service – Home Office ministers have resumed answering parliamentary questions about prisons and there has been a review of the organization and running of the agency (Prison Service, 1997). Labour condemned Michael Howard's use of the 'policy'–'operations' distinction to wriggle free of responsibility over the Derek Lewis affair, but there remains considerable scope for tensions and confusion in the relationship between ministers and agencies in such highly controversial policy areas. One big item of unfinished business hanging over from the Conservative years is in fact a rethink of the convention of ministerial responsibility (Public Service Committee, 1996), but it is not clear how willing or able the Labour government will be to tackle this problem. Labour had criticized the Conservatives for operating on the basis that no minister need ever resign for any policy failure – will that accusation be one day flung back in its face?

Labour had mocked John Major's Charter but had accepted the idea of charterism and its themes of quality, responsiveness, customer-empowerment and better public services (Labour councils in the 1980s pioneering some of the new ideas). The old top-down Fabian paternalism was thus finally buried, and a party identified with public sector employees acknowledged that 'a public bureaucracy can be a vested interest just like any other', as Blair put it. The charter approach was also seized on as a way of making limited resources go further. The talk under the new government was of 'refocusing' and 're-energizing' the Charter programme. A big consultation and ideas-gathering exercise was launched in September 1997, and a 5000-strong People's Panel will be used to find out what people think about public services and their delivery. The relaunch came in June 1988, with the new 'Service First' programme. In some ways this was just a relabelling and repackaging job developing established ideas and themes, but there was a potentially important new emphasis. This stressed 'the more effective use of resources' rather than the old 'value for money' mantra, and on promoting cross-sectoral working coordination and 'partnership' in service-delivery ('seamless government' has become the new buzz-word). One cannot see the Treasury under its new masters being any more responsive than it was under the old ones to the idea of quality-driven public expenditure increases, however.

Even before becoming Labour leader, Tony Blair made clear that while opposed to the 'commercialization' of public services, he believed that it was in many ways 'valid to import market mechanisms' into the way they were run and for government to take on the role of 'guarantor and not . . . provider' (*FDA News*, January 1994). Abandoning the pre-election pledge of a moratorium and an independent review, the Labour government announced that market-testing and contracting-out will continue where they offer best value for money, but they will not be pursued as an article of faith (Clark, 1997, p. 12). Privatization is also still very much on the agenda, Gordon Brown ordering a review of departmental assets (found to total £300 billion) which will facilitate the sell-off of surplus property, land or other holdings to bolster the coffers. In part this is newfound ideological flexibility, but it is largely a financial, Treasury-driven process. The spending squeeze and frozen departmental 'running costs' will continue, together with a tough line on pay increases, and the Comprehensive Spending Review set targets for annual 'efficiency improvements'.

The pressure to 'do more with less' means Labour is proceeding with schemes it had previously condemned, to the dismay of the civil service unions. The go-ahead has been given for more privately financed jails, for instance, and for the sale (and leaseback) of the Social Security property estate (including 700 local benefit offices) to a private consortium, a move which may now be copied by other departments. Computer systems have been sold and the Benefits Agency medical services transferred to the private sector. Ministers are talking of making more use of public–private partnerships and the Private Finance Initiative. 'Outsourcing' of government operations looks likely to expand (*The Times*, 15 August 1997).

Although Labour advisers are floating radical ideas to wipe £3.5 billion (10 per cent) off the cost of running the Whitehall bureaucracy and argue that more staff reductions are possible, making pointed remarks about 'the myth that no more can be cut' (Byrne, 1997, pp. 23–4), ministers prefer to enthuse about a 'revolution in public services' (*The Times*, 11 February 1998). They say that they want to end the 'forms and queues' perception of bureaucracy. Inspired by Clinton and Gore's Reinventing Government programme in the United States, Blair has talked about a drive for 'Simple Government' and set a target that by 2002, 25 per cent of dealings with government can be done by a member of the public electronically, using telephone, television or computer-links. A *Better Government* White Paper has been promised, inaugurating moves towards what ministers like to call 'joined-up government', aiming to break down entrenched boundaries and introduce more client-focused approaches. A new 'government direct' agenda is opening up and we are likely to see more schemes like the Child Support Agency's planned abandonment of routine work in local offices and a switch to a seven-days-a-week telephone service. 'You can deal with your bank by phone 24 hours a day, why not government?' say insiders. The private sector is setting the standard in customer expectations, and Whitehall sees the need to respond. Plans for smart cards to get access to government services and pay benefits are being considered; high-street information kiosks with electronic forms and touch-screen functions are possible; some functions could be contracted out to local government; there could be a network of one-stop shops (amalgamating local offices) where people could conduct all their official business.

The big problem is how all this brave talk will work out in practice when the resource constraints are so tight. What incentives can be introduced to keep the good people and maintain the staff morale and motivation needed to deliver 'better government' (charter mark Oscars and gushing ministerial speeches only go so far)? Performance-related pay (which Labour now backs) may actually be counterproductive and demotivating. There are major 'human resource' management issues to be faced here. But it is clear that a new phase in the Whitehall 'management revolution' started by the Tories in the 1980s is only just starting.

CONCLUSION

Labour ministers were quick to set a new tone in Whitehall, talking about the importance of the public service ethos and how much they valued the key role of the civil service in the government of the country (Clark, 1997). There were also some important symbolic gestures, such as overturning the union ban at the GCHQ spy centre, throwing open the doors of the Foreign Office to hundreds of school-children and students in an effort to counter the old-school-tie image and encourage a wider range of applicants, and the highlighting of the under-representation of blacks and Asians at senior levels in the service.

At the same time it is clear that New Labour is not going to put the clock back. Thanks to Margaret Thatcher, the bureaucracy is more effectively subject to ministerial control and direction than it was twenty or thirty years ago. Blair intends to keep the politicians in the driving seat. Labour also knows that it cannot afford to halt the management revolution, given the need to squeeze as much as possible from every public-sector pound spent. Indeed, the efficiency drive may intensify.

Peter Mandelson (1997, p. 12) has put the machinery of government reforms introduced since the 1997 election on a par with the 'great modernizing thrusts to the administrative machine' made in the past century only in time of war. They may be only a first instalment. In addition, devolution to Scotland and Wales (and possibly the English regions), FoI, a bill of rights, parliamentary reform and – possibly – proportional representation will have a major impact on the constitutional and political environment in which the civil service operates, and bring further changes to its role and character. The civil service of 2002 (or 2007) could look very different to that of 1997.

9 New Labour and the Decentralization of Power
Peter John

What is the impact of the Labour Government on the territorial distribution of power in the British state? The question is interesting for several reasons. First, every standard political science text states that Britain is a centralized country because the executive controls a sovereign Parliament. Unified political parties have an ability to command a majority of seats in the legislature which means that, once elected to office, they can generally push through what policies they like, through the executive's control over appointments and the parliamentary timetable. Thus, unlike in some European countries, not only do elected local authorities or other territorial organizations have no constitutional right to exist and must find a legal power backed by Parliament to act, they usually deal with a united and powerful executive. Thus a combination between Parliament's legal authority, the lack of constraint on party government and executive coherence centralizes power in Britain. Given that a unified Labour Party was elected in 1997 with a large majority, why should it act any differently to its predecessors? On the other hand, Labour has given executive powers to parliaments in Scotland and Wales which will be hard to repeal. Most of all Labour is keen to reform the very British constitution, which centralizes power, and the electoral system, which sometimes creates large majorities in Parliament. Thus it is an open question whether the move to a territorial division of powers in Britain marks a change from the normal pattern whereby the executive based in power in London exercises power over the politically weak periphery.

The second reason why Labour's stance toward decentralization is interesting is that local government lacks political power in the British state. In Jim Bulpitt's (1983) formulation, there exists a 'dual polity', a separation between central and local elites, which means that local government is not entrenched into national politics as in other states. There are no local leaders who hold powerful positions in the legislature and few who do so in the national party. This political separation of central and local government weakens local democracy as it removes the automatic protection of local interests and denies local areas privileged access to central government decisions. The separation between national and local government reached its apogee during the years the Conservatives were in office when, at the end of the 1980s, there were few local councils controlled by the governing party and where central–local government relations were an arena for intense party conflict. The question which arises is whether policy-making under Labour is likely to be markedly different. One change is that the new post-1997 parliamentary Labour Party has many formerly locally elected leaders who might be able to speak for local interests. In addition, there may be greater access of local government to central government, particularly as many of Labour's policies, such as welfare to work, require local government as the main implementing organization.

The third reason why the decentralization of power is an interesting subject after 1997 is because of the history of the Labour Party in and out of government. Notwithstanding the experiments with municipal socialism in the 1920s, which were anyway seen by their advocates as precursors of policies a government would follow nationally, Labour has generally been a centralist party. It has aimed to gain a majority of seats in Parliament and to implement a programme to reshape the economy and social life. Even though it has its citadels of Labour-run councils in the north of the county, the party has never come to articulate decentralization because of its mission for change. Most of all, during the first half of the twentieth century the party created a machine which would sit neatly in government with a potential Prime Minister and Cabinet who could drive the executive. This mission required unity and a centralization of power in the party organization (Sharpe, 1982). Thus it was usually Labour which took power from local authorities, such as during the 1945–51 Labour governments.

Ironically, as many studies of party organizations have noted (e.g. McKenzie, 1964), the Conservative Party was the party of decentralization, as it represented the shires and small towns, was linked to the Independents, and resisted centralization, such as comprehensive state schooling in the 1960s. It is the Conservatives which give much independence to their local party organizations over finances, policy and the selection of candidates, whereas in the Labour Party power rests with the party leadership and the National Executive Committee. Yet, during the 1980s, the Conservatives centralized local government, introduced controls of finance, removed functions and limited local discretion. There even grew up a culture of Conservative hostility to the supposed inefficiency of local authorities in favour of consumers and unelected micro-agencies.

In contrast, Labour became the party of local democracy, controlling more and more councils and defending local government from marketization and privatization. Moreover, the geographical base of Labour's national electoral support shrank into the periphery and even strengthened in Scotland, Wales and in the North, so that Labour represented London and the South less and articulated the voices of the economically and culturally marginalized regions. The question that arises after 1997 is whether the Labour Party can uphold its faith in territorial politics in office. On the one hand, Labour had to fulfil the electoral promise of decentralization developed while out of power, to meet the emotive demand for a less centralized government and to reward supporters of the party who remained loyal in the 1980s. Moreover, when Labour articulates the language of constitutional change, it may become less wedded to a 'top-down' approach to policy-making. On the other hand, once the rhetoric of partnership between centre and locality has broken down, the opposition parties capture political control of more councils after local elections and the excitement of devolution has ebbed, Labour could become just as centralizing as its predecessors. With its large majority, Labour relies on the marginal seats of constituencies in the south; many of its local-council-leader new MPs stood down from local office and are anxious for ministerial posts; and Labour regards achievement of its manifesto aims as keenly as any government.

The final reason why Labour's stance on decentralization is interesting for political scientists is because of the effects of the 18 years of Conservative policies for local government. The excess of centralization and the inefficiency of introducing quasi-markets for public services suggests a policy of rapprochement with local government is opportune, and indeed the final years of the Second Major government saw some softening of the conflict in central–local government relationships. It would be expected that the Labour government would find it easier to govern with the rhetoric of partnership with local government. Nonetheless, as some writers have pointed out (Stoker, 1991), the disputes and policy innovations of the 1980s were much more than a testament to the potency of neo-conservatism. They marked a fundamental break with the politics of the expanding welfare state and saw the implementation of competition into economic and public life. The logic of state reform meant that the institutional foundations of local government, which had been consolidated by the expansion of the welfare state during the twentieth century, were eroded by marketization and fiscal austerity. The greater role of the private sector in government, the introduction of new management ideas, probably would have emerged whatever party was in power in the 1980s. The implication of this argument is that Labour must carry on with the programme of reform, and a return to an earlier age of central restraint and local professional autonomy is hardly a plausible option. Thus some element of central control and leadership in institutional restructuring is implied by the forces of political modernization and international economic competition.

The politics of decentralization do not follow a predestined course under the government elected in 1997. Depending on how the analyst interprets the British political tradition, the politics of constitutional change, the history of centralism in the Labour Party and the causes and effects of the politics of the 1980s affect what to expect from the 1997 government, both in terms of informal politics and from the policy changes. What is most interesting of all is that the course of decentralization while Labour is in office is useful evidence for interpretations of British politics, both before and during the 1990s. Even a short assessment of the experience of one year in office can help resolve some intellectual disputes about the British constitution and the importance of the statecraft followed by political parties and their leaders.

LABOUR AND DEVOLUTION

The linchpin of Labour's projects of decentralization and constitutional reform is Scottish devolution. The electoral promise to create a parliament with tax-raising powers is deeply entrenched in Labour's programme. The measure potentially changes the distribution of power in the state and could trigger greater decentralization and the extension of regional government. Even though the effects of devolution are potentially profound, they are mediated by the origins of Labour's commitment to constitutional change, and may be a self-contained policy promise which pays off old debts but leaves intact a more conservative strategy for the rest of the country.

The origins of Labour's manifesto promise go back to the Labour governments of 1974–79. These minority administrations were highly vulnerable to the rise of the Scottish nationalists which threatened Labour's precious seats in Scotland. The rise of the Scottish nationalists challenged moribund and undynamic local Labour parties with a more radical, dynamic and romantic agenda. So the commitment to devolution was launched, and nearly reached the statute book in 1979. The simple rationale was that, if parliament gave some form of elected regional autonomy to Scotland, the concession would dish the Scottish Nationalists who would not be able to argue so convincingly that Britain was centralized and that Scotland had little independence. Scottish voters would be assuaged by their assembly and would refrain from voting for the independence party. While much has changed during the 1980s and 1990s, this simple logic seems to explain the Labour Party's commitment to devolution. Even though the light of the nationalists temporarily dimmed in the early 1980s after the failure of the devolution proposals in the 1979 referendum and when North Sea oil ceased to be a political issue, the Scottish National Party regained its electoral support, particularly as it cannily adopted proposals for greater links to the European Union. The pressure of a more dynamic party competitor pushed Labour into consideration of constitutional issues. While Labour benefited from the electoral demise of the Conservatives during the Thatcherite experiments of the 1980s, it could not afford to sit back. Labour had to come up with a coherent strategy to respond to the demands of the periphery. These party-political factors came together in the remarkable cross-party cooperative venture of the Constitutional Convention which laid the foundations of Labour's policy on Scotland.

Even if the Blair government would have liked to renege on its commitment to Scottish devolution, electoral factors locked it into the constitutional strategy. It might thus appear that Labour's agreement to the Scottish parliament was a reluctant accession to electoral politics rather than a willing leap into a new constitutional era. This ambivalence might appear to be shown by the *volte-face* in June 1996 over the referendum on the Scottish parliament. Rather than offer a simple yes or no choice, the Labour leadership proposed a two-question ballot, one to give assent to the assembly and the other to decide whether it should have tax-raising powers. This event could reveal the extent to which Labour saw Scotland as a special problem rather than as a marker for further constitutional reform. Yet, rather than show Labour to be reluctant devolvers, the decision shows a neat political manoeuvre which ensured wider acceptance for the eventual outcome, gave Labour a greater reputation for financial prudence and highlighted the commitment to more democratic choice. The radical nature of the Scottish proposals, particularly in the White Paper *Scotland's Parliament*, show that it is difficult to see Scotland as a self-contained policy issue as the proposals relate to the wider wish to distribute power and engage in constitutional reform. The significance of the change is shown by the extent of the functions being handed over. The Scottish parliament has the power to make the law of Scotland in devolved areas and holds to account an executive headed by a first minister which operates in a way similar to the United Kingdom government. The Scottish Parliament and executive are responsible for the wide range of domestic matters, including health, education and training, local government, housing, social work, economic development, transport, the law and home affairs, the environment, including the natural and built heritage, agriculture, fisheries and forestry, and sport and the arts. There is an array of supervisory powers over other bodies. Unlike the proposals of 1978 the UK Parliament has transferred all the Scottish Office's powers to Scotland. The executive participates in European Union decision-making affecting Scotland and, as mentioned, the parliament has the power to increase or decrease the basic rate of income tax set by the UK Parliament by up to 3 pence.

It is true that the devolution to Wales is rather less far-reaching than in Scotland with fewer functions transferred and the absence of tax-varying powers. However, Wales has always been more integrated into English administration, and the Welsh Office is much younger than its Scottish counterpart. Moreover, as the narrow referendum result shows, Welsh public opinion is not so favourable to a separate democratic identity. Rather than showing the weakness of Labour's constitutional impetus, the Welsh proposals show the salience of the new politics while being tempered by the circumstances operating in each part of the UK. In addition, the powers allocated to the Assembly are not meagre. It has at its disposal the £7 billion budget currently assigned to the Welsh Office, and allocates resources from it to public services in Wales. The Assembly also sets policies and standards for those services; oversees the work of unelected public bodies; and makes detailed rules and regulations through secondary legislation within the framework laid down in Acts of Parliament. The Assembly is able to debate all issues of concern in Wales and it gives equal status to the English and Welsh languages.

THE ENGLISH REGIONS

The test of New Labour's commitment to decentralization is the fate of the proposal to create elected regions in England. With such meagre reforms it is easy to be cynical. Thus regional development agencies, designed to promote sustainable economic development and social and physical regeneration and to coordinate the work of regional and local partners in areas such as training, investment, regeneration and business support, seem to match the bodies in Scotland and Wales but without the direct democratic component. The creation of regional chambers, composed of local authorities and other representatives gathered together on a voluntary basis, to monitor the agencies in areas covered by the government offices for the regions would seem to be the most minimum democratic reform possible. The measure adopts the top-down and technocratic aspects of regionalism rather than decentralizing power. As with Scotland and Wales, there is a high degree of political pragmatism in the progress of the reform, but such caution need not indicate that Labour rules out a commitment to more radical decentralization should future conditions permit. The cynical view does not do justice to the blend between statecraft and constitutionalism which characterizes the Labour Government's policy experiments.

To understand the context of the reforms, it is important to know how the regional political movement developed with the Labour Party, particularly in the north of the country. Labour's regionalism was driven by the impact of greater economic recession in some regions more than others; a resistance to the centralizing policies over local government in the 1980s; a reassertion of cultural identity which was entrenched in northern Labour parties against market-based policies emanating from the south-east; and a response to the strengthening of the unelected regional state. Regionalism found its expression in consultation documents in the late 1980s and early 1990s (e.g. Labour Party, 1987, 1991), if not in manifesto commitments. It was not until the 1992 general election that Labour returned to a formal commitment to regional devolution, but the Labour Party leadership did not pursue its regional government commitments with much conviction in the 1992 election campaign. From that time Labour gradually committed itself to a slow, but nevertheless perceptible programme of political regionalism over the first term of the new administration. The refinement of the Straw proposals on regional devolution after consultation (Labour Party, 1996a) has removed some of the main hurdles for political devolution, with the disappearance of an initial insistence on a mainly unitary local government structure as a precursor to elected regional assemblies, and the broadening of the acceptable tests of popular support for elected assemblies to reflect the multi-stage, multi-track approach that was seemingly successful in Spain. Alongside this process, the final report of the Millan Commission (Regional Policy Commission, 1996) has produced a substantial analysis of the economic case for regional devolution and a methodology for the integration of the long-held Labour Party aspiration for English regional development agencies along with the political process of devolution. In this context, the 'U-turns' of the Labour leadership on the issue of a Scottish referendum can be seen as an attempt to integrate the process of Scottish devolution with the longer-term, more challenging idea of extending decentralization in Scotland first to its neighbours in the north of England and then, more problematically, to the south of the country.

Along with the regional chambers and the regional development agencies, are the special reforms for London which, like other regions, is run by a government office. What happens in London could have knock-on effects for the rest of the country. Thus the directly elected mayor, the assembly of 25 members, elected under a mixture of first-past-the-post and party list electoral systems, could be replicated in other regions. Moreover, the mayor and assembly have responsibility for transport, economic regeneration, crime, fire and emergency services, environment, land-use planning, arts, sport and health. More than £3 bn has been transferred from existing budgets to new bodies controlled either directly or indirectly by the mayor, such as the police committee which ended 170 years of the metropolitan police reporting to the Home Secretary. Even if the mayor and assembly have to work under the control of central government departments, it is hard to believe such a dramatic shift of responsibilities does not represent a major shift in power from the centralization of metropolitan governance in the Thatcher years and could enhance further democratization in other areas. As with Scotland and Wales, Labour's policies show a curious blend of radicalism and caution which reflect both a commitment to some constitutional change but a wish to see it bed down and to allow for either retreat, consolidation or extension.

LOCAL GOVERNANCE

Locally elected authorities suffered the ravages of the Thatcher years more than any other civic or political institution. It will be a mark of New Labour's constitutionalism whether the centralization of power can be reversed. As with London, Wales and Scotland, it is easy to provide a cynical gloss on the reform promises, as this author did shortly before the 1997 election (John, 1997). The argument runs that Labour has inherited some policy proposals it could not get out of, but in the main it extended the Thatcherite project and continued central controls. In opposition Labour tried to keep a careful balance between rewarding its members in local government who wished for new freedoms and financial security after the years of Conservative rule and the need for policy responsibility and fiscal restraint in the face of a national media obsessed by the machinations of Labour London and metropolitan local councils. After all, the turning-point of the fortunes of the Labour Party in the 1980s was leader Neil Kinnock's public refutation of Labour-controlled Liverpool City Council policies at the Labour Party Conference of 1985. As well as an electoral calculation, the moderation of Labour's main policy document, *Renewing Democracy, Rebuilding Communities* (1995), and the subsequent watering down of many of its commitments reflect the selective acceptance of slices of what was once regarded as the Conservatives' policy agenda and is also testament to the power of the ideological revolution which is likely to live far beyond the Conservative governments of the 1980s and 1990s. Thus Labour's plans for 'best value' and local performance plans have little to distinguish them from the value-for-money proposals pushed by the Audit Commission since 1988, and strongly encourage councils to retain competitive tendering, albeit in the context of a partnership between local and central government. Indeed, the proposal to give powers to the Audit Commission and to the secretary of state to overhaul inefficient services goes beyond the policies of the Conservatives. Other policies contained in the Labour policy document, *New Labour, New Life for Britain* (1996b), were carefully qualified so they did not give away any hint of irresponsibility.

However, the cynical view does not do justice either to the substance or the spirit of Labour's reforms for local government when in office. It would be implausible to expect a massive transfer of power under a recently elected government with a national manifesto and, given the media's obsession with local government excesses and malpractice, it is difficult to relax the reins of power. As with the regions and devolution, given the context and the low level of public interest in local politics, there have been progressive reforms. For example, even though the review of local government finance did not fully relax the capping of local government expenditure and did not give back control of business rates to local government, there has been a softening of central powers in the proposal that central government warns councils that they may be spending unreasonably. The giving of the power to vary an increment of the business rates, while not a return to the pre-1990 system of local government finance, represents a modest move in the direction of greater local responsibility and autonomy. The proposal to put large spending increases to a referendum cannot be characterized as centralizing, but is in keeping with the democratic experiments of New Labour. In addition, the government proposes to abolish most capital finance controls, though with some significant exceptions.

While central government appears to be taking a strong directive role through policies, such as New Deal, in fact local authorities, through the Local Government Association, lobbied hard to have a role in the policy experiments. While it appears that central government has been heavy-handed with changes in planning rules which seem to allow building on green-belt land, in fact the issue is highly complicated with much involvement of local bodies and professional associations. While it seems that the move to 'best value' centralizes through the new power for central government to intervene in the worst cases of failure, this is a normal form of reserve power, and the precise legal language is a consequence of the judicialization of central–local relations during the 1980s rather than evidence of a desire to intervene. The Government's intention to introduce elected mayors also appears to centralize. After the failure in the House of Commons of the private members bill introduced by Lord Hunt in the second chamber, which would have introduced new forms of executive management in local government on application by the local authority, the government has moved to a more compulsory system which requires local authorities to introduce a new constitutional structure. Yet it is surely on these constitutional issues that central government needs to take the lead and experiment as the existing system is defended by those who are part of it. After all, every legislative change for local government could be regarded as centralizing because it involves the initiative and sanction of central government, but what counts is the extent to which new legislation is consistent with healthy and vibrant local democracy. In future years it will be interesting to find out if the introduction of elected mayors in the UK is still regarded as centralizing. Though the proposal to create regional boards to supervise ethics in local government appears to be a centralization of power, it could herald the end of the draconian legal rule of surcharge which makes local councillors directly responsible for any loss of funds deemed by the district auditor.

As education is the policy arena within which the government wishes to achieve the most, it appears that the centre has taken a directive role. Education Action Zones resemble areas taken from local education authorities, much in the same way as the Conservatives introduced urban development corporations to kick-start regeneration. In fact these zones are local clusters of schools – usually a mix of not more than 20 primary, secondary and special schools – working in a partnership with the LEA, local parents, businesses, TECs and others. The partnership is designed to encourage innovative approaches to tackling disadvantage and raising standards and there are at first only 25 zones envisaged, attracting about £500 000 each.

The Local and Regional Government Group in the Department of the Environment, Transport and Regions has pioneered a spirit of democratic experimentation through the series of regional briefings led by local government minister Hilary Armstrong and academic Professor Gerry Stoker. The discussion has been of democratic renewal, improving turnout, experiments in new forms of participation and decision-making, such as community forums, citizens' juries and electronic technologies, captured in the government's Green Paper *Modernizing Local Government* (1998). Local government also plays a key role in the Prime Minister's thinking about modernization, summarized in his pamphlet, *Leading the Way* (1998). The importance of a dynamic local government is that it helps deliver or is key to many aspects of the government's programme.

While the cynical approach to the Labour Government should be tempered by examining the detail of their policies, the conclusion about locally elected government under New Labour should not be unduly sanguine either. With the exception of Scotland, abandoning decentralization would not harm Labour, and if control over local government served another political interest, Labour would not hesitate to act. The context-dependent status of Labour's commitment to local government was indicated by Tony Blair in the same pamphlet which stressed its importance. He warned local government that 'if you are unwilling to or unable to work to the modern agenda, then the government will have to look to other partners to take on your role' (Blair, 1998). There is no doubt that central government believes that the independence of local government depends on performance, and in that sense they are no different from their predecessors save in the types of policies the centre wishes to promote.

CONCLUSION

The implication of the scenarios outlined at the beginning of this chapter is that the Labour Government, with its large majority, programme of change in government and legacy of the political project of the Thatcher years would be happy to exercise strong executive powers over local government, and the decline in local democratic institutions would continue. To an extent the Labour Government is keen to implement its programme decisively and the claims of decentralized politics cannot compete with this aim. Moreover, Labour has inherited much of the Thatcherite agenda, particularly the wish to give powers to the voluntary sector, private interests and micro-agencies; the concern with measuring and evaluating performance; and the belief in competition. Thus central government interest in the detail of local politics and administration has not ceased.

To confound the extremity of the possible scenarios, the first year of the Labour government elected in 1997 displays neither the cynical disregard of decentralized local institutions shown by the Conservatives in their years in office nor the promotion of autonomous local and regional democracies. Instead, the reforms show a number of cautious measures which create new political bodies and give some freedoms to the existing ones. The policies have merged in the context of a modernizing constitutional agenda of electoral reform and experiments with new forms of political leadership. What happens below the level of the nation state is integral to the reforming project. The allocation of new powers to Scotland and Wales, and the reforms in London, underpins an attempt to reshape the landscape of British politics away from traditional representative and purely party institutions to a more flexible and complex state which is adapted to the vicissitudes of the economy, responsive to new policy challenges and appears more in tune with a Britain less wedded to traditional political institutions. It is important for these constitutional experiments to succeed for they are vital to the distinctiveness of the Labour project and offer the promise of further years in office. Labour's commitment to decentralization amounts to far more than the paying of political debts to the Scottish and to northern local leaders; it is part of a quest for political hegemony and legitimacy.

When setting into place its sequence of reforms, Labour shows an acute awareness of the double-edged nature of the concepts of constitutional change and decentralization. If the Conservatives' arrogance toward the periphery led them into extravagant policy follies and contributed to their downfall, Labour are aware that, by letting the constitutional bandwagon roll and by off-loading power to local institutions, they increase their political potency, transfer awkward policy problems to lower tiers of government, and give themselves room for manoeuvre and the ability to manipulate sub-central politics. The reforms so far show there is rarely a divide between political pragmatism and constitutional principles, or between decentralizing or centralizing, as these practices exist together and feed off each other.

10 New Labour, New Local Government?

Hugh Atkinson

INTRODUCTION

Until quite recently, New Labour's policy on local government had rather a low profile. Understandably, much of the constitutional debate had focused on devolution to Scotland and Wales. The situation has now changed. A number of consultation papers and white papers have been published. Various ministerial statements have been made outlining government policy. A preliminary reading of these proposals might give one the impression that local government is about to undergo a renaissance after what has generally been regarded as 18 years of increasingly centralized restrictions imposed by successive Conservative governments.

In its May 1997 General Election Manifesto, New Labour talked of bringing power back to local people by revitalizing civic government and renewing local democracy. In December, Deputy Prime Minister John Prescott, in overall charge of New Labour's local government strategy, announcing changes to the system of local government finance, spoke of his aim 'to build a strong partnership between central and local government'. All this would seem like music to the ears of local government leaders more accustomed to central government strictures.

However, we need to sound a note of caution. There is no doubt that New Labour's policy towards local government is certainly more positive in tone than that of the Thatcher and Major governments. However, as will be outlined in this chapter, there are within the policy a number of uncertainties and contradictions which may undermine New Labour's apparent commitment to revitalize local government.

THE PHILOSOPHY OF NEW LABOUR'S LOCAL GOVERNMENT REFORM

What is the philosophy and rationale underpinning New Labour's policy to local government? For Hilary Armstrong, the Minister for Local

Government, the policy is to be driven by pragmatism, not dogmatism: 'What matters is what works' (*New Statesman*, 25 July 1997). Such a stress on a pragmatic approach is understandable in the context of what has gone before. The attitude of successive Conservative governments to local government reform from 1979 to 1997 was clouded at various times by dogma and an antipathy bordering on hostility toward local government itself, or rather some elements of it. The introduction of the poll tax is perhaps the clearest manifestation of this (Butler, Adonis, and Travers, 1994).

There are, however, obvious problems in pursuing a pragmatic approach if it does not include some kind of vision. There needs to be the imperative of working toward some goal. Yet it would be disingenuous to give the impression that New Labour does not have at least some broad objectives. Indeed Tony Blair has spoken of the need to modernize local government as part of its overall strategy of modernizing Britain (*Guardian*, 3 November 1997). Setting aside what exactly is meant by 'modernizing Britain', what kind of future does Blair have in mind for local government? Speaking at his party's local government conference in January 1998, Tony Blair made it quite clear that New Labour will not tolerate failure in local government, threatening central government action if it deems local authorities are failing. Its decision to send a task force into Hackney Education Authority in London is a good example of this. Yet Blair also talks of creating 'a reborn and energised local government' (*Guardian*, 3 November 1997). Thus the language of centralization and decentralization sit side by side. This paradox in New Labour's local government policy will provide one of the central areas for analysis in this chapter.

1979 TO 1997: THE IMPACT OF LOCAL GOVERNMENT CHANGE

To fully understand New Labour's proposed local government reforms, it is important to look at the context in which they are being introduced and to consider the changing pattern of central local relations since 1979.

1979 saw the arrival in power of a Conservative central government pledged to roll back the state. It identified local government as an area of excessive public expenditure, waste and inefficiency. Central government control over local government finances was radically increased. For the first time a cap, or limit, was placed on the amount of revenue local authorities could raise through council tax. The policy of Compulsory Competitive Tendering (CCT) was introduced which meant local authorities were compelled by legislation to put out to tender a range of services (Wilson and Game, 1998, Ch. 19). In this period a number of functions were removed from local authority responsibility and transferred to what has been termed non-elected local government (Stoker, 1991, Ch. 3).

While Stoker rightly observes that it would be an overstatement to suggest that such changes reduced local authorities to the status of mere agents of the centre, they did mark a fundamental shift in the balance of power between central and local government (Batley and Stoker, 1991, p. 7). Local government, which had previously been regarded by all political parties in Britain as a positive force in the implementation of public policy, came to be regarded by successive Conservative governments at best with suspicion and at worst with hostility. It is against this background that we can best understand New Labour's local government reforms.

NEW LABOUR AND LOCAL GOVERNMENT: PROPOSALS FOR CHANGE

In setting out its proposals, New Labour has been strongly influenced by the work of the Commission for Local Democracy (CLD), which published a policy paper in 1995 entitled *Taking Charge: the Rebirth of Local Democracy*. We can consider New Labour's proposals under four broad headings: constitutional change and central local relations; revitalizing local democracy; service delivery and quality; and reforming local government finance.

Constitutional Change and Central Local Relations

Towards a General Competence Model?
It is important to understand the constitutional position of local government. Its role and influence are clearly circumscribed. Britain has traditionally been described as a unitary political system with effective power residing in the centre at Westminster and Whitehall. This can be contrasted with more decentralized political systems in Europe such as German federalism and Spanish regionalism. However, the creation of a Scottish Parliament and Welsh Assembly are set to change the pattern of central–local relations.

At present, local government in Britain operates on the constitutional principle of *ultra vires* (Chandler, 1996, p. 33; Loughlin, 1997). Put simply, local government can only act in those policy areas where it is allowed by virtue of Acts of Parliament. This contrasts with a general competence model of local government. Here local government is broadly free to act in any policy area provided such activity is not restricted by legislation (Chandler, 1996, p. 34).

The CLD has called for the introduction of such a general competence model for Britain. The implementation of such a proposal could potentially mark a qualitative change in central local relations in Britain. New Labour does appear willing to go some way towards the introduction of this model. It is critical of the present constitutional arrangements for local government which it describes as too restrictive and leaving little room for innovation (*Renewing Democracy, Rebuilding Communities*, 1995, p. 13). It makes a number of proposals. Firstly, a duty would be placed on local government to promote the social, economic and environmental well-being of the communities they serve. Secondly, local authorities could be given new powers to meet local priorities (HMSO, 1998a, Ch. 6).

The introduction of a general competence model would widen the scope for local authorities and limit the 'capacity for central government intervention in local affairs' (Pratchett and Wilson, 1997, p. 19). But the extent to which New Labour is prepared in practice to give new powers to local government is still a matter for contention. Indeed, it concedes that its proposals 'would not extend significantly the scope of what local authorities can do at present' (HMSO, 1998a, Ch. 6).

Local Government and its Place in the Constitution
It has been argued that the institutional underpinnings of local government in Britain are weak (Vernon Bogdanor, *New Statesman*, 6 December 1996). Indeed without a formalized written constitution, the position of local government is not protected within the British political system. Local government does not exist in its own right. As such it can be the subject of fundamental change. The abolition of the Greater London Council in 1986 is the clearest example of this. Such a situation would be most unlikely in the federal political system of Germany where local government has certain rights enshrined in the constitution (Peters, 1993, p. 110).

What is New Labour's response to this situation? Shortly after coming to office, it signed the European Charter of Local Self-

Government. The Charter aims to spell out what should be the relationship between centre and locality. Drawn up under the auspices of the Council of Europe, the Charter has only an advisory status. It does, however, lay down some important principles about the position of local government in the broader political system. For example, Article 2 states that 'the powers and responsibilities of local government must be recognized and laid down in the law, or, even better, in the constitution'. Even if we view the Charter in purely symbolic terms, it could act as a focus for debate on the future of local government and be a catalyst for a strengthened and revitalized local government system.

It is clear, as various commentators have argued, that local democracy cannot be revived without concomitant change in the broader institutions of the British state (Pratchett and Wilson, 1997, p. 25; Loughlin, 1997, p. 33). Reform of the House of Lords could play a key role in this. New Labour is committed to its reform. However, apart from a plan to abolish the voting rights of hereditary peers, its reform policy is still in the process of being developed. One possible approach to reform would be to give local government a major representative role in a new second chamber. Possible models can be found on the European continent. In Germany, for example, its state governments or Länder are represented in the Bundesrat, the upper house of the federal parliament. France's upper house, the Senate, has a strong local government presence.

The introduction of some similar sort of constitutional arrangement in Britain would provide strong evidence of New Labour's commitment to local democracy. A reformed second chamber with strong representation from local government would be an important component in safeguarding the integrity of local government. Whether New Labour is willing or able to take such a step time alone will tell.

Local Government and Democracy

In setting out its local government strategy, New Labour talks grandly of revitalizing civic government and renewing local democracy (HMSO, 1998a, Ch. 1). To achieve this aim it has set out a number of proposals.

Participation, Citizen Involvement and Decentralization
For New Labour, voting in local elections is only part of the democratic process. Community participation and involvement are also

important. Such a participatory view of local democracy marks a departure from the paternalism of traditional Labour politics at the local level with its top-down view of service delivery (Kingdom, 1991, p. 235).

As part of its participation strategy, New Labour puts forward a number of proposals. They include: community forums open to all interested local individuals and organizations, citizen juries, user groups, and advisory panels.

A number of issues arise out of this. Such proposals appear to be an important first step in achieving New Labour's goal of renewing local democracy. However, a number of studies have pointed to the problems inherent in encouraging participation – in particular, how to draw in people who do not usually make their voices heard. Where there have been participation strategies at the local level, there has been a tendency for those best served by them to come from well-organized and existing groups (Burns, Hambleton, and Hoggett, 1994; Mackintosh and Wainwright, 1987). This remains a danger in the current proposals. In an effort to guard against it, New Labour's proposals include regular local opinion polling to check whether the views expressed in the forums outlined above are representative. This is potentially an interesting idea though there are clearly questions about how it would be operated.

New Labour also wants to see decentralization in decision-making: allowing people a role in the shaping of local services. This could include local referendums, tenant management of housing, or user groups monitoring local services. It concedes that there are legal problems at present in the area of decentralized decision-making and wants to see the law clarified so that local referenda can be held and community councils can be set up. If this can be achieved, it opens up the potential opportunity for a radical change in local democracy.

In putting forward its proposals on local democracy, New Labour is not being prescriptive. It argues that arrangements should be best suited to local circumstances. There is clearly value in such an approach. Local initiatives can serve as pilot projects. New ideas and best practice can then be disseminated. Indeed local government is actively engaged in this area. In June 1997, the Local Government Association and the Local Government Management Board jointly launched a Democracy Network for the purpose of disseminating best practice and encouraging innovations in local democracy. Over half the local authorities in England and Wales are represented. One such example of innovation in local democracy is that of directly elected mayors.

Directly Elected Executive Mayors
The CLD recommended that each local authority should have a directly elected mayor and a separately elected assembly (CLD, 1995, para. 4.3). Such mayors would have executive powers. They should not be confused with the present mayoral system in local government, which is essentially ceremonial. New Labour has outlined plans for a Greater London Authority (GLA) with a directly elected mayor for London together with a separately elected assembly (HMSO, 1998b). In addition, pilot projects for directly elected mayors may be introduced in other major cities (HMSO, 1998a, Ch. 5).

These proposals for a separate executive represent a major change in political decision-making at the local level. Proponents of the plans argue that they will enhance local democracy. For the CLD, elected executive mayors would be 'highly visible and thus highly accountable' (CLD, 1995, para. 4.15). The assumption here is that the mayor would be a more conspicuous and active executive of the council who would be associated with specific policies and who would be better placed to provide direct leadership to achieve these policies (Pratchett and Wilson, 1997, p. 20). Cities such as Barcelona and Paris with executive mayors are often held up as examples.

Some Labour local government leaders have expressed reservations. John Harman, leader of Kirklees Council, has warned that the concept of directly elected mayors 'runs against the role and purpose of the elected local representative' (*New Statesman*, 6 December 1996). Concern has also been expressed about the drift towards a presidential style of politics and lack of accountability (Ken Livingstone MP, *The Guardian*, 24 October 1997). Indeed the CLD appears mindful of such potential problems when drawing up its plans. It recommended a number of checks on the directly elected mayor. Thus the separately elected council should have overall responsibility for the budget and policy plans of the authority (CLD, 1995, para. 4.9).

The Greater London Authority
New Labour's plans for London broadly adopt this approach and seek to provide checks and balances (HMSO, 1998b). The abolition of the GLC in 1986 left London without a system of city-wide elected local government. This is a situation unique among capital cities in Western Europe. The creation of the new GLA would clearly change this. However, the Government has been quick to point out that the plans do not mean the return of the GLC. The so-called 'loony left' image

associated with a number of Labour-controlled councils in the 1980s, including the GLC, is something New Labour is very keen to dispel (Lansley, Goss and Wolmar, 1989). The old GLC had a staff of 25 000. The GLA will probably have a core staff of around 200. Its primary function will be one of strategic planning and delivery of services in areas such as transport, traffic and roads, the environment, and urban regeneration. In addition, it will be responsible for the police, the fire brigade, and arts and culture.

The new institution of Mayor of London, the first directly elected political executive in Britain, marks a key change to the political system. Provided the various legislative hurdles can be overcome, the election is expected to take place in the year 2000. At first glance the new office of mayor has the potential for great influence and power. He or she will represent a population of some six million people and be responsible for a budget of some £3 billion. However, the mayor's potential for action is weakened by the fact that 90 per cent of this budget will be provided and controlled by central government. The mayor's position is further weakened by the absence from the proposals for any significant direct tax-raising powers for the new GLA. However, the introduction of congestion charging and parking levies is under consideration (HMSO, 1998b, paras 6.9 and 6.36).

The proposals for the GLA seek to address the concerns of the CLD that the directly elected mayor should be accountable. Thus, while it will be the role of the mayor to propose a budget and put forward strategic policy proposals, the assembly will have the authority to examine and approve these. This understandable desire to introduce some democratic accountability into the equation is not without its problems. Without an effective mediating mechanism, the result could at best be confusion, and at worst policy gridlock.

Non-Elected Local Government
It has been argued that the shape of local government has changed significantly since the early 1980s. Many service areas which tradition-ally have been the responsibility of local government came under the control of non-elected local government bodies, or quangos as they are popularly known (King, 1996, p. 216). These included urban develop-ment corporations, housing action trusts, and grant-maintained schools.

This growth in non-elected local government can in part be explained by a Thatcherite new right agenda which viewed many areas of local government to be inefficient and not responsive to change.

Such growth was actively encouraged by successive Conservative governments as part of a package aimed at restructuring and reforming the practice and performance of elected local authorities (Stoker, 1991, p. 62). New Labour has been highly critical of the increase in non-elected local government since 1979. In the May 1997 General Election, it stated that it would reverse this trend, arguing that non-elected bodies produce problems of democratic accountability. Various commentators share this analysis (King, 1996). At this stage only an initial assessment can be made on its reform of non-elected local government. The existence of non-elected local agencies does hold certain attractions for central government. As Wilson and Game note:

> The presence of such agencies . . . increases the influence of central government departments at the local level – an especially useful device if political control at local level is different from that at the centre. (Wilson and Game, 1998, p. 141)

Stoker notes how the previous Conservative governments viewed such non-elected local agencies as 'being more amenable to their policy influence' (Stoker, 1991, p. 62). For these reasons, New Labour might well find such agencies attractive.

However, there have been some developments. Its proposals for London government should see a number of non-elected agencies come under the purview of the elected GLA. In the field of education, the move from grant-maintained schools to foundation schools will give greater control to local education authorities. This would appear to signal a shift away from non-elected local agencies.

However, proposals for education action zones appear to point in the opposite direction. They were signalled in the General Election, and further spelt out by an announcement from special education adviser Professor Michael Barber in January 1998; the government plans to set up an initial tranche of 25 education action zones. Aimed at deprived urban and rural areas, the professed aim of the action zones is to improve education standards. Although involving local education authorities, the action zones will also have representation from parents, schools, community organizations, local training and enterprise councils, and, significantly, local businesses.

The proposals for education action zones have met with a strong response from a number of Labour local government leaders who thought they were going to have control of the zones. Graham Lane,

Labour education chair of the Local Government Association, in a speech to the North of England education conference in January 1998 stated that the proposals 'could lead to the destruction of local democracy'.

While local education authorities can bid for action-zone status, parent groups and businesses can make their own bids, effectively bypassing local authorities. As the action zones are at a very early stage in their development, it is clearly not possible to offer a detailed analysis of their role. Should Lane's charge prove correct, however, their introduction would appear to fit uneasily with New Labour's pledge to restore local democracy. This would appear to be another indication of the contradiction in its local government policy, increasing the role of local government in some areas while reducing it in others. An explanation for this contradiction may lie in what some have described as 'a lurking fear' on the part of New Labour 'of the so-called loony left in local government' (Adonis and Twigg, 1997, p. 6).

Reform of Voting Procedures
A number of proposals have been made in relation to voting procedures (HMSO, 1998a). As part of its expressed policy of making local councils more accountable, New Labour is committed to the introduction of annual elections for all local authorities. It has also expressed concern at the low turnout in local elections which is on average 40 per cent. It is considering a number of reforms to increase this. These include universal postal voting, weekend voting and more mobile voting booths.

These and other proposals are undergoing consultation with local authorities. Such ideas could be tested in pilot projects. The government has made it clear that an increased role for local government is contingent on an enhancement of local democracy and that includes increased voter turn-out (Hilary Armstrong, *Progress*, Winter 1998).

It has, however, stopped short of proposing proportional representation for all local elections, something strongly advocated by the CLD. However, the assembly of the GLA will be elected by the Additional Member System, a form of proportional representation (HMSO, 1998b, para. 4.13). Advocates of proportional representation argue that its introduction is essential if local democracy is to be renewed (Twigg and Adonis, 1997, p. 11). Others take a more cautious approach. The introduction of proportional representation is likely to produce many more hung councils. Some commentators have argued that while hung councils 'may well have the capacity to make the policy process more democratic in some respects (for example, by preventing one group from dominating the policy agenda) the experience of balanced local government in the UK has been mixed' (Pratchett and Wilson, 1997, p. 21). Other commentators argue many hung councils produce stable and effective government (Adonis and Twigg, 1997, p. 12).

Service Delivery and Quality

The Introduction of Best Value
Improving service delivery and quality is a key element in New Labour's local government strategy. It is introducing a new requirement for local authorities to secure what it calls 'best value' for local people. This will be monitored by the Audit Commission.

To start up this system the local government minister Hilary Armstrong announced in December 1997 the setting up of 37 'best value' pilot projects, 35 of which are local authorities (DETR, *Best Value Update*, December 1997). The Government has set various broad criteria for their success. These include:

- good consultation with service users and others in the local community
- use of measurable local performance indicators and targets to measure performance
- a willingness to share information with other local authorities

The pilot projects will come into effect in 1998 and run for between two and three years. The lessons learnt will then provide the base for a more general strategy.

Compulsory Competitive Tendering (CCT) and the Role of the Private Sector in Service Delivery
The Government has committed itself in the long term to replace CCT introduced in the 1988 Local Government Act with its 'best value' approach. The rationale of CCT was part of the New Right agenda of the Thatcher and Major governments to introduce market forces and private-sector techniques into the delivery of local services. This was a radical departure in local government practice. Supporters of this policy claimed the result was more effective and efficient services. Opponents, including the Labour Party, claimed the policy was too restrictive and often led to falling standards.

New Labour in government has announced a number of changes to the CCT regime. For example, Hilary Armstrong, in a speech to the Local Government Association in December 1997, announced that all the 'best value' pilot local authorities will be offered specified exemptions from CCT (DETR, *Best Value Update*, December 1997). In advance of a broader introduction of 'best value' the Government has announced guidelines on CCT. Firstly, they attempt to provide incentives for local authorities to move to 'best value' Secondly, they aim to give greater flexibility to local authorities in the application of CCT.

This would seem to imply a reduction in the centralization of the Thatcher and Major governments and a renewal of local democracy. However, New Labour has made it clear that it is prepared to intervene directly and decisively in local government should the need arise. Speaking at the Labour Party's local government conference in February 1998, Tony Blair spoke of the 'best value' strategy, arguing that it would not be 'a soft option'. He continued: 'If authorities cannot or will not take the lead, we will have powers to intervene'. The result might be greater restrictions on local government, not less. Thus once again the language of decentralization and centralization sit side by side.

The Role of the Private Sector
The New Labour government's commitment to remove CCT in the longer term marks a change from the policy of its Conservative predecessors. At the same time, however, there is continuity in the role played by the private sector in the delivery of local services. While the 'best value' strategy moves away from the compulsion element of CCT, it nonetheless still envisages a major role for the private sector. Competition in the provision of services will remain an important element of best value (DETR circular 16/97).

Furthermore, in the field of education, described by Tony Blair as the number-one priority for New Labour, the private sector is set to play an expanding role. Business is set to play a key role in the education action zones referred to above. Launching the scheme at the North of England education conference in January 1998, the Government's special adviser on education, Professor Michael Barber, announced that the first five zones which are due to come into operation in September 1998 would include at least one to be managed by a local business. In his speech Professor Barber extolled the virtues of business, arguing that 'Successful companies are uniquely able to manage change and innovation.' Whether these skills can be harnessed successfully in the education action zones will become clearer with time.

One might argue that emphasis on the role of the private sector represents more than a continuity with previous Conservative administrations. While under both the Thatcher and Major governments, there was an emphasis on the role of the private sector in the provision of state education, for example city technology colleges, the education action zones mark a significant extension of this policy. This is a case not just of stealing the Conservatives' policy clothes but of adding some significant accessories!

As a further illustration of New Labour's strong orientation towards the private sector, it is seeking to encourage what it calls 'Partnership Networks' between local authorities and the private sector. Their aim will be to develop best practice in the way local authorities work with the private sector (DETR, *Best Value Update*, December 1997).

Reforming Local Government Finance

The Future of Capping
New Labour has committed itself to keep to the previous Conservative government's spending plans for its first two years in office. In addition, Chancellor Gordon Brown has stressed the importance of keeping public expenditure under control. This would seem to suggest that tight restrictions on local government expenditure are set to continue.

In relation to capping, its policy is somewhat ambiguous. Although it stated in its General Election manifesto that it would 'abolish crude council tax capping', it goes on to state that it will retain 'reserve powers for use in extreme cases'. In announcing the financial settlement for local government for 1998/99, Deputy Prime Minister John Prescott indicated that there would be a slight easing of the capping restrictions. However, the broad capping regime will remain in place for 1998–99.

What will replace it in subsequent years still has to be determined. A Department of the Environment, Transport and the Regions consultation paper, *Modernising Local Government: Improving Financial Accountability*, does provide us with some useful indicators. The paper proposes that in future local authorities would no longer have their spending plans firmly capped. On the face of it this would appear to signal greater autonomy for local government and a greater degree of decentralization within the British political system. However, the

Treasury will still set a broad expenditure figure. Local authorities wishing to exceed this figure would have to gain approval. One proposal put forward in the paper is for council spending plans to be put to a series of mini-referendums. This would mark a radical departure both in terms of local government finance and local democracy. A similar scheme had been considered but rejected by the Thatcher government in the early 1980s.

Many issues arise out of the referendum suggestion. Should there for example be a minimum turnout? Low turnouts could undermine the legitimacy of any vote. There is also the possibility of well-organized but unrepresentative groups influencing the vote. Furthermore, the proposal, if implemented, could produce a great deal of uncertainty in local authority financial planning.

The question of capping again demonstrates the paradox of New Labour's local government policy. At one level it appears to give greater autonomy to local government while at the same time introducing new restrictions. The reasons for this are twofold. Firstly, New Labour is determined to demonstrate its fiscal responsibility. As a consequence, local government expenditure has to be controlled. Secondly, and perhaps more fundamentally, it is suspicious of the capacity of local government, or certainly sections of it, to behave responsibly.

CONCLUSION

New Labour talks of creating a revitalized local democracy but is not yet ready fully to trust local government. The clear message is that until local government is modernized, it will not acquire the degree of autonomy it desires. It is this mistrust which helps to explain the paradox in New Labour's local government policy. On the one hand it seeks to raise the status of local government through mechanisms such as directly elected mayors. Yet at the same time, it has stated its clear determination to intervene directly in individual local authorities if their performance is inadequate. There is a clear potential for a renaissance of local government. Realizing it will be another matter.

Part III

Policy

11 Labour's Economic Policy: Studiously Courting Competence
Colin Hay and Matthew Watson

INTRODUCTION

At the time of writing, with Tony Blair safely ensconced in Downing Street and the Labour Party still exhibiting all signs of becoming the 'natural party of government', it is rather chastening to recall the not-so-distant past. For, after successive electoral defeats in 1983, 1987 and 1992, commentators, pundits and psephologists alike rushed to conclude that Labour was not, nor was ever likely again to become, electable. Consigned to the political wilderness for eternity, Labour would not only have to accommodate itself to the legacy of Thatcherism, but would have to do so in a 'one party state' where it could never again hope to seize the mantle of governmental power (Margetts and Smyth, 1994; King, 1993; Nairn, 1994; *cf.* Heath, *et al.*, 1994). Scarcely five years after this had become something of a prevailing orthodoxy, talk is now of the Conservatives' banishment to the political margins. However premature, heroic and foolhardy such claims, the tables have, for now, been turned.

That this is so owes much to Labour's intervening 'modernization' and its revision of economic policy in particular. Arguably, it was Labour's refusal to adapt to popular perceptions of new economic 'realities' – a refusal made manifest in its continued commitment to Keynesianism in the late 1970s (Fforde, 1983; Artis and Cobham, 1991; Thain and Wright, 1995, p. 19) and its later flirtations with protectionist dirigisme in the early 1980s – that first rendered, and subsequently served to keep, Labour 'unelectable'. Similarly, it has been Labour's long and comprehensive process of review, revision and 'modernization', its acceptance of precisely those 'realities' it had once fought so hard to deny, which is responsible for its electoral rejuvenation (Wickham-Jones, 1996a; Hay, 1997b; Panitch and Leys, 1997). No longer does Labour display the Keynesian instinct of class-compromise economic policy; driven by a gradual capitulation to the mantras of neoliberalism, its policy priorities now reside in a studious courting of capital and an equally studious courting of competence on capital's terms. The extent of Labour's modernization is, then, in economic policy in particular, considerable. Moreover, the significance, indeed centrality, of economic policy to Labour's more general process of renewal can scarcely be overemphasized. However, it is difficult at times to differentiate between the rhetoric of modernization – of a new economic policy for 'new times' – and the reality of economic policy-making. The constraints presented by a globalized political economy characterized by heightened capital mobility, labour market deregulation and ever accelerating speculation on the foreign-exchange markets have come to be seen as circumscribing and delimiting the realm of the politically possible for New Labour across the full range of policy arenas. Accordingly, the period from 1983 onwards might be seen as one in which Labour has, in the course of acquiring the prefix 'new', relinquished much else, 'downsizing' its expectations and aspirations for government (Hay and Watson, 1998). In so doing, it has come to sacrifice on the altar of (perceived) globalization: a positive agenda for welfare reform; an active role for the state in industrial policy; and its commitment to restore an indigenous investment ethic to British capitalism (Watson and Hay, 1998; Hay, 1998). Arguably, it now subscribes to the view that, in an era of globalization, there is simply no alternative to welfare retrenchment, exaggerated moderation in all things, and fiscal probity across the board (Grant, 1998). In short, Labour's modernized macroeconomics appears to have been guided by assumptions that there simply is no alternative to the new neo-liberal orthodoxy.

This makes an assessment of Labour's modernization in economic policy, such as that briefly presented in this chapter, essential for any understanding of the party's more general trajectory in recent years and its prospects for government. Yet it would be a mistake to suggest that Labour's overall modernization strategy has been driven solely by economic concerns. If Labour has, increasingly in recent years, come to regard the parameters of the politically possible as being constrained by changes in an external economic environment, then equally important has been its attempt to revise policy in tune with the (perceived) aspirations and preferences of the electorate. In this chapter, then, we seek to chart the changing relationship between electoral expediency and globalization's perceived logics of inevitability and necessity in the revision of the party's economic agenda in opposition and, subsequently, in government. We conclude by noting the irony of Labour's seeming return in government to systematic wage restraint and fiscal austerity, which surely invites discomforting comparisons with the period 1974–79 when Labour was last in power.

THE CONTEXT OF ECONOMIC 'MODERNIZATION'

If we are to assess the extent of Labour's economic modernization in opposition and the likelihood of that being translated into economic policy 'reality' in government, it is first imperative that we consider the context in which modernization came to be understood as a necessity, and the manner in which that context came to be perceived. Two factors are perhaps particularly significant here: the first largely exogenous and economic, the second largely endogenous and political.

Labour's modernization, we contend, cannot be understood without due consideration of the international political economic environment of the 1970s and, more specifically, the exhaustion of the long period of sustained economic growth that had characterized the 'golden age' of Keynesian social democracy in Western Europe (Marglin and Schor, 1990). The withdrawal of the United States from the Bretton Woods system destabilized the postwar international regime of embedded liberalism (Ruggie, 1982) to such an extent that this period is widely held to be one of crisis. If the crisis in the early 1970s was still latent, it served to expose the global economy to the subsequent oil shock of 1973 following the Yom Kippur war. This had the effect of plunging the western economy into profound recession, shattering many of the Keynesian orthodoxies of the time as inflation and unemployment rose simultaneously. In Britain, successive governments in the 1970s turned increasingly to (quasi-)corporatist strategies as a means to manage accelerating inflation, entreating and subsequently coercing the unions into wage restraint in return for largely unfulfilled promises about tripartite coordination of economic management. First the Heath Government in 1973–74 and, latterly, the Callaghan Government in 1978–79 fell as a direct consequence of the unions' withdrawal from such punitive wage restraint in the three-day-week and the 'winter of discontent' respectively. This served to pave the way towards a Thatcherite future, as corporatism appeared impossible, Keynesianism unmanageable, and the social democratic consensus of the postwar period not only exhaustible, but actually exhausted.

The Conservative Government came to power in 1979 with, if not a clearly developed economic blueprint, then a loosely articulated alternative monetarist economic paradigm. This was combined with an almost religious conviction to loosen what was seen as the tight grip that the unions had established around the throat of a beleaguered and overburdened state. While the strict monetarist rhetoric of the early Thatcher years marked a decisive discursive break with the past, the incoming government's most significant substantive break with the past came six months after its election. Spurred on by the ideological commitment to freeing the invisible hand of 'the market', capital controls were abolished, exposing the British economy in the most direct way to what is now often called globalization.

It is in this context that Labour's modernization must be situated. For it was the perceived obsolescence of Keynesianism, reflected in the exhaustion of the 'Fordist' mode of growth that had come to characterize the postwar period, which led Labour in opposition to identify a qualitatively new world of post-Fordism and globalization. 'New times' were assumed to require a new economic stance, and hence a wholesale modernization of the party's economic policy (Smith and Spear, 1992; Hay, 1994).

Yet this diagnosis did not emerge overnight. Between 1979 and 1983, the party in opposition reacted against the failures of technocracy under the centre-right Wilson–Callaghan governments by moving to a less technicist, more explicitly socialist and interventionist economic policy. Labour now adopted a revised and revamped version of the so-called Alternative Economic Strategy that had earlier been devised by the party's National Executive Committee (NEC). This had, in fact, been an *official* aspect of policy since 1974, albeit one which had been ignored consistently in government (Wickham-Jones 1996b). As Eric Shaw notes:

> defeat at the polls in 1979 transferred the initiative to the left-controlled NEC, constitutionally responsible for policy formulation. It moved with alacrity and embarked on an ambitious programme of policy renewal culminating in the compendious *Labour Programme 1982*. (Shaw, 1994, p. 8)

Protectionism and an introspective anti-European stance became the order of the day as Labour, now under the leadership of Michael Foot, emphasized industrial democracy, capital repatriation and a radicalized 'Keynesianism in one country'. This represented a disavowal of the connections between the British economy and international market forces, emphasizing instead the restoration of a growth dynamic to the British economy through supply-side intervention along collectivist lines. Though such measures had been appealed to rhetorically, they had in practice been thwarted consistently during the Attlee and first Wilson governments (Tiratsoo and Tomlinson, 1994).

It was thus the ignominious electoral defeat of 1983, rather than that of 1979, which was the immediate precursor to Labour's modernization. Within the party, or certainly within the party leadership, the election was seen as a defeat for socialism rather than as a defeat for the Labour Party *per se*. Attention focused both on the manifesto, famously regarded as 'the longest suicide note in history', and on the campaign itself, which, in *The Guardian*'s equally memorable phrase, had seen 'disaster snatched from the jaws of defeat' (30 June 1983). Moderation and modernization now became the dual imperatives, as Labour came to conceive of its task in primarily psephological terms. What also became clear was that if 'Keynesianism in one country' was an electoral liability and the corporatist-Keynesianism of the late 1970s was no longer possible (especially in the new context created by the Thatcher Government's programme of trade union reform), then Labour required a new economic paradigm. It was economic policy that was held responsible for Labour's embarrassment at the hands of the electorate; it was the modernization of economic policy which would now have to restore Labour's electability (Kavanagh, 1997).

THE MODERNIZATION PROCESS

From 1983, then, amid a growing sense that, more than ever before, Britain now approximated a 'one-party state', the Labour leadership set out to effect the necessary transformation which would take the Party from the electoral wilderness to governmental power. Energized by a modernization discourse which stressed the importance of establishing a 'new model party' (Hughes and Wintour, 1990), this odyssey began with the careful construction of a binary opposition between Labour's past and Labour's present. While this tendency clearly predated the 'New' Labour phenomenon, the image being created for popular consumption was, nonetheless, one of a decisive shift from the Party's traditionally class-conscious economic policy. The novelty of the modernizing Labour Party was emphasized most deliberately in its attempts to break down the class antagonisms which had dominated 'Old' Labour's economic policy-making. Perhaps most symbolically given its umbilical links with the trade unions, the party leadership systematically redefined its response to Thatcherite industrial relations policy in a manner consistent with a desire to disembed the party from the wider labour movement. From an initial stance of outright rejection of these reforms and an attendant commitment to wholesale reversal once in government, succeeding iterations of party policy led first to reluctant acceptance and, later still, to open embrace. A policy which initially offered nothing but a threat to the specific class interests of which, historically, the Labour Party was itself a manifestation, subsequently presented an opportunity for a modernized party to re-embed itself within a new alignment of class forces. First, the party extended a series of olive branches to the umbrella organization for organized industrial capital in Britain, the CBI, before embarking on an even more high-profile campaign to woo financial interests operating in the City (Wickham-Jones 1996a).

Two overriding concerns dominated the reformulation of Labour Party policy as the modernization process unfolded; one was psephological, the other economic. Scarred by the experience of four successive General Election defeats, a period of prolonged self-reflection culminated in Labour openly identifying itself as 'the party of the past' (Hill, 1993), the political embodiment of the failed class compromises of the postwar welfare settlement (Hay and Watson, 1998). Such assumptions – and, moreover, the 'inevitable' subsequent period of creative destruction which such assumptions were seen to announce – were animated primarily by perceptions of the electorate's changed fiscal preferences. The politics of 'old' Labour were assumed to be synonymous with the high-taxing, high-spending, redistributive, collectivist social democracy which had been laid to rest by the populist politics of individualism enshrined in Thatcherism. Viewing contemporary reality through the distinctively Thatcherite perspective of increasing fiscal inertia, Labour's modernizers set themselves the task of becoming 'the party of the aspirational classes' (Streeter, 1996) by shedding its high-tax image (Seyd, 1998; Grant, 1998). Hence, the Labour Party moved to revise its fiscal policy goals in the direction of neo-liberal convergence. In its battle to win not only the hearts and minds of Middle England, but also its votes, Labour's studious courting of a reputation for economic competence led it to distance itself from any argument for injecting new progressive elements into the tax system.

In this respect, the domestic constraints upon autonomous social democratic policy-making which are imposed by widespread perceptions of taxpayer revolt (Seyd, 1998) are reinforced by international constraints imposed by globalization. While, in general, the faceless forces of globalization are commonly assumed to narrow the context of the politically and economically possible, they are in particular held responsible for depoliticizing the fiscal agenda. Globalization is assumed to have locked nation-states into a competitive dynamic in which all struggle against one another in their attempts to retain a share of a fixed stock of world capital (Cerny, 1990; cf. Watson, 1998). In an era in which footloose multinationals are assumed to be able to outrun territorially bound national regulators, governments are further assumed to undermine their own competitive position by attempting to activate progressive fiscal policy instruments (Levitt, 1983; Ohmae, 1990, 1996; Reich, 1992; Sachs and Warner, 1995). A state which is seen to use fiscal techniques in order to overextend its scope in a social democratic direction is one which increases its own susceptibility to market retribution in the form of mass capital flight. As such, national economic policy is effectively policed towards low-tax norms by speculative flows of financial funds. Put simply, globalization is assumed to deny national governments the space in which to construct alternatives to the neo-liberal orthodoxy.

However, when subjected to systematic empirical scrutiny, claims for globalization are shown to be routinely overstated (Hirst and Thompson, 1996; Boyer and Drache, 1996; Berger and Dore, 1996). Capital – whether productive, financial or human – fails to flow around the world in a manner which corresponds to a truly global economy (Watson, 1999a). It is the discursive construction of globalization, rather than globalization *per se*, which is driving political change in contemporary Britain. Globalization has been used as a rhetorical device to discipline expectations of the limits of fiscal activity (Watson, 1999b), which in turn has increased the possibility of facilitating lower marginal tax rates through reducing the size of social expenditures and the scope of welfare entitlements. As such, globalization acts as a convenient *post hoc* rationalization for a logic of tax-cutting which the Labour Party had already internalized. While it is thus misleading to suggest that globalizing tendencies have forced a wholesale reappraisal of the Party's policy goals against its will, the notion of a 'quantitative leap' in Labour's economic policy-making is in some senses still valid. Yet the novelty of Labour's new economic policy is distinctively political in character, and is to be understood in terms of its acceptance of neo-liberal demands for fiscal inertia in line with perceived electoral necessities. It is to the details of this policy that we turn in the next section.

BIPARTISAN CONVERGENCE

Labour's industrial policy has undergone significant revision and an effective emasculation in recent years – a process accelerated since 1994 by the resolution of a growing conflict between its Treasury and Trade and Industry teams in favour of the former. Thus, despite continued reference to the structural weaknesses of the British economy – the shortfall of dedicated capital and long-term strategic investment in particular – New Labour retains little in the way of concrete proposals which might address this distinctively British pathology (Hutton, 1996). Where once the party emphasized the crucial strategic role that the Department of Trade and Industry (DTI) would have to play in the rejuvenation of Britain's manufacturing economy, requiring its elevation to super-ministry status, it has since undergone a complete *volte-face* and now proposes to expand the role of the Treasury such that it will encroach significantly into the existing remit of the DTI. Proposals for a National Investment Bank that might provide investment capital on competitive terms to British industry have been dropped. Proposals for Regional Investment Banks, introduced in 1994 and based on similar principles, have now been subjected to a similar fate. This leaves New Labour with no proposals to address what it still identifies as the principal structural weakness of the British economy – its investment shortfall. The sole remaining aspect of the regional industrial strategy developed under the tutelage of Robin Cook (as Shadow Secretary for Trade and Industry) and Labour's Industry Forum is its commitment to regional development agencies. Yet, in so far as these merely build upon and institutionalize existing arrangements, Labour seems effectively to have vacated the industrial policy arena, emphasizing instead macroeconomic conservatism and fiscal stability (Watson and Hay, 1998).

Here, too, the general trajectory of Labour's reforms is one of convergence on an agenda increasingly circumscribed by the tenets of neo-liberal economics. Labour's current economic policy is a catalogue of abandoned commitments and political U-turns. Where, as recently as 1992, the party identified the principal means of economic management as supply-side intervention, in clear contrast to the Conservatives' fiscal conservatism and control of inflation, it now conceives of economic management as providing 'a robust and stable framework of monetary and fiscal discipline' (Labour Party, 1995). Competition policy, once justified principally in terms of its contribution in protecting employees from the consequences of deregulatory practices, is now recast in terms of its role in promoting flexibility and enhancing profit margins. Where, in 1992, Labour identified increased public expenditure as a top priority, by 1996 it would come to chastise the government for an increase in welfare spending at a time of falling unemployment. It now pledges itself in government to 'no new public expenditure' without corresponding reductions in existing departmental budgets. Where Labour sought significant reform of Britain's financial institutions and the development of, first, a National Investment Bank and, subsequently, a network of Regional Investment Banks as the means by which investment in the domestic productive economy could be raised, it can now only echo the Conservatives' faith in private–public partnership and foreign direct investment. As recently as 1994 the party proposed an increase in the top rate of taxation to 50 pence in the pound and an end to the ceiling on national insurance contributions (effectively raising the top rate of taxation from 40 to 59 pence in the pound); it now proposes a reduction of the bottom rate of taxation to 15 (and ideally 10) pence in the pound, while quietly dropping any commitment to reform of the national insurance system. Where, in 1992, Labour's principal economic goals were to raise investment in the domestic economy, to boost productivity and to reduce long-term unemployment, by the 1997 election its primary aims were to control inflation and to promote macroeconomic stability. The Keynesian consensus of the postwar period would appear to have been replaced by the neo-liberal consensus of the post-Thatcher period.

Such policy modifications, revisions and U-turns may be born of a combination of pragmatism and astute political strategy. Yet their consequences are surely to reaffirm and consolidate an emergent bipartisan consensus on economic, industrial and competition policy which will, for the foreseeable future, remain couched within, and circumscribed by, the now dominant neo-liberal paradigm.

POLICY IN POWER

Indeed, the Labour Government's unwillingness to challenge the central claims of the neo-liberal orthodoxy has been demonstrated repeatedly since the 1997 election. Moreover, in the moments in which it has displayed the radical edge which Tony Blair promised before the election, it has done so in ways which show the new government to be more orthodox in strict neo-liberal terms than its Conservative predecessor. By breaking with the conventions of the immediate past and working within below-inflation increases in public spending (Labour Party, 1997) as a means of driving its debt reduction programme (Brown, 1997), Labour's Treasury team has clearly adopted a more strictly observed 'rules-based' policy than the Conservative Treasury team it replaced (on the 'rules versus discretion' debate, see Kydland and Prescott, 1977; Calvo, 1978; Barro and Gordon, 1983). Furthermore, its disavowal of discretionary macroeconomic management was made even more apparent in the decision, taken within a week of assuming office, to cede operational responsibility for the control of interest rates to the Bank of England. The actions of New Labour in power point to the realization of the tendential depoliticization of macroeconomic policy implicit in its neo-liberal rhetoric. Therefore, any argument that New Labour's campaign pledges on the economy were designed merely as an election tactic and, as such, will subsequently be sacrificed on the altar of a renewed and reinvigorated social democratic economic policy (McAnulla, 1998; Smith and Kenny, 1997), appear, at best, to be wishful thinking. Indeed, the rhetoric of the new Prime Minister implies as much. Blair's pre-election pledge that 'We run from the centre and govern from the centre' (Blair, 1997a) – sentiments reiterated immediately after the election as 'We were elected as New Labour and we will govern as New Labour' (Blair, 1997b) – suggest that the government's commitment to neo-liberal orthodoxy is likely to endure.

Thus, it is within the context of an apparently long-term conversion to the demands of a neo-liberal economic policy that the Labour government's actions should be understood. In this respect, there are both clear similarities and marked differences between the economic policies of the Labour governments of Blair and Wilson–Callaghan. The social and economic consequences of a comprehensive fiscal austerity package aimed at balancing the public finances through reducing state expenditures resonate just as strongly at the end of the 1990s as they did at the end of the 1970s. However, monetary constraints were imposed upon economic policy two decades ago merely as a temporary crisis-management technique. They were designed primarily to offer some semblance of short-term stabilization to the economy, with a longer-term view that a 'holding operation' (Harrison, 1980, p. 390) of this sort was necessary if the space was to be created for a renewed British Keynesianism. By contrast, the monetary constraints which are presently being imposed on the economy owe nothing to the *ad hoc*ery and short-termism which characterized the Wilson–Callaghan governments' response to the enveloping crisis of the 1970s. Nor do they owe anything to a contemporary Keynesian instinct. Instead, they are an integral part of the current administration's long-term, strategic and distinctively neo-liberal plans for managing the economy.

Driven initially by the perceived electoral necessity of reinventing the Party's reputation for 'tax and spend' politics, New Labour's commitment to reducing both private taxation and public expenditure subsequently seems to have taken on a new dimension. For, consistent with its general acceptance of neo-liberal orthodoxy, these psephological concerns appear to have been augmented by a normative commitment to reducing the role of the state in terms of social and economic regulation. Perhaps most significantly, successive Labour leaderships have fundamentally redefined the Party's understanding of 'the market'. Where once in Labour's thought 'the market' represented little more than the embodiment of the alienation felt by those in Thatcher's Britain who were denied an active role in economic life, the Party's new Clause Four actively extols the virtues of 'the enterprise of the market and the rigour of competition'. In both the rhetoric and actions of New Labour, it is now clear that 'the market' is assumed to be the most efficient allocator of economic resources.

Set in this ideational context, as New Labour readily admits, the economic role of government amounts to little more than helping business to help itself. To this end, Labour's conversion to the politics of fiscal conservatism should be viewed, in Gordon Brown's words, as a desire to create 'a credible framework for monetary discipline' (Brown, 1995). For, it is only once such a framework has been established, New Labour believes, that the private sector will be guided by the 'invisible hand of the market' to engage in 'the long-term investment that is essential to sustain growth' (Brown, 1996). Thus, 'fiscal rules', the Chancellor has argued, 'reflect not only [the government's] commitment to prudence today but the importance of investment for tomorrow' (ibid.). In line with the consequences implicit in such arguments, the new Chancellor used his first budget to float his deficit-reduction plan (Brown, 1997). Reminiscent of the first Thatcher Government's medium-term financial strategy, this programme aims to reduce the structural budget deficit in a non-inflationary way by setting prescribed, and steadily diminishing, limits for both public borrowing and public expenditure. Hence, the new Labour Government has instituted the first overtly 'rules-based' policy in Britain since the Thatcher Government ended its monetary targeting experiment in the early 1980s. Moreover, in an attempt to ensure the success of such a policy, it has moved to depoliticize monetary policy relations by externalizing responsibility for the control of interest rates. The Bank of England has been instructed to set interest rates in a manner which is commensurate with price stability, and these formal price-stability targets in turn prevent the government from reducing deficit ratios via unanticipated inflation.

CONCLUSION

As we hope to have demonstrated in this chapter, Labour's revisions to economic policy have been crucial to its more general process of modernization since the General Election of 1983. Two distinct imperatives have come to guide this process of modernization and policy reform: the first, and initially dominant of these, was psephological – expressed in Labour's desire to project itself as the natural party of economic competence; the second, and increasingly prominent, has been the logic of neo-liberal convergence that globalization is seen to conjure. Though distinct, these twin imperatives are mutually reinforcing in that the logic of globalization has come to be seen by New Labour as necessitating precisely the measures likely to reinstil confidence in Labour's economic competence. Accordingly, Labour has come to espouse in opposition, and to adopt in government, a competence understood in neo-liberal terms. This is reflected in a studious advocacy of a predominantly 'rules-based' policy, encompassing fiscal austerity, public-sector wage restraint, the staged management of welfare retrenchment and the prioritization of inflation over unemployment as the primary concern of economic policy.

In this respect, New Labour's management of the economy serves to invite discomforting comparisons with the period 1974–79. Of course, much has changed in the interim. Whereas the terms of economic management of the late 1970s were seen to be mired in crisis, those today exhibit all the signs of an unquestioned and unquestionable 'common sense'. The dual impact of Thatcherism and globalization in the intervening period should not be downplayed in accounting for this apparent paradox. In particular, the position of the trade unions has altered markedly. In the late 1970s, wage restraint, fiscal tightening and welfare retrenchment were entirely dependent upon the acquiescence of the trade unions. However, the barrage of anti-union legislation in the 1980s, much higher levels of unemployment across the advanced capitalist economies and, more significant still, New Labour's acceptance of the inevitability of this new *status quo*, have conspired to change all this. Wage restraint has now been facilitated in the absence of incomes policies; fiscal tightening and welfare retrenchment enabled without the prospect of a political backlash from organized labour. The Thatcher governments' emasculation of the collective power of the trade unions may well make it more straightforward than it was twenty years ago to displace the consequences of neo-liberal economics on to labour. Yet the current absence of popular political countermovements to this tendency should not lead us to overlook the austerity measures being imposed on large sections of the population by present Labour Party policy.

12 Women, Gender and New Labour
Sarah Perrigo

Perhaps the most powerful and enduring symbol that New Labour had really transformed itself into a modern party were the numerous pictures of the 101 Labour women elected to Parliament that appeared in the press following the election in May 1997. In many ways the election can be seen as a watershed for women in British politics. Not only did women's representation in the House of Commons virtually double from 9.2 per cent in 1992 to 18.2 per cent in 1997 (24 per cent of the Parliamentary Labour Party) but the new cabinet contained five women and another 15 were in the government. The election also signalled a breakthrough in the relationship between the Labour Party and the female electorate. For the first time in its history, with the possible exception of 1987, the party closed the gender gap. Labour secured an equal number of votes from women as from men and in fact the swing to Labour among women at 11 per cent was significantly greater than among men at 8 per cent.

The changes that have occurred in the Labour Party in the late 1980s and 1990s in relation to women have been the result of a process of interaction between those committed to the modernization project and women activists who had been mobilizing in the party throughout the 1980s to make gender a salient political issue. Labour's support for women and its willingness to contest the entrenched masculine hegemony in the party, has been conditioned, and will probably continue to be conditioned at least in part, by electoral considerations. New Labour's ability to represent itself as a modern party in tune with the aspirations of the British electorate at the end of the twentieth century has required it to divest itself of its male-dominated image. In order to do so the leadership has had to contest important and entrenched vested male interests in the party. Increasing women's representation has become a powerful symbol of New Labour's modernity. In turn the modernization process and the reform of the party has been helpful to women wishing to make gender a salient political issue. It has opened up spaces and allowed women to construct alliances that were not present before. It is doubtful if the party would have taken the stance it did to increase the representation of women if women themselves had not organized so effectively. In the first part of what follows the meaning of New Labour for women is explored. While New Labour is an ambiguous and contradictory project there is no doubt that under Blair the party is committed to fundamental and radical change which challenges the exclusionary and closed culture of the party. Not only can this benefit women but it makes increasing the representation of women and women's issues a crucial index of success of party transformation. If Labour is to be genuinely inclusive then it must promote gender equality. The second part then reviews the action of the party to date to promote women and tackle gender issues both through government and in the party.

First it is necessary to give a brief discussion of the party and women before party modernization began and the struggles that took place to put gender on the political agenda in the 1980s in order to provide a context for the substantive arguments that follow.

WOMEN AND 'OLD' LABOUR

The Labour Party in 1979 was an extremely traditional, hierarchical and closed organization. What Drucker has called its ethos, its ways of working, the behaviour of its members were archaic, ritualistic and formalistic. It appeared 'stuck in the past' (Drucker, 1979). Despite enormous changes in society in the postwar period the structure and organization of the Labour Party had remained virtually unchanged since 1918. Its federated structure and complicated system of delegated democracy and bureaucratic, rule-book, way of doing business was unwelcoming to newcomers and difficult for individual members to influence without a long apprenticeship. The party was neither a typical mass membership party, nor was it very democratic. Although the party formally assigned sovereignty to the membership through the annual conference, in reality the party was ruled by a coalition of parliamentary and trade-union elites; a situation normally secured by the operation of the union block-vote at conference and the close working relationship of the union and parliamentary leadership on the National Executive Committee (NEC).

Though formally committed to equal opportunities between men and women, the party paid little attention to gender issues until women began to mobilize themselves in the early 1980s. The party remained extremely male-dominated at all levels. In 1979 although women constituted around 40 per cent of the membership they constituted a mere 3 per cent of MPs and 11 per cent of conference delegates. Gender issues were conspicuous by their absence from the mainstream of party policy and conference debates. The culture of the party reflected this male dominance. It was deeply imbued with traditional and conservative notions of gender difference and separate spheres, more appropriate to the 1920s than the 1970s, the effect of which was to privilege the male as the political actor and to marginalize women members. Definitions of class and political priorities themselves reflected the interests and experiences of men and made it extremely difficult for those who wished to raise issues of importance to women. Though factional and ideological differences in the party were rife, neither left-wing socialist discourses of class and politics nor the discourses of more pragmatic 'Labourism' recognized the relevance of gender divisions in their debates or the issue of women's inequality to socialism. The changes in women's lives that had occurred in the 1960s and 1970s had virtually no impact on party attitudes at this time. The impact of the women's movement on the politics of the Labour Party was minimal and largely negative. The one notable exception to this was the support that some women Labour MPs and the TUC gave to the National Abortion Campaign in its fight to retain the 1968 Abortion Act (Randall, 1979). Feminist ideas were, in general, viewed with grave suspicion as divisive and a threat to class solidarity.

In the early 1980s, then, ideology, culture and organization all constituted formidable barriers to women wishing to influence the party as women.

WOMEN'S MOBILIZATION AND PARTY MODERNIZATION, 1983–95

From the early 1980s women began to mobilize in the party to challenge male hegemony (Perrigo, 1996). The ways in which they did so were inevitably circumscribed by the party and its structures and practices. Initially mobilization was strongly inspired by feminist ideals; women utilized the women's organizations of the party in an attempt to give women a collective voice in party affairs. They allied themselves with the left in the campaign for internal party democracy.

However, as the party began to reform itself after 1983, women activists proved themselves adroit at adapting their strategy and seizing new opportunities to press their claims. In the period before the 1987 election, particularly though the organization of the Labour Women Action Committee (LWAC), they widened and deepened their campaign, influencing a broader section of women in the party, a number of Labour women MPs as well as some trade-union leaders who were themselves facing pressures to respond to the demands of an increasingly feminized work force. They were therefore well placed after 1987 when the leadership began a much more radical reform of policies and practices to influence the new agendas.

After 1987 LWAC were quick to utilize the increasing attention paid by the party to quantitative and qualitative research into the views and attitudes of the electorate. The findings of such research demonstrated that the party image was a significant problem. Research suggested that the party continued to be seen as insular, backward-looking and in the pocket of the unions (Shadow Communications Agency [SCA], 1987). This led to the radical overhaul of policy though the Policy Review. From the point of view of women, the findings provided crucial ammunition. The SCA research identified Labour's male-dominated image as constituting a particular problem. Women, who generally held values more congruent with Labour, nevertheless viewed the party in a negative light. This view was reinforced after the 1992 election when polling data identified a significant gender gap (Hewitt and Mattinson, 1992). This provided a favourable context for the success of the women's campaign in the period between 1987 and the general election of 1997. Increasing the representation of women became a key concern, and success a potent symbol, of Labour 'modernity'. LWAC dropped its demands for collective representation and began a vigorous campaign in the constituencies and unions for positive action to increase the individual representation of women. In this period Labour introduced a women's quota for all party delegations, the NEC and for all officer-posts in the CLPs. It also introduced a quota in the new policy forums set up after 1992 and for the Shadow Cabinet. Of even greater significance, the party, with the strong support of John Smith, introduced a quota system through the all-women short-lists for parliamentary selections in half of all marginal and safe vacant seats for the 1997 election. In order to do so the leadership had to face the entrenched hostility of many in the party, including senior Labour politicians such as Roy Hattersley and Neil Kinnock. It was the quota system that resulted in the unprecedented number of Labour women MPs being elected in 1997 even though the policy of all-women short-lists was abandoned in early 1996 after a tribunal declared them illegal under the Sex Discrimination Act.

UNDERSTANDING NEW LABOUR FROM THE PERSPECTIVE OF WOMEN

Both within the overtly political and the academic literature the meaning and significance of New Labour is strongly contested. Among a range of interpretations the process of modernization has been viewed as signifying a decisive shift to the right, a triumph for revisionism, a betrayal of socialism, an instrumental response to successive electoral defeats and a truly radical project. In fact the changes that have occurred are not easily explained in such terms. The process of 'modernization' has been nowhere as linear or as coherent as some of the literature suggests. Smith and Kenny have argued persuasively that although particular interpretations of Labour Party politics in the 1990s offer valuable insights they do not capture the complexity and the ambiguity of the changes that have occurred (Smith and Kenny, 1996). Unidimensional explanations can be misleading both from the point of trying to assess the general significance of New Labour and from the perspective of women. This is clearly apparent if we examine two of the most influential perspectives on 'modernization'.

One influential approach to modernization has interpreted the process as signifying an unambiguous shift to the right, associated with a capitulation to capitalism and an acceptance of Thatcherism. Arguments for this are adduced not just from changes in policy but also from interpretations of internal party reforms which are seen as unequivocally centralizing power in the hands of the leadership and severely curtailing the power of constituency activists (Panitch and Leys, 1997; Heffernan and Marqusee, 1992).

A second important approach, using a Downsian analysis, tends to see the changes in instrumental rational terms; as being dictated by the need to maximize votes in the face of successive electoral defeats. The party on this view has increasingly moved from being a programmatic party to a party of accommodation where change is dictated by the overriding desire to deliver what the electorate wants. Evidence for this is seen in the party's increased professionalism, its close attention to opinion polls and focus groups and its increasing separation from the unions and the traditional working class (Shaw, 1995).

Both these approaches capture elements of New Labour but fail to analyse important aspects of the Labour Party in the 1990s. The first approach views change in the party almost exclusively through the lens of left and right in which the architects of modernization are the right and those hostile to it are the left. The second sees change in purely instrumental terms. They both, in consequence, neglect the potential radical aspects of New Labour and the ways in which changes in the party have opened up spaces for a range of radical and new agendas and different voices.

The challenge to the party's ethos, ideology and practices that New Labour presents cannot be explained in simple right and left terms. In fact, as several writers have noted, many of the so called 'modernizers' have been heavily influenced by the New Left of the 1960s and 1970s (Smith and Kenny, 1996; Sassoon, 1997). The importance given to civil society, the development of public/private partnerships, civil liberties and to more open government all demonstrate the influence of New Left thinking. Neither can the commitment to constitutional reform, the signing of the Social Chapter, the minimum wage, and the use of quotas to increase women's representation be easily explained simply as accommodation to the preferences of the electorate.

From the perspective of women neither the right–left analysis or a purely instrumental approach captures the extent of the new opportunity-structure provided by New Labour. Neither the left nor party traditionalists were ever really interested in promoting women or contesting the ethos and culture of the party that has proved so inimical to the representation of women and their interests. Many of the changes that occurred under Kinnock that benefited women may well be best explained by instrumental rationalism. However, the nature of the changes that have occurred under Blair, albeit sometimes contradictory and ambivalent, suggest a much more radical vision of party change than anything envisaged by Kinnock. Despite all the changes that occurred under Kinnock, he remained steeped in the party and its traditions. Under Blair's leadership we have witnessed an unprecedented assault on traditional thinking and a breaking out of the ideological timewarp. His attack on 'dogma' and his openness to new solutions to old problems all have much to offer to women for whom old Labour was far less radical or progressive than it claimed to be.

His attempts to transform the culture and ethos of the party are also of crucial importance to women. Initiatives for party renewal, an expanded membership, new methods for debating policy and a genuine attempt to get the party to look outwards and connect with those outside the party all reflect Blair's desire to develop a much more pluralistic identity for the party. This also signifies an ongoing commitment to issues of representation, not for instrumental purposes but because it is central to Blair's vision of party transformation.

At the same time the contradictory aspects of New Labour must be taken into account in any assessment of their impact on women. There are aspects of New Labour which may well serve to limit the potential widening of the political opportunities for women. For example, there is a real ambivalence in Labour's stance towards the family and the role of women in society. On the one hand, New Labour appears to stress the values of individual autonomy for women and equality for women in the workforce. On the other hand Blair himself has supported the idea of the 'traditional family' and 'family values' (Hall, 1995). The attack on dependency and a 'dependency culture' appears particularly aimed at women and lone parents and conflicts with other values of care, the importance of parents, community and interdependency.

The government's cautious economic policy and a reluctance to interfere with an employer-defined notion of labour-market flexibility and to encourage 'family friendly' employment practices simply by persuasion rather than through legislation may well leave women's inequalities in the workforce substantially unchanged.

A further contradictory aspect of Blair's Labour Party, of particular importance to women, is between a commitment to openness and democracy and at the same time the extraordinary centralization and control of political debate and the insistence on the tightest party discipline that has occurred under his leadership. Communication between Blair and the membership is predominately one-way. Policy is formulated in plebiscitary fashion without any real dialogue or debate. If the culture of the party is to be radically transformed in ways that women can benefit from, then spaces for real debate and dialogue must be opened up. There is evidence that, despite the increases in membership, many members remain highly ambivalent about Blair's project and the concerns and priorities of many members remain unreconstructed (Smith and Kenny, 1996; Seyd and Whiteley, 1992). The noticeable absence of women MPs in many of the regions where Labour is strongest suggests that the transformation of culture and ethos is far from complete.

NEW LABOUR IN GOVERNMENT

The Issue of Representation

There are two questions that need to be explored: what is the likely impact of the increased number of women MPs and what are the prospects for further developments to increase women's representation? The actual impact of the increase of women in the present parliament is difficult to assess. There is little recent empirical evidence on the attitudes and behaviour or women politicians in Britain and the evidence from other countries is inconclusive. Some research stresses women's similarity to men and others women's distinctive contribution to political life. It is clear, however, that gender is only one factor influencing the behaviour of politicians. Party, ideology and class are all important factors in determining political behaviour and as Pippa Norris notes:

> Even if women politicians enter politics driven by different goals there are strong institutional constraints on how individuals can challenge the dominant party agenda or parliamentary procedure without being marginalized. (Norris, 1996)

This may be particularly significant in New Labour where a premium is placed on party discipline and loyalty. Only one of the newly elected women voted against the government on the withdrawal of extra child-benefit to lone parents despite the fact that many of them privately were extremely unhappy with the policy.

Using data from the candidate survey of 1992, Norris argues that, on a range of policy areas, party affiliation is the greatest predictor of attitudes. However, this does not mean that gender is irrelevant. She found that there was a strong gender gap on a number of important women's rights issues which could impact on private members bills, legislative amendments and the process of policy formation (Norris, 1996). A significant number of the new women elected in 1997 list women's rights and equal opportunities among their main areas of interest, which suggests this remains the case.

If we examine the backgrounds of the new Labour MPs they are overwhelmingly highly educated professionals resembling closely their male counterparts. However, there are signs that a significant number of them are beginning to organize as women. They have begun to have regular meetings chaired by a new MP, Lorna Fitzsimmons, and Joyce Gould. A new leadership campaign team has been appointed to link the work in Parliament with the party in the constituencies and to reach out to the wider community. Another new MP, Bev Hughes, has been appointed to the team with the specific brief of developing campaigning among women. The chairs of the Labour parliamentary women's group and Bev Hughes liaise regularly with the ministers for women. These initiatives over time may well give Labour women MPs as a group more power and influence in party debates and the formulation of policy.

While the actual impact of the new Labour women remains uncertain at this time it is clear that efforts to increase women's representation will continue. The NEC has set up a Parliamentary Selections Working Party which is considering methods for the selection of candidates for the Scottish and Welsh assemblies, for Europe and for the House of Commons. An important brief of the committee is to ensure that women are fairly represented on all these bodies.

For the Welsh and Scottish elections it has been decided that gender balance will be ensured through the twinning of constituencies for selection purposes with each pair of constituencies selecting one man and one woman. This proposal has attracted relatively little opposition or controversy in Scotland. This is partly because these assemblies are new and there is not a problem of incumbency, but also because in Scotland women have been involved from the late 1980s in arguing for gender balance and fair representation for those traditionally excluded from political office and have succeeded in attracting widespread cross-party support (Brown, 1996). The same cannot be said for Wales, where the issue has been much more controversial. This illustrates the significant impact women's mobilization can have in making parties receptive to the importance of 'fair' representation. Until the Scottish Women's campaign neither the Scottish nor Welsh Labour parties were advocates for promoting women.

The party faces more difficulty in increasing women's representation in Europe than in the new assemblies for Scotland and Wales. At present there are 13 Labour women Members of the European Party (MEPs) out of a total of 62. There is a marked regional disparity with no Labour women MEPs north of the Humber.

The government agreed in July 1997 to introduce proportional representation for the European elections, using a regional lists system. Any transition to the new system poses real problems for Labour in its desire to increase the number of women MEPs. Firstly, the use of a proportional system is likely to reduce the overall number of Labour

MEPs. Secondly, the party wants to avoid a situation, which could be extremely unpopular, of deselecting a sizable proportion of existing MEPs in order to make room for more women. The party has therefore adopted a transitional arrangement to be used for one election only. Each existing European Constituency Party will be required to nominate one man and one woman using a membership ballot. All nominated candidates will then be interviewed by a regional panel made up of NEC members and key members within each region. The panels will select and place in order the required number of candidates for each region. The panels are required to ensure that the list is composed of high-quality candidates and that the list is representative of the party. A commitment is given to ensuring there is at least one woman on each regional list and that women are fairly represented at the top of the lists (National Women's Office, 1997).

The most thorny problem is posed by selection for Westminster. The working party has yet to address this issue, though a selection process was due to be approved by the 1998 party conference. While quotas remain illegal it is very difficult to ensure gender equality under the single-member constituency first-past-the-post system. At the same time the evidence suggests that without positive action local parties will continue to select significantly more men than women. There is at present a marked regional difference with Scotland, Wales and the North of England having very poor female representation. As these are areas of Labour's strongest support and safest seats, if this imbalance is not rectified then the commitment to increasing representation at Westminster will be difficult to achieve.

Party Renewal and the Future of the Party Women's Organizations

Under Blair's leadership the party has placed a strong emphasis on expanding the membership and developing changes to the structure and working of the party to make it more representative of the membership, to develop new processes for the development of policy and to make the party both more friendly for new members and to reconnect the party with local communities. The 1997 conference adopted the *Partnership in Power* document which involved changes to the structure of the NEC and to Annual Conference as well as the establishment of a new rolling programme of policy-making. All of the new bodies have a quota for ensuring women's representation.

As part of the strategy for 'party renewal' the NEC is at present conducting a review of the women's organizations under the title

Building a Healthy Women's Organization and is consulting members on possible changes. There is a view that the women's sections as presently constituted are not representative of women in the party. Research carried out by the National Women's Officer in 1995 suggested that women's sections were declining in number and even where they existed were composed of only small numbers of women and that their activities appeared unfocused. Changes have already been made to the structure and function of women's conference, both regional and national, in an attempt to attract more women and to make them more high-profile through the attendance of senior politicians. The new women's conferences are open to any woman member who wishes to attend, are structured much more informally and are designed to offer training and information to women as well as discussing particular policy areas. There is evidence that the new format is popular and has succeeded in attracting new women (author's interview with National Women's Officer M. Russell, March 1998). However, the changes, and the consultation process, have not gone without criticism.

The women's organizations played a very important part in enabling activist women to effectively mobilize in the party. Their maintenance and their revitalization will be crucial to continued progress of women's politics in the party. However, it is clear that some women fear that the changes are the prelude to the closure of the women's organizations and view the consultation as part of a leadership strategy to disempower activists generally. This evident distrust with the motives of the leadership suggests that the attempt of New Labour to transform the culture of the party is far from complete and that some women activists share with their male 'comrades' a deep antagonism towards the kinds of changes proposed by Blair. If the women's organizations are to be revitalized, to be effectively representative of the views of women in the party and outside, then the party leadership needs to seek ways of dispelling this distrust. It can only do so by resolving the stark inconsistencies between the centralization of political debate and the desire for party renewal in ways that allow the membership a more active role in party affairs.

Delivering Policy for Women

A key test of the importance the party places now on gender issues will be the priority it gives to women's rights issues and its success in integrating a women's perspective into the policy-making process.

The 1992 election was fought on a manifesto commitment to a separate Ministry for Women. In 1995 a consultation on the nature and function of government machinery for women was established by Clare Short, at that time the Shadow Minister for Women, which resulted in the abandonment of the idea of a separate ministry and the decision to appoint a Minister for Women with cabinet status. This resulted in the appointment of Harriet Harman as the Minister for Women after the 1997 election. A Cabinet sub-committee was also established, chaired by Harriet Harman, with the specific task of coordinating the women's agenda across government departments. Other important initiatives included the establishment of a Women's Unit within the Department of Social Security and the appointment of Joan Ruddock as Parliamentary Under-Secretary of State for Women to assist Harman. Baroness Symons was given the role of spokesperson on Women in the House of Lords.

It is too soon to assess what will be the long-term impact of these new initiatives. They suggest a serious commitment to women and are a significant advance in comparison to the arrangements that existed under the previous Tory administration. The success of the new arrangements will depend on whether the Prime Minister and the new women's minister prioritize the work of the women's unit and the Cabinet sub-committee. Even with commitment the work of the unit will face substantial obstacles not least from the Whitehall culture which, as Sophie Watson has recently argued, remains extremely exclusionary (Watson, 1994). The laudable aim of 'mainstreaming' women's needs across departments and the development of women's units in all departments will also prove difficult when departments tend to be both gender-blind and to defend their own territory. Of even greater significance are the changes to public management systems, introduced by the Tories, but generally accepted by the new government. They have resulted in both central and local government being administered more and more on the lines of private businesses with the use of external agencies, purchaser–provider splits and Compulsory Competitive Tendering (CCT). As several writers have pointed out, the new public management makes it much more difficult to develop effective equal opportunities through either central or local government (Margetts, 1996; Forbes, 1996). Certain changes recently announced by the government may mitigate the worst effects of CCT. The introduction of 'Best Value' into local government, for example, widens the criteria for judging an authority's performance and significantly includes equality issues in both employment and service delivery (Local Government Association, 1998).

The government is also currently considering strengthening the Sex Discrimination Act and the Equal Pay Act. The Equal Opportunities Commission has produced a consultative document which recommends the amalgamation of the SDA and the Equal Pay Act into a single statute and incorporates European Community law. It also recommends the strengthening of equality legislation through the shifting of the burden of proof in discrimination cases and the inclusion of sexual harassment (EOC, 1998).

Developing policy for women is not easy. Women are not a monolithic entity and have a diverse range of interests depending on age, class and so on. However the Ministers for Women have identified three areas for priority: childcare, the development of 'family friendly employment' and combating violence towards women. The government has already begun to make progress on some of these issues. The development of a national childcare strategy, including the increase of nursery provision and after-school clubs, will undoubtedly help women as will tax credits for childcare and the adoption of the EU directives on working time and parental leave.

At the same time there are discernible confusions and some real contradictions in government policy as it relates to women and family life. First, as noted earlier, there are mixed messages about 'the family'. On the one hand, there are welcome signs that the government recognizes that families are diverse and that it is not the job of government to moralize or use the tax and benefits system to encourage certain 'traditional' kind of families. Recent budgetary changes with significant increases in child benefit and benefits for poorer families with children under 11, paid for by reducing the married tax allowance, suggests that for the government what matters is tackling child poverty regardless of family form. On the other hand ministers continue to moralize about the family and to blame a variety of society's ills, including crime, truancy and drugs, on working mothers, lone parents and 'dysfunctional' families.

This contradiction is also apparent in the government's emphasis on 'welfare to work'. The welfare-to-work strategy is clearly designed to encourage women, particularly lone mothers, to undertake paid work. This, however, conflicts with New Labour's stated commitment to a more caring and compassionate society. It tends to undervalue the unpaid caring work of women and to stigmatize those lone parents who choose not to take paid work as welfare dependants. As Jean Gardiner has recently written:

> Providing women with access to jobs and childcare must be part of a strategy to deal with women's and children's poverty. But we also need to reconsider the balance between family and social care, and between paid and unpaid work. (Gardiner, 1997)

This means that the government needs to pay more attention to issues of working time and redefining labour-market flexibility to help carers if the objective of developing 'family friendly employment' policy is to be achieved.

Issues around women, care and family responsibilities are not easy for any government to deal with. As Sassoon notes: 'to equalize responsibilities between men and women requires a long-term perspective and involves a profound change in values beyond the scope of government' (Sassoon, 1997, p. 661). However, government can contribute to that change and though there are signs that the present government is moving slowly and tentatively in this direction many feminists would be critical of the lack of a more coherent policy in this area.

CONCLUSION

It is too soon to give an authoritative assessment of the prospects for women under New Labour. Certain developments indicate the possibility of real progress. For the first time a British government has a distinctive women's policy agenda which can be built upon and developed. The commitment to increasing women's individual representation will clearly continue and will impact on party politics. Whether increasing the number of women representatives leads them to act collectively on behalf of women or whether they simply enlarge the range of voices heard in Parliament remains an open question, but in either case the prospects for women's politics will be enhanced. The internal changes and the stated aim of Blair to create a culture and ethos in the party that is inclusive and open offers women in the long run a chance to gain some genuine equality with men in the party.

However, progress will be severely hampered if the leadership fails to resolve some of the central contradictions in New Labour. The contradictions and ambiguity of New Labour and in particular the authoritarian and centralized nature of Blair's leadership constantly threatens to undermine the attempt to create a new kind of party which is open and inclusive. The constant stress on the need for party discipline, imposed from above, further alienates the active membership from the process of reform and stifles debate and dissent. Without an active and committed membership it is difficult to envisage a more democratic politics emerging in the Labour Party. Without a committed and enthusiastic female membership who are able and willing to press the claims of women the new 'opportunity structure' provided by New Labour will be in danger of becoming an empty shell.

13 New Labour's European Challenge: from Triumphant Isolationism to Positive Integration?

Russell Holden

In the 1997 General Election, Europe will be remembered as an issue which split the Conservative losers rather than one which inspired the New Labour victors. However, within months of acquiring office it has returned to dominate Labour's political and economic agenda. For a government keen to tout its claims of modernity and progressiveness it has become an issue from which it cannot hide. Thus Europe presents a notable challenge to a party that appears resistant to making a firm commitment to European integration. This is despite acknowledging the fact that policy on Europe intersects with the two most critical issues of party leadership: namely, economic policy and party unity (Shaw, 1994). At the same time the Party is also keen to restore the credibility lost by its Conservative predecessors in the eyes of its European Union (EU) partners.

Parties that wish to govern competently for any length of time have to engage with realities and this necessitates the provision of leadership. On matters European the gauntlet thrown down by the European treaties, the institutions and member states is evident, yet the response to them by the current government is far too ambivalent. This chapter will seek to explain the detail, nature, and reasoning behind the response. In so doing, substantial attention will be devoted to the Chancellor's October 1997 statement to the House of Commons, and the government's participation in a series of important meetings between May and December 1997 as these provide the clearest statements of intent on their part. Although it took on the mantle of Presidency of the Council of Ministers at the start of 1998, this provides little more than an opportunity for symbolic gestures as much of the agenda for discussion is preprogrammed, while the time available to make any real impression on the policy-making process is limited. If anything, the opportunities presented for making an impact are far more evident in the domestic political setting as the Presidency is more often about tone than content.

THE CHALLENGE PRESENTED

Clearly the pressures on New Labour both in opposition and government to make a dramatic stance on Europe are very different to those that confronted Blair's immediate predecessors. The Parliamentary Labour Party (PLP) now only has to contend with external pressures in respect of the impact of the Union on policy concerns because as a result of internal reform and reorganization the Party has become sympathetic to Europe. Domestically the European device has been used to promote Party renewal and modernization, and although these gains have to be consolidated, the Party now only has to consider the independence of action it could have if it chooses to remain a peripheral rather than an active player in shaping the course of a changing continent. As Stephens (*Financial Times*, 15 December 1997) has stated, Britain has moved from 'Triumphant Isolationism' yet it is far from clear what it is moving towards and why. This task is made all the more complex by the difficulty in reconciling fears of interference in domestic policy-making with the possibility of being politically, economically and socially sidelined. As Dunleavy (1991) states, the government needs to think far more in terms of policy, that is 'preference shaping' rather than 'preference accommodating', yet the populist policy motivations of the government have resulted in it being driven more by expressions of public reservation over Europe, and the desire of the Labour Party to maintain the domestic political consensus. These are not the most effective means for promoting positive integration, yet Labour has long struggled to repel Conservative charges of selling out British interests to foreigners.

The challenge therefore revolves around the willingness of the government to fully enter into the spirit and programme of European integration, duly accepting all its implications, most notably in terms of policy commitment and the pooling of sovereignty. In many respects the government is now presented with a set of choices that are as far-reaching as those of forty years ago, and consequently it needs to be aware of both previous decisions and their implications on national performance and status. In responding to this challenge any attempt at understanding the response must consider statements of intent and behaviour in the context of economic policy, changing foreign-policy priorities, the evolving domestic agenda, and the concerns and prejudices of public opinion. This helps to explain the evidence of tactical rather than strategic thinking by New Labour on European concerns, and the lack of a follow-up to the renunciation of the Social Chapter opt-out undertaken by the government in its first days in office, although Blair's speech to the European Parliament in June 1998 appears to contradict this view.

NEW LABOUR PERSPECTIVES

It was clear to Blair at the outset of his leadership that the sympathetic European disposition of Kinnock and Smith had to be continued as this had contributed substantially to the regeneration of the PLP, as Shaw (1994) rightly claims. The party was now increasingly viewed as safe, pragmatic and prudent by the electorate. Most importantly of all it had constructed an acceptable and non-controversial economic policy and it was acquiring, as Norton suggests, the attributes of a party of governance (King, 1998), changes which themselves were inspired by the European imperative. However, he also acknowledged that progress was to be based on pragmatism rather than principle, realizing that the electorate expressed misgivings regarding the European Union, confirmed by the findings of the 1996 British Social Attitudes Survey. In order to overcome this it became evident that it was wiser to make progress on issues less controversial than EMU, preferably where publicly identifiable policy dividends could be identified, notably in the spheres of regional and social policy and the single market, where national interest was protected and tangible benefits evident.

At a tactical level this enabled the Party to tackle the longer-term issue of remoulding public opinion. In the interests of party unity and potential electoral appeal the leadership clearly wished to avoid adding Europe to the list of policy areas where clashes could arise between the membership and the public. The areas most likely to generate hostility were those concerning changing economic and welfare matters where the party leadership was showing itself willing to challenge core Labour values. Clearly the appointment of Robin Cook as replacement for Jack Cunningham as Shadow Foreign Secretary in October 1994 helped to placate some of the reservations both in the ranks of the PLP and the public, as Cook did not have a record of longstanding unquestioning support for the EU. It was Cook who injected populism into Labour's European thinking which has become much more evident since May 1997, most notably through the notion of an 'ethical foreign policy'. However, he equally acknowledged the dangers of isolation at the same time as noting the difficulties of introducing a single currency without economic convergence, a message that was later to be strongly endorsed by the Chancellor of the Exchequer in his statement to the House of Commons on 27 October 1997. These were messages that the party conveyed in its submission to the Inter-Governmental Conference, whose final deliberations it attended as a party of government.

By May 1997 the PLP had a new constitution, new policies, new internal structures and a new image essentially as a consequence of the direction provided by the Blair leadership, though he duly acknowledged the efforts of Kinnock in particular. It was Kinnock who masterminded the policy overhaul on Europe (Holden, 1997), a commitment that New Labour has done little to alter. The lack of attention devoted to Europe in the five key election pledges confirms the low rank that it had in popular thinking. In pursuit of electoral victory the PLP chose to move towards the position of the median voter as part of its 'Downsian' strategy to broaden its electoral appeal; the European issue therefore merited delicate handling, as it straddled domestic concerns over government mishandling of relations with its European neighbours, with the need to avoid offering any radical proposals. Thus, like the Conservatives, Labour chose a safe route on EMU by promising a referendum on whether Britain should join a single currency, ignoring the clear contradiction between offering the electorate a referendum while seeking to preserve parliamentary sovereignty.

In relegating the European question to a lesser status, the PLP could maximize its strategy which, as Sanders (King, 1998) observes, played on three elements, each of which reflected a perceptive reading of public mood. These were the need to display competent party leadership, fiscal and monetary conservatism demonstrating policy convergence with the main opposition party, and a clear determination not to favour special interests. This constituted the nature of a newly modernized party, with a clearly defined vote-maximizing strategy. New Labour clearly conceived an election strategy in which the objective was to contest the campaign on the basis of a limited number of carefully costed and cautious commitments that included economic and budgetary campaign pledges based on existing government spending targets.

Following the election the Foreign Secretary made it clear that Europe was at the top of his agenda (Anderson and Mann, 1997) indicating that a new era was to begin which involved the rapid visiting of member-state capital cities by Cook and the new Minister for Europe. In so doing the government was seeking to realize the intentions signalled by Blair in an address to the Federation of German Industrialists: 'Britain should take its proper place in Europe . . . . I intend to lead a new Labour government that will provide a fresh start in Britain's relations with Europe' (June 1996). This ideal was used in the conduct of negotiation and diplomacy at a series of key meetings throughout 1997 where the government could capitalize on the goodwill prevailing in the member states.

The leadership task was eased as the government did not have to concern itself with Parliamentary worries in view of the size of its Westminster majority, the lack of any penetrating dissent on Europe within the PLP, and the reality that in the short run the EU clearly has no intention of advancing the integration process while it struggles to put the final details of EMU in place. These were luxuries denied to recent governments. However, the lifting of these constraints only serves to generate expectation; little thought had been devoted to the issue of the conflicting ideas on the integration process offered by the Maastricht Treaty. Labour still had to resolve whether this implied a democratic, decentralized, federal-style Union or a championing of intergovernmentalism preserving the sovereignty of existing nation-states. The latter suited the idea of preserving the consensus that the PLP evidently favours.

RESOLVING EMU ENTRY

Clearly the abandonment of the Exchange Rate Mechanism in 1992 did not totally determine the result of the last election, although it severely damaged the Major government, and set the parameters for Labour in the conduct of the one policy crucial to its overall objective of vote maximization. In this context a responsible economic policy was pivotal. Clearly from this point onwards Europe dominated political and economic debate. In many respects the PLP could not afford to differ much from the government in respect of its economic strategy, yet the level of internecine strife within Tory ranks made it easier for the Labour leadership to defer on European matters, enabling it to gauge the mood of public opinion and construct its stance accordingly.

Much of the conflict that has divided the PLP since the late 1970s concerned economic policy, and the issue of EMU membership embodies the next stage of economic policy, moving on from previous failings and outdated prescriptions of previous Labour governments. Therefore, in going beyond Triumphant Isolationism, old core values had to be challenged; yet Europe conceivably represents one issue too many for both elements in the party and among the electorate fearful of wholesale policy change and party transformation. At the same time its overlap with foreign policy concerns serves only to complicate matters, slowing down any thoughts of rapidly pushing the concept of positive integration.

After much deliberation and media pressure the Chancellor made a key statement to the House of Commons on 27 October 1997 which, aside from the European meetings between last May and December, provides the clearest indication of government thinking. Prior to May it had been preoccupied with fears over Euroscepticism and claims of supposed independence granted following the freedom from German monetary policy constraints secured with the suspension of ERM membership in 1992. However, after four months in office it was time to declare intentions on an issue that provides the clearest benchmark against which true commitment to positive integration can be measured.

If there was a desire to provide leadership in the EU, the tone of the Chancellor's statement clearly put an end to that objective by opting to play a domestic hand in preference to a European one, using the issue to consolidate and build public goodwill, acknowledging the longer-term need to adjust public opinion on Europe. Above all else, it was a case of ensuring that, as the Chancellor argued: 'The economic benefits of joining for business and industry are clear and unambiguous.' The domestic agenda was seen as a greater imperative though the government did not choose to identify explicitly the link between Europe and the domestic constraints in place as a consequence of the Maastricht convergence criteria. These detail a number of macroeconomic criteria which governments have to meet if they wish to qualify for EMU. Thus, despite the claims of modernity and progressiveness, Europe was not the issue on which the PLP chose to underpin its policy prescriptions. It was clearly avoiding the declaration of a new policy position that graduated beyond Triumphant Isolationism. This was a case of preference-accommodation, moulding party policy to suit perceived public opinion, rather than preference-shaping, seeking to persuade the public towards the party's preferred option. Europe was still deemed as peripheral to the vote maximization process, at least while public opinion was being shifted from its position of deep misgiving over Europe. However, it appears that the government had not accorded the time and consideration that the issue merits, opting to view EMU almost purely through the lens of domestic policy tests. What the Chancellor achieved on 27 October was a clever balancing act in terms of mastering the competing strands of domestic opinion. Although he clearly indicated that Britain would not be part of the 'first wave' of EMU entrants he did declare the government's willingness to participate albeit on certain conditions. However, this intention had already been declared by Tony Blair in the House of Commons as far back as March 1995 (*New Statesman*, 31 October 1997). The difference between 1995 and 1997 is that this time Labour stated that there were no constitutional bars to entry. However, the much-proclaimed tough choice that the Chancellor acknowledged as being necessary was not made. When will the economic benefits of membership to the British economy be clear and unambiguous? This could give the government the option of a longer-term postponement, which, however unlikely, provides a chance to respond to events, changing political contexts, and a sceptical public shaped by an island mentality, a press tinged with Euroscepticism, and a relatively thriving economy. Although any government has to be conscious of these factors, New Labour appeared to be controlled by these elements, and to be to some extent guilty of political cowardice.

The government was willing to indulge in an element of 'constructive engagement' over Europe yet it was not prepared to indicate either how it was going to contribute to the success of EMU or provide a target deadline for entry. The tone of conduct was different to that of the previous government yet the recent record of non-cooperation, which had extended to Labour supporting the Tory government over its handling of the beef crisis, remained unchallenged. This indicates a lack of commitment to the European ideal that would temper fears about the success of the project. More significantly it demonstrates a lack of commitment, with the British government tradition of using Europe as an issue for short-term tactical purposes continuing. From a policy of 'wait and see', the British government has moved to a position of 'prepare and join'. In declaring that the time for practical preparation has begun (Brown, House of Commons, 27 October 1997), Labour has not provided a ringing endorsement of European integration, while the wrangles over the role and activities of the new Committee X, largely generated by Britain, did little to help foster improved relations with our EU partners. The handling of EMU reflected a neglect of the political dimension of the issue in favour of concentration purely on the economic elements and their domestic implications.

FOREIGN POLICY INFLUENCES

The European issue ties in with concerns over foreign policy even though it has been transposed into more domestic concerns underpinned by anxieties over insecurity, national pride, and the preservation of sovereignty and national identity. European policy has to be viewed in the context of a wider set of international priorities and obligations and against a rapidly changing international political system that the British government is involved in at a level beyond her status as a middle-ranking power. This requires a consideration of the imperatives of foreign policy, whether they have they changed, and if so why?

In seeking to explain current government behaviour, a historical context is necessary. Since the last century, the reality and concept of the 'balance of power' has been embedded in UK foreign policy, seeing policy as seeking and resulting from the manoeuvring of strong states in relation to each other. While British interest in Europe was thus directed to maintaining a balance of power, Britain continued unchallenged as an empire-builder or, as Parker suggests, Britain became 'A lion in the world, and a sheepdog in Europe' (1997). This stance was legitimized by geopolitics that ensured Britain's peripheral status in relation to the European landmass and its desire to remain on close terms with the US.

In the postwar era the UK has faced the dual problem of coming to terms with its decline on the world stage, and subsequent retreat from past glory, and the rise of the Common Market and development of European Union. The response by Conservative and Labour governments has been to bask in the nation's global reach, military strength and membership of global organizations rather than to meet the challenge. Consequently governments have been preoccupied by insisting that Britain matters more diplomatically, economically and politically than it really does, without fully recognizing how the European Community could be used to secure increased stature in Europe and worldwide influence. This has continued into the 1990s with elements on both the left and right of the political spectrum maintaining that Britain could cope effectively alongside an integrated Europe while being free of its obligations. However, this has to be reconciled with the reality that Britain cannot afford to deny itself a place in a group whose decisions have a massive impact on the state's economic well-being and preservation of security, where the Franco-German alliance remains critical to the success of the venture, rather than the outdated diplomatic concept of preserving the balance of power. This is the reality that the British electorate was prepared to accept when they voted substantially in favour of continued membership of the Community in 1975.

Europe has to feature prominently as a foreign-policy concern simply on the basis that the Cold War era has passed, while the growing importance of the Asian 'tiger economies', despite their current problems, to the member states has shifted attention to a new region. As the EC, and more latterly the EU, has continued to acquire policy competences it has become a more influential global actor. Thus it is interesting to note the new Foreign Secretary's desire to tackle 'The sterile, negative and fruitless conflict between the UK and its European partners' (*Financial Times*, 9 May 1997).

Yet the challenge that remains is one of determining where the real destiny of the UK lies, as part of an interdependent Europe where economic concerns increasingly take precedence over purely political ones, or as an independent state struggling in an ever more globalized economy. The Chancellor's statement indicates a tendency towards the latter, although it appears to be based upon caution and possible ignorance.

In some respects Britain can maintain her 'sheepdog' role by ensuring economic openness to Europe and the rest of the world while criticizing some European intrusion into domestic concerns, as the Thatcher and Major administrations attempted, with mixed fortunes. However, conflict soon arose on the back of Europe's increasing policy responsibilities, which threaten a strong central state, hence the insistence on the insertion of the subsidiarity principle by the Major government at Maastricht.

Since last May the government has sought to claim a clear European strategy which Ministers will happily articulate and the public will accept. However, reality indicates something different. From the Noordwijk meeting in preparation for last June's Amsterdam summit onwards a populist message has been pushed. This demanded a focus on publicly identifiable benefits such as the promotion of employment opportunities, the acceptance of European social regulations and the agreement to promote the increased flexibility of labour markets. It also necessitated a protection of British interests in the spheres of immigration, asylum and tax regulation.

The government has had ample opportunity to indicate a sense of real commitment to positive integration particularly with the passing of the Delors–Kohl–Mitterrand axis. The end of this era enables Britain to convey its interest in EMU, thus convincing its neighbours of its serious attitude to the project, yet it has not chosen to take advantage of this opening. Now that the political decision on the future membership of EMU has been taken, Britain is in a weaker position compared to others taking part in EU policy-making, notably within the Economic and Finance Ministers Group (ECOFIN), and will be on the sidelines alongside less influential member states. Thus the key to the government's foreign policy should be to accept the Union as a fully fledged political entity seeking to guarantee and secure the economic well-being of some 360 million inhabitants, rather than merely providing a free trade zone and single market. This would place the UK in that rare position of being able to frame rather than respond to an existing agenda for the first time since the mid-1980s when it strongly advocated the Single Market programme. This would indicate progress from the end of Triumphant Isolationism to something more positive. However, the outcome of the Brussels summit (May 1998) has confirmed Britain's distance from the centre of policy-making in the most critical element of policy integration even though the problems at the summit were not of the United Kingdom's making.

What is also striking is the unwillingness to pick up on the federalist arguments in view of the domestic constitutional reform programme underway. This could be an effective device for portraying to the public the link between domestic and foreign policy concerns, and could help in the process of shifting public opinion toward a more favourable stance on European integration.

PLAYING THE DOMESTIC CARD

Blair pledged that the British presidency would be used to make Europe work for the people, hence the commitment to a set of 'People's Priorities'–namely peace, prosperity, progress and partnership (*Financial Times*, 5 January 1998). This indicates the continuing use of Europe as a domestic policy device. The independent research organization Demos (February, 1998) has stated that more concentration should be placed on encouraging public enthusiasm rather than institution-building in generating public goodwill towards the EU.

In purely practical terms this has been undertaken through the heavy promotion of the enforcement of single-market rules simplifying relevant legislation and removing obstacles to the free movement of goods and services, and dealing with crime by means of coordinated efforts spread across more than one member state. However it remains uncertain what this approach is offering. In the search for a second term of government it is shrewd, yet in terms of earning the backing and support of fellow European colleagues it does little to undermine longstanding perceptions of British aloofness. If the government was keener to offer true leadership, this would involve the initiating and devising of new ideas combined with a blend of authority, inventiveness and sense of true commitment to integration. This could help to convince the electorate of how the policy-making concerns of the EU of which Britain is part could help to address traditional domestic concerns such as those of unemployment, the value and dangers of new technology and, most crucially of all, inequalities of wealth and opportunity. However the evidence continues to point to government still lacking a realistic perception of the importance of the EU to the UK. This limited view would be rejected if the government devised a clear, detailed and long-term vision for the future of the Union which included a defined role for the UK. Yet Labour is now struggling with the rigours and complexities of government which make it all the more difficult to apply the recommendations of Opposition. As Moisi remarks, this implies the urgent need to accept that 'Europe is not simply a means towards an end, but an inherent value, an end in itself' (*Financial Times*, 9 December 1997).

PUBLIC OPINION

Clearly the sentiments of public opinion are crucial to government yet even more so to New Labour which places great emphasis on identifying and responding to the 'people's needs'. Yet unless it intends to absolve itself of leadership responsibilities on this key issue, it clearly has to determine and lead public opinion and engage in 'preference shaping', rather than merely respond to it.

In some respects the scepticism over Europe can be quickly eased by the media choosing to focus on an alternative issue. Since last May media concern has reduced substantially as correspondents have been deprived of details of internal struggles within the ruling party over fundamental issues but this does not remove underlying misgivings over principle and detail. Neither does it mean that the majority of public opinion can be won over to vote for a single currency in three to four years. Scepticism can only be overcome by convincing the public initially of the relevance of integration, the dangers of isolation and in moving to positive integration by indicating that being pro-British does not equate with being anti-European, a task ideally undertaken by the Minister for Europe. Thus the challenge is to win over public opinion rather than to be driven by it. In moving beyond Triumphant Isolationism the public has to be convinced that the country is now undeniably European, an issue that could have been addressed a quarter of a century ago, and one that has to be addressed urgently by a self-proclaimed modernizing government. The challenge remains one of how this government can accept this reality as the horrors of Black Wednesday and the related criticisms of the German government are still evident in public thinking. The public prefer to support a political system that is seen to address their needs and priorities but with the EU not recognizing national boundaries, this remains an obstacle rather than the opportunity. Secondly, people identify with a regime that has a clear sense of direction, and they still find it difficult to determine what the EU is seeking to do particularly since the departure of Jacques Delors as Commission President and the realization of many of its initial objectives. Lastly, legitimacy rests on a shared sense of identity and destiny, yet the EU is perceived as being more concerned with what divides rather than unites its members. This requires the Labour leadership to fully explain the rationale of the EU, and its value to the UK, particularly in terms of the strong link between the failure of European integration and the maintenance of domestic prosperity. A real indication of commitment to Europe is necessary, one that extends beyond the good intentions expressed by the Foreign Secretary in his speech to the Overseas Club and Senate in Hamburg (September 1997), and more recently by the Prime Minister in The Hague (January 1998) and in Paris to the French National Assembly (March 1998).

It could be argued that the government is cleverly trying to redirect public opinion by having as Foreign Secretary an individual who has long had reservations about the Union, though he is clearly now in tune with the Party leader. Although never a hard-core opponent of Europe, Cook has not been in a hurry to fully embrace EMU. Hence his desire to reposition Europe to tie in with public opinion, while stressing the importance of a Europe of independent states that voluntarily come together to boost cooperation.

CONCLUSION

The significance of the European challenge presented to the new government was, and remains, immense. However, their commitment to addressing the issue is masked by doubt. Despite the limitations connected to the presidency of the Council of Ministers, during its six-month tenure in 1988 the New Labour government was reluctant to reveal a positive strategy on integration. Keynote speeches such as those in The Hague (January 1998) and to the French National Assembly (March 1998) have been full of positive European rhetoric yet scant on policy detail, while the behaviour of the government during the recent Gulf Crisis served to undermine some of the good-will expressed by many European government spokesmen towards New Labour during their first months in office.

Whether New Labour is really addressing the challenges of Europe depends on when reactive politics will be replaced by a positive mood emboldened by longer-term thinking, vision and a strategy that extends beyond the desire of a second term in office. The ultimate test of whether New Labour moves in this direction will be in how it projects its own policy position which the electorate can understand, judge and use to reassess their own views. The electorate is likely to think differently once they are presented with a relevant agenda that provides tangible benefits and does not threaten the survival of the nation-state.

Clearly the strength derived from their Westminster majority enables the government to place Europe low on its list of immediate concerns, yet it is commitment to EMU that signifies the true value of Britain's European credentials. This would imply a full acceptance of the sentiment that European integration is an end in itself rather than a means to an end. Fortunately Britain was able to escape the worst of the damage that the poor handling of the Brussels summit and the appointment of a Governor for the European Central Bank could have generated through the happy coincidence of timing with Labour's first anniversary in government – but an important lesson from this must be drawn with so-called tough decisions having to be made. The worst excesses of Euroscepticism may have passed (Mori poll, February 1998), but much is still required on the part of New Labour in meeting the European challenge, at home as well as abroad. However, the appointment, in the government's first reshuffle, of Joyce Quinn as Minister of Europe is clearly a very positive sign that New Labour is alive to its continuing European challenge.

14 The Blairite Betrayal: New Labour and the Trade Unions

Peter Dorey

INTRODUCTION

Ernest Bevin famously remarked that the Labour Party grew out of the bowels of the trade union movement, but today, it is New Labour which seems to view the trade unions as excrement. Although both Neil Kinnock and John Smith pursued a number of worthy and welcome reforms which 'loosened' the Labour Party's organizational and financial links with the trade unions, New Labour, under the leadership of Tony Blair, has sought to go significantly further, leading to speculation that it is only a matter of time before the Labour Party and the trade unions formally announce their 'divorce' from each other.

In the run-up to the 1997 general election, many trade union leaders became concerned about various comments and apparent equivocations from Labour leaders over the party's trade union and industrial-relations policies. However, these union leaders sought to comfort themselves with two particular explanations for New Labour's increasing ambivalence over such policies.

Firstly, they assumed that much of it was merely rhetoric intended to defuse Conservative allegations about the likely effect of a Labour victory at the polls. Secondly, and following directly on from this assumption, trade union leaders anticipated that once New Labour was firmly installed in office, with a comfortable parliamentary majority, and a 'mandate' from the electorate, then the party's pre-election equivocation and caution over its attitude and approach towards the trade unions would be discarded, with Ministers no longer needing constantly to be on the defensive.

Since its landslide victory in May 1997, the Blair government has indeed evinced a remarkable degree of boldness in its attitude towards the trade unions, but not the boldness which union leaders envisaged. On the contrary, instead of abandoning its coolness towards the trade unions, the Blair government has, in many respects, intensified it.

Trade union leaders have discovered that when Tony Blair and his 'modernizer' colleagues insisted that the trade unions would enjoy no favours or privileges under a Labour government, this was not merely intended to assuage the fears of Middle England in order to persuade them to vote Labour; it actually reflected a determination by New Labour to distance itself from the trade unions, a determination which has apparently been reinforced by electoral success.

TONY BLAIR'S INHERITANCE

Since becoming leader of the Labour Party, Tony Blair has accelerated the process of reducing and weakening Labour's historic links with the trade unions. This process was actually initiated back in 1983, when Neil Kinnock, the then newly elected leader of the Labour Party, sought – unsuccessfully – to introduce one member, one vote (OMOV) for the selection of the Party's prospective parliamentary candidates. Two years later, Kinnock announced that the Thatcher government's legislation concerning trade union strike ballots would not be repealed by a future Labour government.

During the remainder of the 1980s, three further initiatives confirmed that the Labour Party leadership was seeking to reduce the role and power of the trade unions. Firstly, the Trade Union–Labour Liaison Committee – formed in 1971 to provide the unions with a role in the formulation of Labour's economic and industrial policies – was steadily downgraded, meeting less and less frequently, and exerting diminishing influence. Indeed, by the end of the decade, the Committee had virtually fallen into abeyance.

Secondly, 1986 witnessed the publication of a Labour Party policy document, *People at Work: New Rights and Responsibilities*, which placed considerable emphasis on the rights of employees to be consulted and informed by management *vis-à-vis* workplace matters. By contrast, there was very little reference to the rights of trade unions *qua* institutions. The Labour leadership was keen to promote the view that the workplace was not (or should not be) an arena of conflict between employers and employees, but, instead, a forum of partnership derived from a shared interest in economic success.

Thirdly, the Labour Party's Policy Review, launched by Neil Kinnock in the wake of the 1987 election defeat, heralded a much more explicit commitment to the market economy, in which consumer interests would prevail over the interests of producers. At the same time, the Policy Review reaffirmed the new commitment to the rights of employees rather than the rights of trade unions themselves. In this respect, Kinnock and his fellow Labour modernizers were pushing the party in the direction of individualism rather than collectivism, which in turn reflected a partial acceptance of Thatcherism.

While Neil Kinnock was primarily concerned with modernizing the role of the trade unions in the spheres of economic policy and industrial relations generally, his successor as Labour leader, John Smith, was more concerned with reforming the party's organizational links with the trade unions. This reflected a widespread view in senior Labour circles that the party's defeat in the 1992 General Election was partly due to public concern – fuelled by Conservative propaganda – that a Labour government would be beholden to the dictates of the unions, and thus incapable of governing in the interests of the whole country.

This view was underpinned by the results of a survey conducted shortly after the 1992 election defeat, by the party's Shadow Communications Agency, which revealed that

> many people were deterred from voting Labour because of its out-dated, strike-prone, cloth-cap image: and the Party's union links presented the biggest single obstacle to reforming that image (Kellner, 1992).

Indeed, some trade-union leaders, such as Gavin Laird, leader of the Amalgamated Engineering & Electrical Union, claimed that the Labour Party's close links with the unions were an important factor contributing to the 1992 election defeat. This in turn prompted Laird to wonder whether it might be in the interests of both the Labour Party and the trade unions for the two organizations to 'divorce' from each other (*The Independent*, 2 August 1993).

In this context, John Smith secured support at the 1993 Annual Conference for three main reforms intended to reduce the role and influence of the trade unions within the Labour Party: reduction and restructuring of the unions' block vote at Labour's Annual Conference; the introduction of OMOV for the selection of the party's parliamentary candidates; and reorganization of the electoral college for the election of the party leader, reducing the unions' share from 40 per cent to a third alongside Labour's PLP and constituency Labour parties.

When Tony Blair was elected Labour Party leader in July 1994, following the untimely death of John Smith, he immediately made it clear that the process of modernization would continue apace, not least with regard to the Labour Party's relationship with the trade unions. Indeed, Blair has evinced even more determination to distance the Labour Party from the unions, while simultaneously marginalizing them *vis-à-vis* economic and labour market policies. In so doing, Blair reiterated the perspective that the Labour Party 'has struggled against a perception that it had too narrow a base in its membership, finance and decision-making' (Blair, 1996, p. 16).

EMBRACING THE MARKET

An early indication that the trade unions would continue to be marginalized under a New Labour government was provided by Tony Blair's emphatic endorsement of 'the market' and the primacy of private enterprise. Notwithstanding the irony that New Labour was lauding the market just as the electorate was becoming increasingly disenchanted with the negative aspects of unbridled market forces and the socially destabilizing effects of the relentless pursuit of short-term profits, Tony Blair has consistently made clear his belief in the importance of the market economy, and the concomitant values of competitiveness, labour market flexibility, and profitability. Indeed, less than a year after becoming Labour Party leader, Blair was declaring that 'Thatcher's emphasis on enterprise was about right' (*The Sunday Times,* 23 April 1995).

A similar perspective has been advanced by arch-modernizer, Peter Mandelson, who believes that, partly as a consequence of the success of certain Conservative policies,

> Britain can now boast some of the world's most successful companies. The problem is there are just not enough of them. The quality of management has improved . . . and the 'British' disease of bad industrial relations and frequent strikes has been almost eradicated (*The Observer,* 24 December 1995).

Blair's lauding of the market in general, and of enterprise in particular, went rather further than Labour's previous modes of social democracy, for whereas hitherto Labour governments had upheld a mixed economy, in which there was a 'partnership' between the public and private sectors of the economy, and a concomitant neo-corporatist partnership between government, trade unions' and

employers' representatives, Tony Blair has made clear that nationalization is no longer an objective of the Labour Party and that,
instead, the role of the free market and private enterprise are now
permanent and paramount. This, in turn, entails a further downgrading and distancing of the trade unions, symbolizing as they do
the collectivist ethos of 'old' Labour, and perceived as an impediment
both to the much-vaunted labour market flexibility and 'management's right to manage'.

'FAIRNESS, NOT FAVOURS'

On his first full day as Labour leader, Tony Blair declared that under
any future Labour government 'Trade unions will have no special or
privileged place. They will have the same access as the other side of
industry.' Blair reiterated this point at the TUC's 1995 Annual
Conference, when he informed delegates that 'We have an obligation
to listen, as we do to the employers. You have the right to persuade,
as they do. The decisions, however, rest with us . . . we will govern for
the whole nation, not any interest within it.' He had made the same
point in his speech to the 1995 Annual Conference of the Transport &
General Workers' Union (TGWU), insisting that

> There was a time when a large trade union would pass a policy and
> then it was assumed Labour would follow suit. Demands were
> made, Labour responded and negotiated. Those days are over.
> Gone. They are not coming back. Today, trade unions will of course
> be listened to. So will employers. But neither will have an armlock
> on Labour or its policies. We seek to govern for the whole nation.
> Persuasion is in. Demands are out.

Yet since New Labour's landslide election victory on 1 May 1997,
many trade unions have been dismayed by the extent to which Blair
seems far more concerned to heed the views and advice of business
leaders and employers rather than the aspirations of the trade unions
and their members. This is not what trade union leaders envisaged
when Blair talked of the trade unions being listened to on the same
basis as employers, or pledged that the unions would be treated with
'fairness'.

On numerous occasions, Tony Blair has displayed a clear preference
for listening to, and appointing to significant political posts, senior
figures from the business world, while flagrantly disregarding trade

union leaders. Whereas previous Labour prime ministers have offered
Cabinet posts to senior trade unionists – Clement Attlee's cabinets
included Ernest Bevin and George Isaacs, while Harold Wilson's post-
1964 Cabinet included Frank Cousins and Ray Gunter – Tony Blair
has revealed a clear preference for business leaders, as evinced by the
appointment of the BP chairperson, Sir David Simon, as Junior
Minister at the Department of Trade & Industry. Elsewhere, Tony
Blair had wanted the chief executive of Whitbread, Peter Jarvis, to
chair the Low Pay Commission (charged with determining a statutory
minimum wage), but was obliged to back down after fierce opposition
from some of his own ministerial colleagues.

NO REPEAL OF CONSERVATIVE (ANTI-)TRADE UNION LEGISLATION

The extent to which New Labour has embraced much of the
Thatcherite agenda is further indicated by Blair's stance on trade union
law, where he has been even more emphatic than his two predecessors
that the bulk of the 'employment' legislation introduced by the
Conservatives since 1979 will remain on the statute book. According to
Blair: 'keeping laws about ballots before strikes and restrictions on
mass picketing . . . is common sense' (*The Sunday Times,* 23 April 1995;
Blair, 1996, p. 132). Meanwhile, the 1996 policy document *New
Labour, New Life For Britain* insisted that 'The key elements of the
trade union legislation of the 1980s – on ballots, picketing and industrial action – will remain' (Labour Party, 1996b, p. 14). This much the
trade unions expected. What they did not anticipate when Blair
became party leader was that a Labour government might go even
further than the Conservatives in some areas of industrial relations,
possibly pursuing no-strike deals in parts of the public sector, for
example (Mandelson and Liddle, 1996, p. 152).

New Labour did promise the trade unions a few positive proposals in
the run-up to the 1997 general election – most notably on the issue of
union recognition – but even this was increasingly subject to ministerial
prevarication and procrastination following electoral victory.

Furthermore, Tony Blair proudly proclaimed that whatever legislative changes were introduced on behalf of the trade unions, Britain,
under a New Labour government, would still have a 'more restricted
trade union legislative framework than any country in the western
world'.

REPUDIATION OF INCOMES POLICIES

A further indication that the trade unions would not enjoy *insider* status under a Blair government is the party leadership's repudiation of incomes policy. Although there have been occasional references to some form of National Economic Assessment, involving Labour ministers, trade union leaders, and employers, which would seek to place pay negotiations in the context of what industry and the country could afford, the dominant discourse has been that of 'responsible' bargaining between employers and employees, 'responsible' in this context clearly referring to criteria such as profitability and competitiveness.

Although Blair's repudiation of incomes policy is entirely explicable in terms of embracing of the market, this is not the sole explanation. Also important is the acknowledgement by Blair and his fellow Labour modernizers of the extent to which the economic structure and the concomitant character of the labour market have altered since the 1970s, when the Labour Party was last in office. Large-scale Fordist industry has contracted, along with trade union membership, while the service sector has expanded, as has the number of small- or medium-sized firms. In both of these areas, trade union membership tends to be much lower than in the older Fordist industries.

Similarly, trade union membership tends to be lower in the private sector, a point which assumes particular significance in the context of the Conservatives' privatization programme during the 1980s and 1990s. Furthermore, incomes policies in the past implied the existence of a *national* economy to which such policies could be applied; in the era of globalization and multinationals, the notion of a national economy is highly questionable, and thus renders even more problematic the pursuit of incomes polices.

One further development of the last fifteen years which militates against a national incomes policy is the trend towards decentralization of pay bargaining through such phenomena as cost centres at local level, or the breaking-up of public services into smaller units, such as NHS Trusts or the 'agencification' of the civil service. There has also been a trend towards individual contracts and performance-related pay in many industries and professions, a trend which further undermines the efficacy of incomes policy determined through tripartite forums at national level. Even some senior trade union leaders acknowledge the apparent futility of seeking to reintroduce incomes policies in the light of changes in the structure and character of the labour market since the 1970s. As the General Secretary of the TUC, John Monks, acknowledges:

> The ability of a relatively small number of national union officials to deliver pay restraint has been changed because the structure of bargaining has been changed. Leaving aside the public sector, the labour market is much more decentralised. So I don't think the old tradeoffs are relevant. (Monks, 1995, p. 4)

In the context of these changes, New Labour evidently deems it pointless to seek to determine pay via discussions between ministers, trade union leaders and employers' representatives. In the context of the economic and labour market changes referred to above, New Labour believes that 'Centralised incomes policies are no longer appropriate.' Indeed, it is suggested that 'New Labour should promote increased flexibility in the setting of employee rewards that genuinely relate pay to performance' (Mandelson and Liddle, 1996, pp. 80–1).

However, there is one further reason why New Labour eschews formal incomes policies, namely the realization that such policies were instrumental in creating the impression under previous Labour administrations that economic policy was effectively determined by the trade unions. More importantly, though, previous incomes policies embroiled Labour ministers directly in wage disputes, and thereby undermined public confidence in the Labour Party's governing competence and statecraft.

However, the Chancellor, Gordon Brown, has signalled his determination to be 'tough on public sector pay' as part of New Labour's commitment to restraining public expenditure. With regard to the public sector, therefore, New Labour again invokes the discourse of Thatcherism, warning that pay increases will have to be linked to increases in productivity or improved efficiency, otherwise they will invariably result in higher unemployment and push up interest rates. In the absence of a formal incomes policy, wages in the public sector are thus to be restrained by coercion, while private-sector wages are to be curbed, as far as possible, by exhortation, backed ultimately by the discipline of the market.

Needless to say, however, no such restraint is to be imposed on business leaders. On the contrary, 'competitiveness' continues to mean holding down the wages of ordinary working people while simultaneously permitting business leaders to pay themselves exorbitant salary increases, often totally unrelated to the criteria of profitability and productivity to which their employees are subject.

PARTNERSHIP IN THE WORKPLACE

Blair has also reinforced the industrial-relations perspective which Neil Kinnock had increasingly promoted (which is perhaps not surprising in view of the fact that Blair was Labour's Shadow Employment Minister during the last two years of Kinnock's leadership), namely that the relationship between employers and employees should be seen in terms of partnership, rather than conflict. Furthermore, New Labour invokes the term 'partnership' with regard to relationships within the workplace, rather than with reference to the relationship between the state and industry, or government and trade unions. It is claimed that 'an efficient workforce must be ... treated as partners in the enterprise', there being 'no place for the outmoded view of the relationship between employer and employee as one of master and servant'. Nor, it is emphasized, is there any place for the notion of 'institutional conflict between unions and management' (Mandelson & Liddle, 1996, p. 25; see also Labour Party, 1996, pp. 14–15).

This new notion of industrial partnership underpins the emphasis on the 'rights and responsibilities' which employers and employees have towards each other, and thereby reinforces the extent to which the discourse of rights has been divorced from the notion of trade-union immunities. It is the rights of employees which New Labour emphasizes, rather than the rights of trade unions *qua* institutions, although one of the rights which Labour espouses is the right to join or form a trade union. Yet, this particular right was itself subject to considerable equivocation after New Labour's election victory.

REFORMING THE FINANCIAL LINKS

With regard to the financial relationship between the Labour Party and the trade unions, Blair has so far announced two initiatives. Firstly, he has proposed that instead of sponsoring Labour MPs, trade unions should be invited to sponsor constituency parties, particularly in marginal constituencies, although it should be borne in mind that, particularly since the 1970s, the relationship has increasingly been 'not between the individual and the union, but the constituency party and the union'. In other words, even prior to Blair's announcement, trade-union sponsorship of Labour MPs effectively entailed payment to the party rather than payment to an individual (Fisher, 1996, p. 74). What

was more notable about Blair's proposal, therefore, was the suggestion that trade union sponsorship ought to be targeted primarily on
marginal constituencies.

Part of the impetus for this proposal was the establishment of the
Nolan Committee, whose remit included examination of the financial
links between MPs and 'outside interests'. Although this aspect of the
Nolan Committee's deliberations was primarily prompted by allega-
tions of financial impropriety levelled against certain Conservative
MPs, Blair evidently felt it expedient to pre-empt potential criticism of
trade union sponsorship of numerous Labour MPs. He also con-
sidered that such a move would render both himself and the Labour
Party less vulnerable to the charge of hypocrisy when accusing the
Conservatives of 'sleaze'.

The second proposal mooted by Blair with regard to the financial
relationship between the Labour Party and the trade unions was a
pledge that a Labour government would introduce a system of state
funding for political parties. Although the specifics have not yet been
elaborated upon, it is clearly intended that such a measure would
greatly reduce, if not eradicate, Labour's financial dependence upon
the trade unions, and in turn, enable it to fend off Conservative taunts
that Labour is 'in the pocket' of the unions.

Indeed, Labour's financial dependence upon the trade unions has
already begun to diminish somewhat, although the trade unions remain
the single largest source of income for the Labour Party. Even so,
Labour received a total of £7 855 000 from the trade unions in 1991, but
this figure had reduced to £6 924 000 in 1993, and to £6 686 000 in 1994.
Put another way, whereas in 1991, trade union funding constituted
63.3 per cent of Labour's total income, it had declined to 49.1 per cent
by 1994; from nearly two-thirds to less than half.

FURTHER REDUCING THE BLOCK VOTE

Meanwhile, Blair has sought to maintain the momentum of John Smith
in reforming the organizational and financial relationship between the
Labour Party and the trade unions, with the objective of loosening the
links between the two bodies – although Blair sought to persuade the
TUC's 1995 Annual Conference that the relationship he was seeking
was not one of greater distance but 'more clarity'. Blair has proved
particularly keen to pursue the reduction in the trade unions' share of
the vote at Labour's Annual Conference in order to bring it down to

50 per cent (the target which John Smith had originally stipulated), a move which has been described as 'a necessary *first* step in modernizing the party–union link' (Mandelson and Liddle, 1996, p. 225, emphasis added). Blair has been able to point to the fact that in the first year of his leadership, Labour Party membership increased by 100 000, thereby taking it beyond the threshold of 300 000 which was to be the trigger for reducing the trade union's share of the vote at Labour's Annual Conference to 50 per cent.

Indeed, it is entirely conceivable that sooner or later – and probably sooner – Tony Blair will seek to abolish the trade unions' block vote altogether. This would surely be a logical extension of the recent policy of reducing the size of the block vote in order to extend the principle of OMOV, so that Labour Party policies are formally determined or approved by the ordinary members on an individual basis.

AMBIGUITY OVER A MINIMUM WAGE

Blair's stance on all of the above issues rendered his position *vis-à-vis* a statutory minimum wage prone to particular scrutiny by the trade unions. When he first became Labour leader, Tony Blair was firmly in favour of a statutory minimum wage. Afterwards, however, he appeared increasingly cautious, with his professed support for a statutory minimum wage qualified by emphases on the need to be 'flexible' and 'sensible' in implementing such a measure.

When Blair became Labour leader, the Labour Party was formally committed to a minimum wage which would initially be set at half average male earnings, thereafter increasing to two-thirds. However, two particular issues subsequently arose, namely the precise figure at which the minimum wage would be set, and how extensively it would be applied.

Many of Britain's key trade unions, such as the GMB, TGWU and UNISON, had called for a minimum wage of at least £4 per hour, with some unions insisting on an hourly rate of £4.15. Indeed, the TUC's 1995 Annual Conference had been expected to endorse the figure of £4.15 per hour. However, this conflicted with the Labour Party leadership's insistence that the precise figure would only be determined after recommendations by a Low Pay Commission to be set up by Labour in government. This divergence led the TUC General Secretary, John Monks, to warn the trade unions of the damage which might be done (both to their relationship with the Labour Party, and Labour's election prospects) if they formally endorsed the figure of £4.15. Consequently, a compromise was secured whereby delegates endorsed a minimum wage based on half of median male earnings (yielding a figure in the range £3.60–4.15), a decision which Blair hailed as 'evidence of a far more mature relationship between trade unions and the Labour Party'. Yet this compromise – and Blair's warm words – did nothing to allay trade union suspicions that the Low Pay Commission insisted upon by the Labour leadership would result in both a lower figure than they wanted, and a delay in implementation of a minimum wage.

In fact, when the Low Pay Commission presented Tony Blair with its report, at the end of May 1998, it recommended a minimum wage of £3.60 per hour. This figure was a serious disappointment to many trade unions, but was warmly welcomed by employers' representatives. This fuelled trade union suspicions that New Labour – particularly Tony Blair himself – was far more sympathetic to the views of employers that to those of trade unions.

The second issue which arose over New Labour's formal commitment to a statutory minimum wage concerned exemptions. In particular, the Labour Party often indicated that young workers might well be excluded from the implementation of a minimum wage (*The Times*, 20 June 1996). This shift followed lobbying by employers and industrialists over the costs and possible job losses which might arise if young employees were covered by a minimum wage. In view of its commitment to tackling youth unemployment, the Labour leadership took seriously the warnings of employers that the universal application of a minimum wage might deter them from recruiting young workers. Consequently, the Low Pay Commission recommended that workers aged 18 to 21 (inclusive) should be entitled to a minimum wage of just £3.20 per hour.

TRADE UNION RECOGNITION

Alongside the haggling over the level at which the statutory minimum wage would be set, the issue which evinced the greatest tension between the Blair government and the trade unions was that of statutory trade union recognition in the workplace. Prior to its election victory in May 1997, New Labour was formally committed to introducing a statutory right for trade unions to be formally recognized by employers when a ballot of the workforce confirmed that a majority of employees were in favour of forming or joining a trade union, or having their existing union 'recognized' by management for collective bargaining purposes. This was a commitment included in Labour's election manifesto, and apparently supported fully by Tony Blair himself (Blair, 1996, p. 45).

After the election, however, this commitment was subject to increasing equivocation and qualification, with the Blair Government seemingly conceding to the counter-offensive launched by the CBI against statutory trade union recognition. Whereas New Labour originally declared that a trade union should be permitted and/or recognized if 50 per cent of employees voting in a secret ballot supported it, they faced intense pressure from the CBI to modify the proposals so that 50 per cent of all those eligible to vote – rather than 50 per cent of those who actually vote – must support a trade union in order for it to be legally recognized by employers.

Furthermore the CBI argued that before such a ballot was conducted, it should be proven that at least 30 per cent of the workforce wanted a ballot in the first place. Then, the CBI argued, it should be employers who determined precisely which group of workers were to be balloted over union recognition. The CBI also argued that companies employing fewer than 50 workers should be exempt from any legislation concerning trade union recognition.

When the *Fairness at Work* White Paper was published in May 1998, it proposed that 40 per cent of the workforce would need to be in favour before a trade union became 'legally recognised'. Furthermore firms employing 20 workers or less will be exempt from legislation on trade union recognition, a caveat which will affect over 5 million employees. What was most notable about union recognition was how grudgingly Tony Blair approached the issue, and the disdain with which he viewed the trade unions themselves.

'GAINS' FOR THE TRADE UNIONS?

It would be wrong to suggest that New Labour and the Blair Government have completely reneged upon all their commitments towards the trade unions since May 1997. In response to allegations of betrayal, ministers could readily point to the signing of the Social Chapter, the restoration of trade unions at GCHQ, the establishment of the commission to determine the minimum wage, the appointment of trade union officials to various advisory committees in Whitehall, and the contacts or dialogue established between ministers and trade-union leaders. None of these are to be dismissed as meaningless, and they have certainly been welcomed by the trade unions after 18 years of unrelenting Conservative hostility and exclusion.

Yet neither should the significance or impact of such measures be exaggerated. The signing of the Social Chapter, along with the restoration of trade union rights at GCHQ, while welcome, can also be seen as largely symbolic. The Conservatives always vastly exaggerated the significance and likely impact of the measures enshrined in the Social Chapter. Furthermore, Tony Blair has himself made clear that he will oppose any measures emanating from the European Union which are deemed to undermine labour-market flexibility or competitiveness.

Meanwhile, although Tony Blair has indeed met trade union leaders at 10 Downing Street, he only held three such meetings during his first four months as prime minister, with some union leaders complaining that such meetings appeared to be a 'dialogue with the deaf'.

Certainly, a number of commentators have suggested that business leaders are shown much more respect and courtesy when they meet Blair, and that Blair is actually much more comfortable when meeting representatives from the business community as opposed to trade union leaders (Bell, 1998; Milne, 1997a; Wintour, 1997). Indeed, the Chairperson of the CBI, Sir Colin Marshall, claimed that Tony Blair and business leaders shared a 'largely mutual philosophy' (*The Guardian*, 28 May 1998).

A PARTING OF THE WAYS?

The disdain with which Tony Blair appears to view the trade unions has reactivated the question of whether the Labour Party and the unions will formally disengage, to become two separate and independent entities. The issue of Labour's links with the trade unions, and the impact this might have on the party's electoral fortunes, was originally alluded to by Croslandite revisionists during the late 1950s and early 1960s, for whom the Labour Party's 'cloth-cap' image was deemed a serious obstacle to securing support among the expanding middle classes: white-collar workers, managers, scientists and technicians.

The question of whether the Labour Party and the trade unions ought to 'divorce' was once again raised during the time of John Smith's reforms of the organizational links between Labour and the unions. Advocates of 'divorce' insisted that Labour 'cannot hope to convince the electorate that it will pursue the public interest when it is tied to sectional pressure groups' (Walsh and Tindale, 1992, p. 10). It was suggested that by virtue of its links with the trade unions, Labour was widely seen as a party concerned primarily with the interests of trade union members in particular rather than workers generally, a crucial distinction given that less than half of the labour force in Britain now belongs to a trade union, and with the interests of producers rather than consumers. According to Walsh and Tindale: 'Up to one third of voters who were once Labour supporters do not vote Labour because of the union link', while trade union 'domination makes the task of winning over floating Liberal Democrats immeasurably harder' (ibid., p. 10).

In a society in which strongly unionized manufacturing industry has been increasingly replaced by a largely non-unionized service sector, and in which individualism seems to have superseded collectivism, Labour's continued links with the trade unions were deemed by such commentators to be historically anachronistic and politically damaging. It was even suggested that the Labour Party's links with the trade unions were based on 'money, power and a certain corruption. To cement the whole thing, there is a strong lashing of sentimentality' (Lloyd, 1988, p. 37).

Proponents of such perspectives therefore claimed that the Labour Party ought to sever its ties with the trade unions, and thereafter treat them as just one of any number of groups and organized interests in society who would be consulted from time to time. It was claimed that 'The only way that the [Labour] party can modernize itself is to start from a clean sheet ... it is time to break the link' (Dewdney, 1992, p. 4).

By making this break, it was alleged that the Labour Party would be able far more readily to broaden its electoral appeal so as to win support from non-trade-unionists, sections of the middle class and consumers. Freed of its financial and organizational ties to the trade unions, the Labour Party could 'champion the cause not just of organized labour, but of all labour' (ibid. p. 11). Endorsing this perspective, Dennis MacShane MP has declared that: 'The separation of unions from formal party politics is now an imperative' (MacShane, 1993, p. vii).

It might immediately be countered that as these views were most prevalent in the wake of the Labour Party's 1992 election defeat, they have since been invalidated by the resounding electoral success of New Labour on 1 May 1997, which apparently proved that Labour's organizational and financial links with the trade unions were not, and are not, an obstacle to winning a general election. Indeed, it might even be argued one of the factors underpinning the Labour Party's phenomenal victory in 1997 was the prevalence of job insecurity – particularly among many former Conservative voters – coupled with a perception that the balance of power in industry and the workplace had swung too far in favour of employers.

Yet this does not appear to be the interpretation which Tony Blair and his fellow New Labour modernizers subscribe to. On the contrary, they appear to believe that the Labour Party's electoral popularity owes much to its embracing of the market, and its concomitant distancing of itself from the trade unions, coupled with its pledge that there will be no repeal of the Conservative's anti-trade-union legislation. Indeed, such a perspective seems to legitimize a further loosening of Labour's links with the trade unions, and a further marginalization of the unions from policy-making within the Labour Party, the logical conclusion of which would be a complete and irrevocable parting of the ways.

One of the most notable indications that this is precisely what many senior figures in New Labour desire was provided at the TUC's 1996 Annual Conference, when the party's employment spokesperson, Stephen Byers, revealed to journalists that Tony Blair wanted to effect a complete divorce between the Labour Party and the trade unions. Furthermore, Byers intimated that an incoming Labour government might invoke a public sector pay dispute as the pretext for instigating a formal and final separation between Labour and the unions.

Although this scenario has not so far materialized, there have been other indications that New Labour's modernizers envisage a complete break with the trade unions in the foreseeable future. For example, Tony Blair has made clear his desire to see the trade unions' traditional organizational link with the Labour party replaced by one whereby trade union members join the Party as individuals (*The Guardian*, 30 July 1997).

Meanwhile, the 1997 document *Labour into Power*, which enshrined New Labour's proposals for intra-party reform, included measures to reduce trade union representation on the party's National Executive Committee (Labour Party, 1997a).

TRADE UNION ANXIETIES INCREASE

As one would expect in the light of New Labour's increasingly con-
temptuous stance towards the trade unions, some unions themselves
have begun to voice criticisms of the Blair government, with Derek
Hodgson, of the Union of Communication Workers (UCW), con-
demning those 'who want partnership with the banks, the credit companies, the media magnates, with captains of industry . . . but not, it
seems, with unions' (*The Observer*, 7 September 1997), while John
Edmonds, the TUC President, has warned that if Tony Blair reneges
on New Labour's election commitments to the trade unions and ordinary working people, then his government would face demonstrations
and rallies similar to those held by the Countryside Alliance, with
Edmonds explaining that: 'I noticed that the Government seemed to
be impressed by 100,000 people walking through London wearing
green Barbour jackets and waving foxes' tails', before suggesting that
if New Labour failed to deliver its election pledges to the trade
unions, then it would face even bigger marches and public protests by
union members (*The Guardian*, 13 March 1998).

Meanwhile, some union leaders – including Alan Johnson of the
UCW and John Monks, General Secretary of the TUC – have themselves started to wonder whether the time might soon be ripe for a
looser or more distant relationship between the trade unions and the
Labour Party (Johnson, 1997, p. 13; see also Milne, 1998, p. 15).

CONCLUSION

The scale of New Labour's betrayal of the trade unions is becoming
ever clearer. On a range of issues, most notably the level at which the
minimum wage was set, and the equivocation over union recognition,
the emerging record appears to be one of backtracking, and a clear
preference for ascribing greater importance to the views and reservations of the CBI. Accompanying these deeply disconcerting moves
has been the Blair Government's announcement that the public
sector will continue to be subject to a pay-freeze, with any increases
being introduced in two stages, one in April, and the remainder in
December.

Further evidence that the trade unions were to be treated with con-
tempt by New Labour was provided in March 1998, when Tony Blair
made clear that he would oppose a proposed EU directive requiring

employers to establish consultative forums within the workplace in order to facilitate social dialogue. Like his Conservative predecessors, Blair's resistance to such an initiative was couched in the rhetoric of labour-market flexibility and subsidiarity.

While there is nothing new in the sorry spectacle of Labour governments failing to deliver their pre-election pledges to the trade unions, the first year of the Blair government has been remarkable for the extent to which Labour's already minimal commitments to the unions have been downgraded, delayed or diluted. Indeed, the fact that New Labour's pre-election pledges to the trade unions were so modest makes their subsequent downgrading and dilution even more offensive.

In its concern not to alienate Middle England, New Labour appears willing to permit its approach to the trade unions effectively to be determined by employers' organizations such as the CBI. Thus, while the Chancellor, Gordon Brown, is increasingly being compared favourably with Lloyd George, Tony Blair is beginning to conjure up the spectre of Ramsay MacDonald. The British Labour movement is being betrayed by its political leaders yet again.

15 New Labour and Northern Ireland: Bipartisan Consensus and the 'Peace Process'

Mark Hayes

Of all we have done, ask me what has taken the most time, the most effort, it's probably Northern Ireland (Blair, Northern Ireland Office, 1997).

The state of Northern Ireland was set up as a result of the Government of Ireland Act, 1920. Ireland was partitioned with Northern Ireland becoming an integral, yet distinct, component of the United Kingdom with a clearly devolved administration. However, at the time, this 'compromise' was seen by most as, at best, a transitory arrangement. In essence Northern Ireland was created on the basis of crude demographic mathematics to ensure a Protestant majority, and as a result the state was dominated by the ideology of Unionism. The Northern Ireland Parliament at Stormont had legal and administrative competence over wide areas including law and order, electoral arrangements, education and aspects of economic and social policy. In fact a convention was soon established by which questions concerning matters under the auspices of Stormont should not be raised at Westminster. In effect the Catholic minority were trapped within a state to which many held no allegiance and which was dominated by an antagonistic ideology. This so-called 'Orange state' was characterized by the extent to which it institutionalized Protestant supremacy and deprived the minority Catholic community of basic civil and political rights. This has been well documented and there is no need to reiterate the point here (Farrell, 1992). When Catholics demanded their citizenship rights in the 1960s they were cynically and brutally rejected by the Protestant-Unionist state. This situation precipitated widespread social conflict and armed resistance which persisted for well over twenty-five years.

In Northern Ireland society was and is ethnically segmented. The core issue was and is one of ethno-national identity and the conflict revolves around the respective constitutional claims which reflect those allegiances. The fact is that the legitimacy of the Northern Ireland state has never been fully established. Consequently the 'troubles' in Northern Ireland have continued remorselessly, apparently impervious to political solutions. Moreover, there is no doubt that government policy, with regard to Northern Ireland, has generally reflected a pervasive pessimism about what could be achieved within the context of a divided community. Policy choices have been effectively constrained by a constitutional zero-sum game whereby any concession granted to one community has precipitated pronounced anxiety in the other; and the outcome, almost inevitably, has been a process of reciprocal reaction. In constitutional terms a qualitative improvement in the position of both communities is all but impossible, and there has been little or no scope for genuine compromise. Hence efforts to resolve the 'crisis' have invariably been tentative and incremental, and, as Cradden has said, policy-makers have in turn been 'disinterested or exasperated' (Cradden, 1996, pp. 71–87).

In the final analysis, however, the most important consideration for British policy-makers has been to sustain the integrity of the state against those forces that refused to accept 'legitimate' authority in Northern Ireland. This, in reality, has meant the prioritization of crisis control and containment. Security policy has dominated the political agenda. This has been true for the Labour Party as much as the Conservative Party.

There is no doubt that Labour Party policy has been characterized by the extent to which it has sought to sustain a bipartisan consensus on Ireland. Ever since the outbreak of the 'troubles' the overriding concern of Labour Party politicians has been to protect the state and, more specifically, avoid the accusation that they were or are somehow 'weak' on terrorism. In adopting this approach the Labour Party, in effect, endorsed the Conservative perspective and underscored the political position of Unionism by reiterating the sanctity of Northern Ireland's status within the United Kingdom. The logical corollary of this position has been the delegitimation of Nationalist perspectives, particularly Republicanism, which has been perceived as little more than a clandestine criminal conspiracy.

These general observations about the nature of the Labour Party's approach to Northern Ireland are powerfully reinforced if we take even the most cursory glance at the historical record. In the first instance Labour supported partition and the ratification of the 1921 'agreement'. Moreover, it was the postwar Labour government that passed the Ireland Act in 1949, Section 1 (2) of which reiterated that

> In no event will Northern Ireland or any part thereof cease to be part of His Majesty's dominions and of the United Kingdom without the consent of the Parliament of Northern Ireland (quoted in Cunningham, 1992, p. 30).

This effectively copper-fastened partition and the Government of Ireland Act, 1920. Throughout the years of discrimination in housing and employment, and while elections were gerrymandered to the benefit of the majority Protestant Unionist community, the Labour Party was guilty of serious neglect. It was the Labour Party in 1969 that sent in the British Army to 'support the civil power' after the riots in the Bogside (Bell, 1983, p. 108). During the brief moment of optimism which followed the deployment of troops Callaghan made certain promises in Derry (27–9 August 1969) about supporting communities that were deprived of freedom and justice. These proved to be hollow incantations since Stormont remained intact and troops were utilized to, in effect, stabilize the Unionist regime (Rose, 1996, pp. 88–101).

Within a few weeks of Labour's February 1974 election victory the Ulster Workers' Council strike by Loyalists destroyed the power-sharing Sunningdale agreement. Put simply, the Unionists called the Labour government's bluff and Wilson's administration did nothing. Indeed it was Merlyn Rees, the abortive Constitutional Convention notwithstanding, who began the process of 'criminalization', ending special-category status for prisoners, which precipitated the so-called 'blanket protests' and subsequent hunger-strikes by Republicans. It was Roy Mason who followed through the process of 'Ulsterization' and claimed he would 'squeeze the IRA like toothpaste'. (It could be argued that the Labour Government fell as an indirect result of problems in 'Ulster'. Gerry Fitt refused to support the government in a vote of confidence in 1979 because of the revelations contained in the Bennett Report on police brutality). It is certainly worth remembering that it was the Conservative Party that abolished Stormont (1972) and signed the Anglo-Irish Agreement (1985). Thus the record of Labour administrations indicates that they have never really sought to escape from the severe constraints imposed by a security agenda and a pervasive culture of containment and control (Newsinger, 1995, pp. 83–94). To borrow an aphorism, being 'tough on terrorism' has always been easier than being 'tough on the causes of terrorism'.

Even in Opposition, and free of the onerous responsibilities of office, the Labour Party has never really pursued an interest in radical or imaginative solutions. Indeed Labour has been anxious not to create difficulties for the Conservatives even when there might be legitimate grounds for criticism. For example, the Labour Party never seriously questioned the conduct of the military authorities after Bloody Sunday in January 1972 or the handling of the hunger-strikes in 1981. However, after the 1981 Conference, the Labour Party adopted a position of 'unity by consent' with regard to Ireland. This policy reorientation was undoubtedly a reflection of more pro-Nationalist sympathies at the grassroots constituency level. Indeed during the 1980s it might be argued that, given the shift in prevailing nuances, bipartisanship was fraying at the edges somewhat. Labour voted against the renewal of the Prevention of Terrorism and Emergency Provisions legislation (for a short time) after 1983–84; and some disquiet was expressed at measures restricting the right to silence and media coverage. Indeed when the Labour Party appointed Kevin McNamara as spokesman on Northern Ireland in 1987, it was considered a reflection of a more proactive Nationalistic perspective. Under McNamara's stewardship a paper entitled 'The Options for a Labour Government' was circulated confidentially which envisaged a breakdown of inter-party talks in circumstances unfavourable to Unionists and, moreover, considered the desirability of an imposed Anglo-Irish Framework 'tantamount to joint authority between London and Dublin' (Aughey, 1997, p. 251). However, these tentative moves toward a more ambitious approach were abruptly terminated after the success of Tony Blair and the emergence of 'New' Labour.

After Blair became leader of the Labour Party, McNamara was replaced by Mo Mowlam in 1994. Mowlam was promoted to Shadow Northern Ireland Secretary following the Shadow Cabinet elections in October 1994. Mowlam was a Kinnockite modernizer who subsequently prospered under the leadership of John Smith; she was also one of the earliest declared supporters of the Blair succession. Although Mowlam was evidently energetic and affable, there was little doubt that she was given the portfolio in order to check the discernible pro-Nationalist drift under McNamara. It can certainly be argued that since Blair took over, despite initial signs of dynamism and a more proactive style of government, and regardless of occasional rumblings at constituency level and the odd dissident backbencher, the Labour Party has conformed even more rigidly to a Unionist agenda.

New Labour has adopted a cautious and consensual approach. Party leader Tony Blair reiterated early on that he was not going to 'play politics' with the peace process; and Mowlam was concerned to avoid emphasis upon the 'unity by consent' position for fear of alienating the Unionists. Although Mowlam maintained that 'generalised activity is not a substitute either for real policy or for determined engagement with a politics of discussion and negotiation' (Mowlam, 1996b, p. 15) the Anglo-Irish Declaration and Joint Framework documents were to remain the foundation of any prospective peace process. In Opposition she claimed that Labour would be constructively critical with regard to the handling of marches, policing, fair employment, civil rights and economic development. Mowlam was keen to emphasize the need for a negotiated settlement and stressed Labour's rejection of violence (Mowlam, March 1996a, p. 8–9). It is in the context of this cautious approach in Opposition that we can evaluate the development of the so-called peace process and Labour's orientation toward it.

There is no doubt that the so-called 'Irish peace initiative' transformed the prospects for a settlement in Northern Ireland. In effect the Republican movement made significant concessions in the attempt to articulate a peaceful diplomatic strategy constructed around a configuration of forces sympathetic to Irish nationalism (the 'pan-Nationalist front'). In essence the Republicans, in reevaluating their strategy, were drawn into an alliance with the forces of constitutional nationalism (the Dublin regime and the SDLP). By doing so Republicans had moved significantly from their longstanding commitment to a unitary (32-county) Gaelic socialist state, and the emphasis was shifted toward 'cultural pluralism', 'parity of esteem', and an 'agreed', 'inclusive' Ireland. The administration in Dublin evidently took these moves seriously and felt that there was scope for some kind of accommodation. Albert Reynolds approached John Major on the assumption that progress could be made. The outcome was the Joint Declaration for Peace ('Downing Street Declaration') of December 1993, which in turn precipitated the IRA ceasefire of August 1994.

Unfortunately, despite initial progress, the process lost momentum largely because of British equivocation. John Major refused to clarify parts of the Downing Street Declaration; insisted on a three-month 'quarantine period' after the ceasefire; emphasized the word 'permanent' in relation to the cessation; sanctioned the release of Lee Clegg; belatedly focused on the issue of decommissioning of arms as a precondition for talks; and called for Forum elections after the publication of the Mitchell Report. All of this appeared to indicate a

reluctance to engage the Republicans-Nationalists in the serious business of substantive negotiation. The last significant steps by the Major
administration were to regularize the scrutiny of legislation hitherto
passed mostly through Orders in Council, and agree to the establishment of a Grand Committee for Northern Ireland. These were explicit
concessions to the Ulster Unionists. Of course Major's regime was
constrained by a slim majority and the need to rely on Unionist votes
in Parliament. As Brendan O'Leary has said:

> the Major government walked a fateful path. In the aftermath of
> the IRA's ceasefire, and the reciprocal loyalist ceasefire six weeks
> later, it engaged in important confidence-building measures, but,
> more significantly, began to erect an ever-changing obstacle course
> to inclusive multiparty negotiations (O'Leary, 1997, p. 672).

In short, Major did not display the requisite flexibility. Indeed his
tenure reflected a willingness to manipulate the peace process in
order to secure short-term political advantage. Moreover, New
Labour failed to offer a principled critique of Major's position.
Labour was quite prepared to accuse the government of cynicism and
dishonesty on a range of issues from Europe to the NHS but when it
came to Ireland the Labour Party gave John Major an extraordinary
degree of latitude. Even McNamara was drawn into criticizing Blair
and the party's Northern Ireland team for 'slavishly following everything the Prime Minister does' (quoted in Smyth, 1995, p. 41).

The IRA ceasefire ended in February 1996. The Forum elections
took place on 30 May 1996 at which Sinn Fein received its best-ever
share of the vote (15.5 per cent); and when talks began on 10 June
1996 Sinn Fein representatives were refused entry. Shortly afterwards
the SDLP actually resigned from the Forum in July 1996 in the aftermath of disturbances at Drumcree. Yet, while on a trip to Belfast
before Christmas 1996, Blair was clearly anxious to apportion blame
for the failure of the peace efforts:

> when the IRA ceasefire was called originally, we all took this as firm
> evidence that there was a real desire on the part of Sinn Fein to put
> the past behind it. When it ended, renewed violence did not just
> cause dismay. It caused fundamental doubts about the desire for
> peace. (quoted in Mallie and McKittrick, 1997, pp. 394–5)

Blair was determined not to criticize the government. Indeed in a
speech at the Royal Ulster Agricultural Show on 16 May, shortly after
the election, Blair paid fulsome tribute to the efforts of John Major:

After only a few days as Prime Minister I also began to appreciate fully the scale of his efforts and of his devotion to peace and a political settlement. We offered him bipartisan support in doing so . . . if there is a new opportunity for progress now, it is in large part thanks to him. (NI Information Service, May 1997)

This is an extraordinary interpretation of events prior to the 1997 election given the fact that it was Major's government that had actually squandered a genuine opportunity to reach an accommodation. The Labour Party was elected in May 1997 with an overwhelming parliamentary majority, and Mowlam took up her post as Northern Ireland Secretary on 3 May 1997. There is no doubt that Mowlam brought to the office a personable style which marked a stark contrast to the Tory patricians that had presided over 'the Province' in recent years. It seemed to underscore the existence of a new dynamism and sense of direction. Even Gerry Adams noted that the Labour Government had taken up positions 'in advance' of the previous administration.

However the first real test for Mowlam occurred in July 1997 in Drumcree. Local residents on the Garvaghy Road had long protested about the annual Orange march and Mowlam had engaged in some high-profile interjections to try and secure some kind of workable compromise. In the final analysis Mowlam, after taking advice from the Royal Ulster Constabulary (RUC) Chief Constable, Ronnie Flannagan, conceded that the march should go ahead. Nationalist protesters were unceremoniously removed by the RUC, and the general perception was that the authorities had capitulated to the threat of Protestant violence. Mowlam was accused of duplicity and betrayal by residents' groups and there was widespread rioting in Nationalist areas. There is no doubt that, in the eyes of Nationalists, events at Drumcree seriously undermined the credibility of Mowlam and the new administration.

Nevertheless, there was evidently contact between Sinn Fein and the New Labour government in an attempt to retrieve the situation. During the course of this liaison assurances were apparently given to Sinn Fein with regard to: the timescale for entry into inclusive negotiations (six weeks); the time limit on the talks process (May 1998); the decommissioning issue (to be left to an independent body); and certain so-called 'confidence-building' measures (in relation to prisoners). By addressing these issues, while keeping the Ulster Unionist Party (UUP), the main Unionist party, on board, Blair was able to create the impression that he had manufactured some scope for progress. This perception was powerfully reinforced when the IRA instituted a new ceasefire on 20 July 1997. Given the Labour Party's unassailable parliamentary majority and a new sympathetic Fianna Fail regime in the Republic the IRA evidently sensed renewed potential for an agreed outcome. Consequently the peace process received new impetus. Mowlam concluded that the ceasefire was 'genuine' and met Sinn Fein on 6 August at Stormont; and on 29 August an invitation was sent to Sinn Fein to join all-party talks to begin in September. Significantly, on 9 September Sinn Fein committed itself to the 'Mitchell principles' of democracy and non-violence (*Report of the International Body on Arms Decommissioning*, 24 January 1996, NI Office, 1997). Obviously the fact that the Democratic Unionist Party and the UK Unionists rejected the talks had the effect of undermining the credibility of the process to some extent, but Blair and Mowlam evidently felt optimistic enough to reiterate the target-date for an agreement of May 1998.

Mowlam, however, emphasized that the notion of 'consent' was to be the guiding principle for the talks, and 'sufficient consensus' would have to be reached between the participants; that is, parties representing a majority of each community should concur with the outcome(s). Moreover, the rules made it clear that any party that 'demonstrably dishonoured' the Mitchell principles would no longer be able to participate in the negotiations. The discussions were designed to deal specifically with three 'strands': the totality of relations within Northern Ireland; between Northern Ireland and the Republic; and between Britain and Ireland. On 24 September an Independent Decommissioning Commission was set up under the Chairmanship of General John De Chastelain which was prepared to consider schemes for decommissioning weapons.

As a result of the ceasefire and the talks process certain incremental confidence-building measures were implemented, such as the transfer of prisoners, an increase in prison-leave for offenders, and the reduction of military foot-patrols in certain areas. Although far less than what was demanded by some Nationalists, it did reflect a diminution of the 'terrorist' threat and arguably indicated steady progress toward an agreement. Mowlam also clearly realized that the marching season was likely to precipitate severe difficulties for the government in sustaining the peace process, and while in Opposition she had argued for an independent review of the parades issue. On 17 October the NIO published a Bill designed to implement the recommendations of the North Report on parades which had been commissioned by the previous administration. The Public Processions etc. (NI) Bill entered the statute book shortly before the 1998 marching season. Mowlam saw this as honouring a manifesto pledge to reduce inter-communal tension during the marching season; and the idea of a commission was seen as the most appropriate (impartial) means of avoiding a repetition of events at Drumcree.

There was also legislative activity in other key areas in an attempt to sustain momentum. For example, when introducing the Northern Ireland (Emergency Provisions) legislation Mowlam expressed a keen desire to repeal such measures eventually, but regretted their necessity in current circumstances. As she said:

> some terrorist groups on both sides remain active and I will not leave the security forces nor the criminal justice system in Northern Ireland without the means they need to counter these activities. (Mowlam, in Labour Party NI team, November 1997)

There were three changes, however: removal of the internment provision; police interviews with terrorist suspects to be audio-recorded; and an extension of the power of the Attorney-General to certify some offences out of the 'schedule' to facilitate jury trial, if appropriate, thus reducing pressure on the Diplock system. Subsequently Jack Straw announced the government's intention to produce new measures to replace the Emergency Provisions and Prevention of Terrorism legislation. A joint initiative by the Home Office and NIO, it is apparently designed to respond to the changing nature of 'worldwide terrorism' and honour a manifesto commitment to 'take effective measures to combat the terrorist threat'.

On 24 October 1997 Labour announced the setting up of a Commission to look at ways of recognizing the pain and suffering of victims of violence as a result of the 'troubles', an idea which appears to have originated with Blair himself. The Commission was led by former head of the Northern Ireland Civil Service Sir Kenneth Bloomfield, and called for, among other things, a victims' Ombudsman and memorial, and an annual 'Reconciliation Day'. On 27 November Mowlam set down new objectives for policing with regard to terrorism, public order and crime, especially drug-related offences. 'Performance indicators' were issued to the RUC in the drive to make it more efficient, effective and accountable. On 2 December it was announced that the Oath of Allegiance for RUC recruits would no longer contain reference to the Crown. On 4 December 1997 the Police (NI) Bill was introduced, which was proposed by the previous government in May 1996. Perhaps more significantly, on 29 January 1998, Blair announced an Inquiry into Bloody Sunday under the Tribunal of Inquiry (Evidence) Act 1921, to be chaired by Lord Saville. As well as ongoing legislative measures and policy proposals Blair made the most visible of symbolic gestures by meeting representatives of Sinn Fein on 14 October 1997. On 11 December a Sinn Fein delegation was received at 10 Downing Street, the first since Lloyd George met Michael Collins in 1921. The fact that Blair was willing to take such a high-profile 'risk' for peace seemed to reinforce the impression of a clear disjuncture with the mode of previous governments. Indeed some saw Blair's willingness to countenance direct contact as emblematic of a new approach not just in Ireland but to government in general; a sign that things really had changed. As Hugo Young put it:

> even had (he) not been in hock to the Unionists, Major would never have had the nerve to meet Sinn Fein. Mr Blair's willingness to do so, stripping away the decades of painful sentiment and futile moralizing, was something open to a new leader with a huge majority, and he did not agonize about matching the moment. He did not shrink in this hard circumstance, from his general desire to lead, to be a leader, to stand out there and take the risk, and thereby demonstrate – a driving obsession, this – how utterly unalike he is to the miserable scenes of non-government that went before. (Young, 1997)

Yet this was a most misleading interpretation of New Labour's position which, in reality, was little different to that adopted by previous Conservative administrations. In fact Blair and Mowlam went out of their way to reassure the Unionists. On 3 May 1997 Mowlam stated categorically that

> the people of Northern Ireland have the right to decide their own future and there will be no change to Northern Ireland's status as part of the UK without the clear and formal consent of a majority of the people who live there. (NI Information Service, May 1997)

Blair's first official engagement outside London as Prime Minister was to Northern Ireland where he stated explicitly that his agenda was not a united Ireland. In the *Belfast Newsletter* he acknowledged that

> Sinn Fein's presence at the negotiating table is still very hard for many people to accept. This is entirely understandable, after all the

years of IRA terrorism and the breakdown of the last ceasefire . . . no-one should be naive about the IRA and Sinn Fein.

Moreover, he continued,

Northern Ireland is part of the UK because that is a wish of the majority of the people who live here. Let me make it abundantly clear: it will remain part of the UK so long as that remains the case. That is not just a statement of fact but a commitment to a basic principle of democracy. And I value the Union and Northern Ireland's place within it. (*Belfast Newsletter,* September 1997)

As John Lloyd has explained: 'Blair has done everything he can do but put on an orange sash and a bowler hat' (Lloyd, 1997, p. 25). The Unionists were still being offered the security of the so-called 'triple lock': party negotiations, referendum and Parliament. In effect New Labour has been quite explicit in acting as guarantor for the Unionist position by reiterating the Unionist veto over substantive constitutional reform.

Of course the negotiations themselves were beset with difficulties. Trimble's Unionists refused face-to-face talks with Sinn Fein, even after December 1997 when talks were restricted to two representatives per party. Both Trimble and Maginnis have met convicted Loyalists in the Maze, indeed Trimble 'liaised' with Loyalist killer Billy Wright during the standoff at Drumcree, but they steadfastly refused to engage with democratically elected representatives of the Nationalist community. In fact, the murder of Billy Wright by the Irish National Liberation Army (INLA) in the Maze prison on 27 December 1997 threatened to derail the whole process. As a result of the ensuing crisis Mowlam had to take the not-inconsiderable political risk of meeting convicted Loyalists in the Maze in order to keep the smaller Ulster Democratic Party (UDP), and Progressive Unionist Party (PUP), on board. To some observers this represented an enormous gamble, but if little else it reflected Mowlam's personal commitment to the negotiations. In the event the Loyalists sustained their commitment to the talks. However, when some of the so-called 'retaliatory' killings of Catholics were attributed to the Ulster Freedom Fighters–Ulster Defence Association, the UDP were (temporarily) expelled from the talks, in January 1998, under the terms of the Mitchell agreement (they did in fact jump before they were pushed).

More significantly, in an attempt to assuage 'Unionist fears', Blair produced a new policy discussion document in conjunction with the

Irish government. The *Propositions on Heads of Agreement* (12 January 1998) was the result of some frenetic telephone diplomacy by Blair while on an official visit to Japan. The resulting document was, as a NIO spokesperson put it, 'a bone for the parties to gnaw on'. Nevertheless it certainly reflected Unionist priorities and delighted UUP leader David Trimble. The 'proposals' called for a Northern Ireland assembly, elected by Proportional Representation, with executive and legislative functions; unspecified cross-border links; and an intergovernmental council of the British Isles. In short it downplayed north–south relations (strand two) and undermined the all-Ireland thrust of the *Frameworks for the Future* document produced by the British and Irish governments in February 1995. And when the British government was forced into conceding that the *Frameworks* document had not been abandoned entirely, the UUP explicitly rejected any solution based upon its proposals (indeed Jeffrey Donaldson tore up a copy of the document for the benefit of the media).

Meanwhile there were persistent threats to expel Sinn Fein permanently from the process as a result of violence in Northern Ireland. Mowlam, on the evidence provided by the RUC, and despite claims to the contrary made by Sinn Fein, and indeed the IRA, suggested that the IRA was responsible for the violence. The decision was subsequently made, in February 1998, to expel Sinn Fein from the talks process temporarily for 'demonstrably dishonouring' the Mitchell principles. This undoubtedly heightened the level of cynicism about the whole process in the Republican movement, and there is certainly little doubt that those Unionists who remained in the negotiations sought to dictate the tone and content of outcomes, whilst refusing to countenance the only reform likely to eradicate the causes of the conflict, i.e. substantive political and constitutional change.

Nevertheless, after months of arduous negotiation, and despite pessimistic predictions in some quarters, a multi-party peace agreement was reached on Good Friday, 10 April 1998. At one point, shortly before the deadline, it looked as though the talks would collapse completely. However, the personal intervention of the Prime Minister appeared to stabilize the situation and re-focus the minds of the participants. Tony Blair's high-profile, hands-on diplomacy certainly won him plaudits from across the political spectrum.

The Belfast Agreement itself has several key features. An assembly is to be elected within Northern Ireland (108 members elected by Single Transferrable Vote) from which an executive will be chosen to take decisions on a cross-community basis. A North–South ministerial council will be set up to facilitate cooperation within the island of Ireland on matters of 'mutual interest' such as agriculture, education, transport and the environment. There will also be a British–Irish Council which, although possessing no formal legislative authority, will exist to promote harmonious relationships between the British and Irish governments and the devolved administrations of Scotland, Wales and Northern Ireland. At the same time a new British–Irish Inter-governmental Conference will facilitate bilateral cooperation and subsume the old structures created by the Anglo-Irish Agreement (1985).

The so-called 'Good Friday Agreement' also expressed a commitment to set up a Northern Ireland Human Rights Commission and an Equality Commission. An independent body is also to be organized under the chairmanship of Chris Patten to investigate the issue of policing; and provision was made for the accelerated release of prisoners convicted of scheduled offences (providing they belong to organizations upholding complete and unequivocal ceasefires). The decommissioning of paramilitary weapons was to be dealt with by another independent agency, and the document reiterated the need throughout for all parties to accept peaceful methods in pursuance of political aims. The agreement effectively transcended the Government of Ireland Act (1920). However, more significantly, the Irish government agreed to concede (via a referendum) Articles 2 and 3 of its Constitution which claimed sovereignty over the entire island of Ireland. In effect the Good Friday Agreement underscored British sovereignty in Northern Ireland which will continue until a majority of the North declares otherwise.

The content of this agreement was accepted by all the participants at the multi-party talks, even Sinn Fein (which had to alter its party constitution to allow participation in a 'six county' assembly). Subsequently, after vociferous campaigning (which included collaborative appearances by Blair and Major), the accord was overwhelmingly endorsed by the people of Ireland via referenda held on 22 May 1998 (71 per cent voted in favour in the north, 95 per cent in the south).

On the face of it, as Blair pointed out, it appeared as though the 'burden of history' had been lifted. However, analysis of the underlying purposes and perspectives of the most important political elements reveals that there may yet be severe difficulty ahead. Those Unionists who accepted the Agreement did so on the plausible assumption that it underscored the principle of consent and thereby secured the status of the Union while it is also important to remember that many Unionists and Loyalists (including UUP MPs) actually rejected the settlement and will inevitably seek to undermine proposed outcomes. Many Nationalists and Republicans, on the other hand, stress the 'equality agenda' and view the Agreement as more of a transitional arrangement, the underlying dynamic of which will precipitate a new all-Ireland configuration of some description. While other Republican groupings reject the accord in its entirety as a flawed 'partitionist' framework ('Sunningdale for slow learners'). Certainly there is no doubt that particularly sensitive components in the Agreement could yet precipitate renewed conflict, such as the reform of the RUC, decisions made by the Parades Commission, the decommissioning of weapons or the release of prisoners. In this context the relentlessly optimistic references to the 'endgame' may yet be somewhat premature.

On 15 August the so-called 'Real IRA' exploded a bomb in Omagh town centre killing 29 people and injuring many others. The Labour Government responded to the widespread outrage by recalling Parliament and passing the Criminal Justice (Terrorism and Conspiracy) Act. The provisions of this new security legislation mean that the word of a senior police officer can be taken as evidence with regard to membership of a proscribed organization; refusal to answer any relevant questions during interrogation may be seen as inference of guilt; conspiracy to commit terrorism outside the UK is considered as a specific offence. All of this is but a short step from the discredited internment procedures. However, the precipitate introduction of draconian legal measures is unlikely to solve the political problem of dissident republicanism.

The fact that a multi-party accommodation has been reached may well prove to be very significant. It is far too early to make a conclusive judgement. However, the fact that it was reached at all reflects, primarily, the ideological flexibility of Sinn Fein and the Republican movement rather than the diplomatic dexterity of Mowlam and Blair. In effect New Labour has not deviated substantially from the pro-Unionist course set by Major, with the emphasis on (Unionist) consent and (pro-partitionist) majoritarian democracy. The New Labour government has simply had the good fortune to encounter a Republican leadership willing to countenance a significant diminution of traditional principles and objectives, at least for tactical purposes in the short-term. Whether this particular 'historic compromise' can provide a durable basis for genuine peace in the longer term is an entirely different matter.

16 Conclusion
Gerald R. Taylor

The act which established Tony Blair's control over the Labour Party on his accession to the leadership, and the act which may come to characterize New Labour, was the repeal of Clause Four. Apart from its leadership and electoral significance, it marked the highest watermark so far in the victory of pragmatism over principle in the history of the Labour Party. Pragmatism may become the defining byword for New Labour, but pragmatism is not necessarily itself unprincipled.

From the essays in this collection the underlying structure of New Labour's politics is not obviously discernible. It is not readily apparent what principles, what perspectives, and what vision for the future of Britain are driving New Labour. That said, certain themes are apparent. On a detailed level it is clear that New Labour is making an impression (albeit limited) on Britain's relations with Europe, on the party's relations with the trade unions, and on the position of women and women's issues in British politics. It has made an impact on decentralization, at least in respect to devolution, on local government and generally on constitutional reform. It has made its presence felt in the internal workings of the party, and in the handling of the media. Its impact in Northern Ireland, though superficially impressive, is complex and difficult to assess, as are its handling of the economy; its developing relations with the civil service; the emergence of a replacement for the postwar welfare state; and the application of Christian Socialism or the development of new principles based around concepts such as stakeholder capitalism.

What is clear is that where New Labour has done most and appeared to gain most ground, as with devolution, internal party control, or Europe, it has largely been as a result of tactical astuteness rather than strategic vision. One area where New Labour could make the most radical departure is that of constitutional reform.

This is in itself ironic given Labour's traditional lack of interest in pursuing reform of the British state beyond the rhetorical, Labour's long-standing deference to the character of the British state, and Labour's apparent acceptance of the British state as a neutral mechanism for the implementation of 'socialist' policies. What is, perhaps, even more curious is that New Labour has embarked on a project, substantial in nature, without any clearly expressed perspective on where it wishes to end up. To some extent this may be a positive advantage, allowing New Labour to tread far further down the path of reform than a more openly radical government would be capable. However, it does seem to stretch to a considerable distance the degree of 'trust' we are being asked to provide to New Labour.

There are some apparent contradictions in New Labour's approach. On the one hand, their policies on open government appear very strong and designed to enable access; on the other, manipulation of the media and control of the party seem less than pluralist. On the one hand, devolution and developments in local government offer the prospect of decentralized power; on the other, New Labour has been prepared to use the power of central control to ensure the results it wishes to see. On the one hand, a more positive view of integration with Europe presents the prospect of a new global view; on the other, the goodwill this has generated has been used to lecture Europeans, and others, on the benefits of global competition and market systems.

The problem for reforming administrations is always how to ensure that the public, or sufficient numbers of them, are prepared to travel the road you wish to walk. New Labour seems determined to add to this the fact that nobody is quite sure exactly where this road is leading. The momentum established by a truly stunning electoral victory may be enough to carry New Labour down this road beyond the point of no return. However, it may alternatively be that when the going gets tough and unexpected setbacks are experienced public goodwill for Labour's project, the 'trust' that is required, may rapidly evaporate.

New Labour is certainly changing the nature of British politics. Where this is all leading is, so far, uncertain. It is also far from obvious that New Labour has won the 'hearts and minds' of the British public, as well as their votes. While the fortunes of New Labour, as with the fortunes of Thatcherism, may depend as much on the state of the opposition as of the support for government, it remains to be seen whether Britain can be reformed by stealth. This is particularly the case where those leading the way seem as unsure of the final destination as those who are following. Whether New Labour will be remembered as the most successful and radical reforming government of the twentieth, or twenty-first, century, or whether they will be seen by history as a bunch of confidence-men hoodwinking the public with hollow promises remains to be seen. For some, though, the loss of the comforting certainties of 'old' Labour and conservatism may cause considerable discomfort. We hope this text has gone some way to plotting a map of the altered landscape of British politics.

Bibliography

Adonis, A. and S. Twigg, 1997, *The Cross We Bear: Electoral Reform for Local Government* (London: Fabian Society)

Ainley, P., 1988, *From School to YTS* (Buckingham: Open University Press)

Ainley, P., 1992, 'On the Trail of the Elusive First Job', *The Guardian*, 1 December 1992.

Ainley, P., 1993, *Class and Skill: Changing Divisions of Knowledge and Labour* (London: Cassell)

Ainley, P., 1994, *Degrees of Difference: Higher Education in the 1990s* (London: Lawrence and Wishart)

Ainley, P., 1997, '"All Pigs Flying" – a Consequence of Indirect Management by Outputs in Further Education', paper delivered at 1997 Vocational Education and Training Conference, Huddersfield University

Ainley, P. and Bailey, B., 1997, *The Business of Learning: Further Education in the Home Counties and Inner City* (London: Cassell)

Ainley P., and Corney, M., 1990, *Training for the Future: the Rise and Fall of the Manpower Services Commission* (London: Cassell)

Ainley, P. and Vickerstaff, S., 1993, 'Transitions from Corporatism: the Privatisation of Policy Failure', *Contemporary Record*, December

Albert, M., 1992, *Capitalism against Capitalism* (London: Lawrence and Wishart)

Anderson, P. and N. Mann, 1997, *Safety First: the Making of New Labour* (London: Granta)

Archbishop of Canterbury's Commission on Urban Priority, 1985, *Faith in the City: a Call for Action by Church and Nation* (London: Church House)

Artis, M. and D. Cobham, (eds), 1991, *Labour's Economic Policies, 1974–79* (Manchester: Manchester University Press)

Atherton, J., 1994, *Social Christianity: a Reader* (London: SPCK)

Aughey, A., 1997, 'Northern Ireland', in P. Dunleavy *et al.* (eds), *Developments in British Politics 5* (London: Macmillan)

Avis, J., M. Bloomer, G. Esland, D. Gleeson and P. Hodkinson, 1996, *Knowledge and Nationhood, Education, Politics and Work* (London: Cassell)

Backstrom, P. N., 1974, *Christian Socialism and Cooperation in Victorian England* (Beckenham: Croom Helm)

Barro, R. and Gordon, D., 1983, 'Rules, Discretion, and Reputation in a Model of Monetary Policy', *Journal of Monetary Economics*, Vol. 12

Batley, R. and G. Stoker, (eds), 1991, *Local Government in Europe: Trends and Developments* (London: Macmillan)

Beetham, D. (ed.), 1994, *Defining and Measuring Democracy* (London: Sage)

Bell, G., 1983, *Troublesome Business: the Labour Party and Northern Ireland* (London: Pluto)

Bell, I., 1998, 'Comment', *The Observer*, 22 March

Bender, S., 1997, *After the Windfall: Young People's Prospects in the New Labour Market* (London: The Children's Society)

Benn, C., 1984, 'Secondary Reform: Time to Move on', *Forum*, Vol. 26
Berger, S. & Dore, R. (eds), 1996, *National Diversity and Global Capitalism* (Ithaca: Cornell University Press)
Blackwell, T. and Seabrook, J., 1985, *A World Still to Win: the Reconstruction of the Post-war Working Class* (London: Faber)
Blair, T., 1996, *New Britain: My Vision of a Young Country* (London: Fourth Estate)
Blair, T., 1997a, Speech to the Newspaper Society, 10 March 1997
Blair T., 1997b, Speech to Labour Party Workers, Royal Festival Hall, London, 2 May 1997
Blair, T., 1998, *Leading the Way* (London: Institute for Public Policy Research)
Blumler, J., 1993, 'Elections, the Media and the Modern Publicity Process', in M. Ferguson (ed.), *Public Communications: Themes and Perspectives* (London: Sage)
Blumler, J., *et al.*, 1989, 'The Earnest versus the Determined: a Study of Election News Making at the BBC', in I. Crewe and M. Harrop, (eds), *Political Communications: the 1987 General Election* (Cambridge: Cambridge University Press)
Blumler, J. and M. Gurevitch, 1995, *The Crisis of Public Communication* (London: Routledge)
Boyer, R. and Drache, D. (eds), 1996, *States Against Markets: the Limits of Globalization* (London: Routledge)
Brittan, S., 1981, *How to End the 'Monetarist' Controversy* (London: Institute of Economic Affairs)
Broadfoot, P., 1996, *Education, Assessment and Society* (Buckingham: Open University Press)
Brown, A., 1996, 'Women and Politics in Scotland', in J. Lovenduski and P. Norris, (eds), *Women in Politics* (Oxford: Oxford University Press)
Brown, G., 1995, 'Labour's Macroeconomic Framework', Speech by the Shadow Chancellor to the Labour Finance and Industry Group, 17 May 1995
Brown, G., 1996, Speech by the Shadow Chancellor to the Confederation of British Industry Annual Conference, Harrogate, 11 November 1996
Brown, G., 1997, Budget speech to the House of Commons, 2 July 1997
Bryant, C. (ed.), 1993, *Reclaiming the Ground: Christianity and Socialism* (London: Hodder and Stoughton)
Bryant, C., 1996, *Possible Dreams: a Personal History of the British Christian Socialists* (London: Hodder and Stoughton)
Bryant, C., 1997, *Stafford Cripps* (London: Hodder and Stoughton)
Buchanan, T., 1996, 'Great Britain' in T. Buchanan and M. Conway (ed.), *Political Catholicism in Europe, 1918–1965* (Oxford: Oxford University Press)
Bulpitt, J., 1983, *Territory and Power in the United Kingdom* (Manchester: Manchester University Press)
Burns, D., R. Hambleton, and P. Hoggett, 1994, *The Politics of Decentralisation* (London: Macmillan)
Butley, D., A. Adonis, and T. Travers, 1994, *Failure in British Government: the Politics of the Poll Tax* (Oxford: Oxford University Press)

Butler, D. and D. Kavanagh, 1988, *The British General Election of 1987* (London: Macmillan)

Butler, D. and D. Kavanagh, 1993, *The British General Election of 1992* (London: Macmillan)

Butler, D. and D. Kavanagh, 1998, *The British General Election of 1997* (London: Macmillan)

Byrne, L., 1997, *Information Age Government: Delivering the Blair Revolution* (London: Fabian Society)

Calvo, G., 1978, 'On the Time Consistency of Optimal Policy in a Monetary Economy', *Econometrica*, Vol. 46

Catholic Church, 1996, *The Common Good and the Catholic Church's Social Teaching: a Statement by the Catholic Bishop's Conference of England and Wales* (London: Catholic Bishop's Conference of England and Wales)

Cerny, P., 1996, 'International Finance and the Erosion of State Policy Capacity' in P. Gummett (ed.), *Globalization and Public Policy* (Cheltenham: Edward Elgar)

Cerny, P., 1990, *The Changing Architecture of Politics* (London: Sage)

Chandler, J., 1996, *Local Government Today* (Manchester: Manchester University Press)

'Charter 88' (1991), *Citizens*, No. 1 July (London, Charter 1988)

Clark, D., 1997, 'The Civil Service and the New Government', speech at the QEII Center, 17 June London: Cabinet Office

Clark, H., 1993, *The Church under Thatcher* (London: SPCK)

Clarke, J., A. Cochrane and E. McLaughlin (eds), 1994, *Managing Social Policy* (London: Sage)

Commission for Local Democracy, 1995, *Taking Charge: the Rebirth of Local Democracy* (London: Municipal Journal Books)

Commission on Social Justice, 1992, *Social Justice: Strategies for National Renewal* (London: Vintage)

Confederation of British Industry, 1994, *Thinking Ahead* (London: CBI)

Conolly, J., 1987, 'British Labour and Irish Politicians' *Forward*, 3 May 1913 in *Collected Works*, Vol. I (London: New Books)

Constitution Unit, 1996, *Delivering Constitutional Reform* (London: Constitution Unit)

Cradden, T., 1996, 'Labour in Britain and the Northern Ireland Labour Party 1900–1970' in P. Catterall and S. McDougall (eds), *The Northern Ireland Question in British Politics* (London: Macmillan)

Cripps, S., 1933, *Can Socialism Come by Constitutional Method?* (London: Socialist League)

Crosland, A., 1956, *The Future of Socialism* (London: Cape)

Crouch, C., 1997, 'The Terms of the Neo-liberal Consensus', *Political Quarterly*, Vol. 68, No. 4, Oct.–Dec.

Cunningham, M., 1992, British Policy in Northern Ireland', *Politics Review*, September

Davies, N., 1997, *Dark Heart: the Shocking Truth about Hidden Britain* (London: Chatto and Windus)

Dennis, N., 1997, *The Invention of Permanent Poverty* (London: IEA)

Dennis, N. and A. H. Halsey, 1988, *English Ethical Socialism: from Thomas More to R. H. Tawney* (Oxford: Clarendon Press)

Dewdney, K., 1992, 'Who Runs Labour?' *Fabian Review*, July
Dowding, K., 1996, *Power* (Buckingham: Open University Press)
Draper, D., 1997, *Blair's 100 Days* (London: Faber and Faber)
Drucker, H. M., 1979, *Doctrine and Ethos in the Labour Party* (London: George Allen and Unwin)
Dunleavy, P., 1991, *Democracy, Bureaucracy, and Public Choice* (Hemel Hempstead: Harvester Wheatsheaf)
Dunleavy, P., A. Gamble, I. Holliday and G. Peele (eds), 1997, *Developments in British Politics 5* (London: Macmillan)
Dunleavy, P., H. Margetts, B. O'Duffy and S. Weir, 1997, *Making Votes Count: How Britain Would Have Voted in the 1990s under Alternative Electoral Systems*, Democratic Audit Paper No. 11 (London: Democratic Audit)
Equal Opportunities Commission, 1998, *Equality in the 21st Century: a New Approach* (Manchester: Equal Opportunities Commission)
Evans, M., 1994, 'Constitutional Doctrine and Revisionism in the Labour Party', *Socialist History* No. 4, pp. 33–49
Farrell, M., 1992, *Northern Ireland: the Orange State* (London: Pluto)
Fforde, J. S., 1983, 'Setting Monetary Objectives', *Bank of England Quarterly Bulletin*, June
Field, F., 1996, *Stakeholder Welfare* (London: IEA)
Field, F., 1997, *Reforming Welfare* (London: Social Market Foundation)
Fielding, S., 1997, 'Labour's Path to Power', in A. Geddes and J. Tonge (eds), *Labour's Landslide* (Manchester: Manchester University Press)
Financial Times, 1996, 'Labour Sets Out to Make Similar Look Different' 21 May
Finn, D., 1987, *Training Without Jobs: New Deals and Broken Promises* (London: Macmillan)
Fisher, J., 1996, *British Political Parties* (London: Prentice Hall)
Forbes, I., 1996, 'The Privatisation of Sex Equality Policy', in J. Lovenduski and P. Norris (eds), *Women in Politics* (Oxford: Oxford University Press)
Franklin, B., 1994, *Packaging Politics: Political Communications in Britain's Media Democracy* (London: Edward Arnold)
Fukuyama, Francis, 1992, *The End of History and the Last Man* (Harmondsworth: Penguin)
Gardiner, J., 1997, 'A New Gender Contract?', *Soundings*, Special Issue
Gee, J., 1996, *Social Linguistics and Literacies: Ideology in Discourses* (London: Taylor and Francis)
Geekie, J. and R. Levy, 1989, 'Devolution and the Tartanisation of the Labour Party', *Parliamentary Affairs*, Vol. 42, No. 3, pp. 399–411
Gould, B., 1997, *The Jobs Letter*, 25 August 1997, New Plymouth, Taranaki, Aotearoa/New Zealand
Graff, H., 1987, *The Labyrinths and the Legacies of Literacy* (Lewes: Falmer)
Grant, W., 1998, 'Roundtable on New Labour', Paper presented to the Eleventh International Conference of Europeanists, Omni Harbor Hotel, Baltimore, 26–28 February, 1998
Gravatt, J., 1998, *Funding by Numbers: the Further Education Funding Councils Method and Madness Explained to the World* (London: Lewisham College)
Gummett, P. (ed.), *Globalization and Public Policy* (Cheltenham: Edward Elgar)

Hall, S. *et al.*, 1981, *Unpopular Education: Schooling and Social Democracy in England since 1945* (Birmingham: Hutchinson)

Hall, S., 1995, 'Son of Margaret?', *New Statesman and Society*, 6 October

Halsey, A., A. Heath and J. Ridge, 1980, *Origins and Destinations: Family, Class and Education in Modern Britain* (Oxford: Oxford University Press)

Harden, I., 1992, *The Contracting State* (Buckingham: Open University Press)

Harrison, J., 1980, 'State Expenditure and Capital', *Cambridge Journal of Economics*, Vol. 4, No. 4

Harrop, Martin (1990), 'Political Marketing', *Parliamentary Affairs* 43: pp. 277–91.

Hastings, A., 1991, *Robert Runcie* (London: Mowbray)

Hay, C., 1994, 'Labour's Thatcherite Revisionism: Playing the Politics of Catch-up', *Political Studies*, Vol. 42, No. 4

Hay, C., 1997a, 'Anticipating Accommodations, Accommodating Anticipations: the Appeasement of Capital in the Modernisation of the British Labour Party, 1987–92', *Politics and Society*, Vol. 25, No. 2

Hay, Colin, 1997b, 'Blairjorism: Towards a One-vision Polity', *Political Quarterly*, Vol. 68, No. 4, Oct.–Dec.

Hay, C., 1998, 'That Was Then, This is Now: the Revision of Policy in the "Modernisation" of the British Labour Party, 1992–97', *New Political Science* Vol. 20, No. 1

Hay, C. and Watson, M., 1998, 'The Discourse of Globalisation and the Logic of No Alternative: Rendering the Contingent Necessary in the Downsizing of New Labour's Aspirations for Government: in Andrew Donson and Jeffrey Stanyer (eds), *Contemporary Political Studies 1998* (Oxford: Blackwell)

Heath, A. *et al.*, 1994, 'Can Labour Win?', in A. Heath *et al.* (eds), *Labour's Last Chance? The 1992 Election and Beyond* (Aldershot: Dartmouth)

Heath, A., 1997, 'What was the Effect of New Labour?' *Renewal*, Vol. 5, No. 2

Heffernan, R., 1998, 'Labour's Transformation: a Staged process with No One Point of Origin', *Politics*, Vol. 5.

Heffernan, R. and J. Stanyer, 1998, 'Contesting the News Media Agenda: the Political Communications Strategies of the British Labour Government', Unpublished paper presented to the European Consortium of Political Research Conference, University of Warwick, March

Heffernan, R. and J. Stanyer, 1997, 'The Enhancement of Leadership Power: the Labour Party and the Impact of Political Communications', in D. Denver *et al.* (eds), *Elections, Public Opinion, Parties* (London: Frank Cass)

Heffernan, R. and M. Marqusee, 1992, *Defeat from the Jaws of Victory: Inside Kinnock's Labour Party* (London: Verso)

Hennessy, P., 1998, 'The Blair Style of Government: an Historical Perspective and an Interim Audit', *Government and Opposition*, Vol. 33, no. 1

Hewitt, M. and Powell, M., 1997, ' "Something Happened": Conflicting Descriptions of the New Welfare State', paper presented at the 31st Social Policy Association Annual Conference, University of Lincolnshire and Humberside, 15–17 July

Hewitt, P. and D. Mattison, 1992, *Women's Votes: the Key to Winning* (London: Fabian Tract No. 541)

Hill, D., 1993, then Labour Party Director of Communications, cited in *The Guardian*, 5 January 1993

Hilton, B., 1988, *The Age of Atonement: the Influence of Evangelicalism on Social and Economic Thought, 1795–1865* (Oxford: Oxford University Press)

Hirst, P. and Thompson, G., 1996, *Globalisation in Question* (Cambridge: Polity)

HMSO, 1944, *Employment Policy*, Cmnd 6527 (London: HMSO)

HMSO, 1993, *Review of the National Curriculum for Schools* (London: HMSO)

HMSO, 1995a, *Competitiveness: Forging Ahead* (London: HMSO)

HMSO, 1995b, *Reply by the Government to the Third Report of the Select Committee on the Review of Expenditure on Social Security*, Cmnd 2948 (London: HMSO)

HMSO, 1996, *Review of Qualifications for 16–19 Year Olds: Full Report* (London: HMSO)

HMSO, 1997a, *Higher Education in the Learning Society: Summary Report of the National Committee of Inquiry into Higher Education* (London: HMSO)

HMSO, 1997b, *Your Right to Know*, Cmnd 3818 (London: HMSO)

HMSO, 1997c, *Rights Brought Home: the Human Rights Bill* (London: HMSO)

HMSO, 1 997d, *European Parliamentary Elections Bill*, 27 November (London: HMSO)

HMSO, 1997e, *Scotland's Parliament* (London: HMSO)

HMSO, 1998a, *A Mayor and Assembly for London: the Government's Proposals for Modernising the Government of London* (London: HMSO)

HMSO, 1998b, *Modernising Local Government: Local Democracy, and Community Participating* (London: HMSO)

HMSO, 1998c, *Next Steps Report 1997*, Cmnd 3889 (London: HMSO)

Holden, R., 1997, 'Political Role Reversal: How the Labour Party became Truly European', *Talking Politics*, Vol. 9, No. 3

Holman, B., 1990, *Good Old George: the Life of George Lansbury* (London: Lion)

House of Commons, 1997a, *The Commons Committee Stage of 'Constitutional' Bills*, Research Paper 97/53, 20 May (London: HMSO)

House of Commons, 1997b, *Wales and Devolution*, Research Paper 97/60, 19 May (London: HMSO)

House of Commons, 1997c, *The Referendum (Scotland and Wales) Bill of 1997/98*, Research Paper, 97/61, 20 May (London: HMSO)

House of Commons, 1997d, *Public Expenditure in Scotland and Wales*, Research Paper 97/78, 9 June (London: HMSO)

House of Commons, 1997e, *The Local Elections of 1 May 1997*, Research Paper 97/82, 27 June (London: HMSO)

House of Commons, 1997f, *Scotland and Devolution*, Research Paper 97/92, 29 July (London: HMSO)

House of Commons, 1997g, *Time Spent on Government Bills of Constitutional Significance*, Research Paper 97/97, 1 August (London: HMSO)

House of Commons, 1997h, *Results of Devolution Referendums (1979 & 1997)* Research Paper 97/113, 10 November (London: HMSO)

House of Commons, 1997i, *Devolution and Europe,* Research Paper, 97/126, 4 December (London: HMSO)

House of Commons, 1997j, *The Government of Wales Bill: Devolution and the National Assembly,* Research Paper 97/129, 4 December (London: HMSO)

House of Commons, 1997k, *The Government of Wales Bill: The National Assembly and its Partners,* Research Paper 97/130, 4 December (London: HMSO)

House of Commons, 1971l, *The Government of Wales Bill: Operational Aspects of the National Assembly,* Research Paper 97/132, 4 December (London: HMSO)

House of Commons, 1998a, *The Scotland Bill: Devolution and Scotland's Parliament,* Research Paper 98/1, 8 January (London: UMSO)

House of Commons, 1998b, *The Scotland Bill: Some Operational Aspects of Scottish Devolution,* Research Paper 98/2, 8 January (London: HMSO)

House of Commons, 1998c, *The Scotland Bill: Some Constitutional and Representational Aspects,* Research Paper 98/3, 8 January (London: HMSO)

House of Commons, 1998d, *The Scotland Bill: Tax Varying Powers,* Research Paper 98/ 4, 8 January (London: HMSO)

House of Commons, 1998e, *The Scotland Bill: the Scottish Parliament and Local Government,* Research Paper 98/5 (London: HMSO)

Hughes. C. and Wintour, P., 1990, *Labour Rebuilt: the New Model Party* (London: Fourth Estate)

Hutton, W., 1995, *The State We're In* (London: Cape)

International Body on Arms De-commissioning, 1997, *Mitchell Report,* 29 January (London: Northern Ireland Office)

Jennings, I., 1934, *The British Constitution* (Cambridge: Cambridge University Press)

Jessop, B., 1993, 'Towards a Schumpeterian Workfare State? Preliminary Remarks on Post-Fordist Political Economy Studies', *Political Economy,* Vol. 40

Jobsletter Online, 1997, website http://www.jobsletter.org.nz, 28 August

John, P., 1997, 'Local Governance', in P. Dunleavy, A. Gamble, I. Holliday and G. Peele (eds), *Developments in British Politics 5* (London: Macmillan)

Johnson, J., 1997, 'The Weak Link Takes the Strain', *New Statesman and Society,* 31 January

Jones, G. and C. Wallace, 1992, *Youth, Family and Citizenship* (Buckingham: Open University Press)

Jones, M., 1996a, 'Full Steam Ahead to a Workfare State: Analysing the UK Employment Department's Abolition', *Policy and Politics,* Vol. 24, No. 2

Jones, M., 1996b, 'TEC the Money and Run', *Working Brief,* No. 79, 4/96

Jones, M. and J. Peck, 1995, 'Training and Enterprise Councils: Schumpeterian Welfare State, Or What?', *Environment and Planning,* Vol. 27

Jones, No., 1997, *Campaign 1997: How the General Election was Won and Lost* (London: Cassell)

Jones, N., 1996, *Soundbites and Spin Doctors* (London: Cassell)

Jones, P. d'A., 1968, *The Christian Socialist Revival, 1877–1914* (Princeton: Princeton Press)

Jones, T., 1996, *Remarking the Labour Party: from Gaitskell to Blair* (London: Routledge)

Jordan, B., 1985, *The State* (Oxford: Blackwell)

Kavanagh, D., 1995, *Election Campaigning: the New Marketing of Politics* (Oxford: Basil Blackwell)

Kavanagh, P., 1996, *British Politics: Continuities and Change,* 3rd edn (Oxford: Oxford University Press)

Kavanagh, D., 1997, 'The Labour Campaign', in P. Norris and N. T. Gavin, (eds), *Britain Votes 1997* (Oxford: Oxford University Press)

Kavanagh, D., 1997, *The Reordering of British Politics* (Oxford: Oxford University Press)

Kellner, P., 1992, 'Time for Labour to bid Goodbye to the Unions', *The Independent*

Kelsey, J., 1996, *Economic Fundamentalism: the New Zealand Experiment* (Auckland: University Press)

King, A., 1993, 'Implications of One-Party Government' in A. King *et al.*, *Britain at the Polls 1992* (Chatham: Chatham House)

King, A. (ed.), 1998 *New Labour Triumphs: Britain at the Polls* (Chatham: Chatham House)

King, P., 1996, 'Conclusion' in D. King and G. Stoker (ed.), *Rethinking Local Democracy* (London: Macmillan)

Kingdom, J., (1991) *Local Government and Politics in Britain* (Hemel: Hempstead: Philip Allan)

Kinnock, N., 1994, 'Remaking the Labour Party', *Contemporary Record*, Vol. 8, No. 3

Kitson Clark, G., 1973, *Churchmen and the Condition of England, 1832–1885* London: Methuen

Kydland, F. and Prescott, E., 1977, 'Rules Rather than Discretion: the Inconsistency of Optimal Plans' *Journal of Political Economy*, Vol. 85, No. 3

Labour Party, The, 1982, *Labour's Programme 1982* (London: Labour Party)

Labour Party, The, 1983, *Labour's Plan: the New Hope for Britain* (London: Labour Party)

Labour Party, The, 1987, *Local Government Reform in England and Wales: a Labour Party Consultation Paper* (London: Labour Party)

Labour Party, The, 1988, *Democratic Socialist Aims and Values* (London: Labour Party)

Labour Party, The, 1991a, *Devolution and Democracy* (London: Labour Party)

Labour Party, 1991b, *The Charter of Rights: Guaranteeing Individual Liberty in a Free Society* (London: Labour Party)

Labour Party, The, 1995a, *A New Economic Future for Britain* (London: Labour Party)

Labour Party, The, 1995b, *Renewing Democracy, Rebuilding Communities* (London: Labour Party)

Labour Party, The 1996a, *A Choice for England: Labour's Plans for English Regional Government* (London: Labour Party)

Labour Party, The, 1996b, *New Labour, New Life for Britain* (London: Labour Party)

Labour Party, The, 1997a, *Labour into Power: a Framework for Partnership* (London: Labour Party)
Labour Party, The, 1997b, *New Labour: Because Britain Deserves Better* (London: Labour Party)
Labour Party, The, 1997c, *Partnership in Power* (two documents) (London: Labour Party)
Labour Party, The, 1997d, *Progress*, Winter (London: Labour Party)
Labour Party, The, n.d.a, *Social Justice and Economic Efficiency* (London: Labour Party)
Labour Party, The, n.d.b, *Meet the Challenge, Make the Change: a New Agenda for Britain* (London: Labour Party)
Labour Party Northern Ireland Team, 1997, *Northern Ireland Policy Briefing for the Parliamentary Labour Party* 29 October–10 November 1997 (London: Northern Ireland Office)
Lansley, S., S. Goss and C. Wolmar, 1989, *Councils in Conflict: the Rise and Fall of the Municipal Left* (London: Macmillan)
Lee, F. and S. Harley, 1997, 'Economics Divided: the Limitations of Peer Review in a Paradigm Bound Social Science', unpublished paper, De Montfort University
Leonard, M., 1998, *The Search for a European Identity* (London: Demos)
Levitt, T., 1983, 'The Globalization of Markets', *Harvard Business Review* May–June
Lipietz, A., 1992, *Towards a New Economic Order: Post-fordism, Ecology and Democracy* (Cambridge: Polity Press)
Lipset, S. M., 1962, 'Introduction' in R. Michels, *Political Parties* (London: Free Press)
Lloyd, J., 1997, 'Why it is Good for Unionists to Keep Talking', *New Statesman and Society*, 19 September
Lloyd, J., 1998a, 'Unionists Blow a Warning Whistle', *New Statesman and Society*, 9 January
Lloyd, J., 1998b, 'Parting of the Ways', *Marxism Today*, March
Local Government Association, 1998, *Best Value: a Statement of Objectives* (London: Local Government Association)
Loughlin, M., 1997, 'Ultra Vires, Hail and Farewell' in H. Kitchin, *A Framework for the Future: an Agenda for Councils in a Changing World* (London: Local Government Information Unit)
Lowe, R., 1993, *The Welfare State in Britain since 1945* (London: Macmillan)
Lukes, S., 1974, *Power: a Radical View* (London: Macmillan)
Lukes, S., 1986, 'Introduction' in S. Lukes, (ed.), *Power* (Oxford: Blackwell)
Mackintosh, M. and H. Wainwright, 1987, *A Taste of Power* (London: Verso)
MacShane, D., 1993, 'State of the Unions', *New Statesman and Society*, May
Mallie, E. and D. McKittrick, 1997, *The Fight for Peace: the Inside Story of the Irish Peace Process* (London: Mandarin)
Mandelson, P., 1997, 'Coordinating Government Policy', speech to Conference on Modernizing the Policy Process, 16 September (London: Cabinet Office)
Mandleson, P. and R. Liddle, 1996, *The Blair Revolution* (London: Faber)

Margetts, H., 1996, 'Public Management Change and Sex Equality within the State', in J. Lovenduski and P. Norris (eds), *Women in Politics* (Oxford: Oxford University Press)

Margetts, H. and Smyth, G. (eds), 1994, *Turning Japanese? Britain with a Permanent Party of Government* (London: Lawrence & Wishart)

Marglin, S. and Schor, J. B. (eds), 1990, *The Golden Age of Capitalism: Reinterpreting the Postwar Experience* (Oxford: Clarendon Press)

Marquand, David, 1988, *The Unprincipled Society* (London: Cape)

Marquand, David, 1997a, *The New Reckoning: Capitalism, States and Citizens* (Cambridge: Polity Press)

Marquand, David, 1997b, 'After Euphoria: the Dilemmas of New Labour' *Political Quarterly*, Vol. 68, No. 4, Oct.–Dec.

Marsh, D. and A. Tant, 1989, *There is No Alternative: Mrs Thatcher and the British Political Tradition,* Essex Papers in Politics and Government, No. 69 (Colchester: University of Essex)

McAnulla, S., 1999, 'The Post-Thatcher Era', in D. Marsh *et al.*, *Post-War British Politics in Perspective* (Cambridge: Polity)

McKenzie, R., 1964, *British Political Parties: the Distribution of Power within the Conservative and Labour Parties*, 2nd edn (London: Mercury)

McNair, B., 1995, *An Introduction to Political Communications* (London: Routledge)

McNair, B., 1996, *News and Journalism in the UK,* 2nd edn (London: Routledge)

McSmith, A., 1996, *Faces of Labour* (London: Verso)

Meacham, S., 1987, *Toynbee Hall and Social Reform, 1880–1914* (Yale: Yale University Press)

Mews, S., 1976, 'The Churches', in M. Morris (ed.), *The General Strike* (Harmondsworth: Penguin)

Michels, R., 1962, *Political Parties: a Sociological Study of the Oligarchical Tendencies of Modern Democracy* (London: Free Press)

Miliband, R., 1972, *Parliamentary Socialism: a Study in the Politics of Labour*, 2nd edn (London: Merlin Press)

Milne, S., 1997a, 'Silenced Voices', *The Guardian*, 12 May

Milne, S., 1997b, 'Blair's Blast Sends a Seafront Shiver through the Unions at Brighton', *The Guardian*, 13 September

Milne, S., 1998, 'Will Tony Blair Pay his Dues?', *The Guardian*, 17 March

Minkin, L., 1978, *The Labour Party Conference: a Study in the Politics of Intra-Party Democracy* (London: Allen Lane)

Minkin, Lewis, 1992, *The Contentious Alliance: Trade Unions and the Labour Party* (Edinburgh: Edinburgh University Press)

Monks, J., 1995, 'No Shopping List...', *New Statesman and Society*, 8 September

Mount, F., 1992, *The British Constitution Now* (London: Heinemann)

Mowlam, M., 1996a, 'The Fourth Strand No-one Can Now Ignore', *Northern Ireland Brief*, March (London: Northern Ireland Office)

Mowlam, M., 1996b, 'Labour will be Supportive but not too Silent on Northern Ireland', *New Statesman and Society*, 19 July

Nairn, T., 1994, 'The Sole Survivor', *New Left Review*, Vol. 200, special issue

National Women's Office, 1997, *National Women's Office Training Conference 1997, Evaluation Report* (London: Labour Party)

Newsinger, J., 1995, 'British Security Policy in Northern Ireland', *Race and Class*, Vol. 37, No. 1

Nicholls, D., 1994, *The Pluralist State*, 2nd edn (New York: St. Martin's Press)

Norman, E. R., 1976, *Church and Society in England, 1770–1970* (Oxford: Oxford University Press)

Norris, P., 1996, *Electoral Change since 1945* (Oxford: Blackwell)

Northern Ireland Office Information Service, 1998, website http://www.nio.gov.uk/

Offe, C., 1974, 'Structural Problems of the Capitalist State, Class Rule and the Political System: On the Selectiveness of Political Institutions' in C. Von Byme (ed.), *German Political Studies*, Vol. 1 (London: Sage)

Ohmae, K., 1990, *The Borderless World: Power and Strategy in the Interlinked Economy* (London: Collins)

Ohmae, K., 1996, *The End of the Nation State: the Rise of Regional Economies* (New York: Free Press)

O'Leary, B., 1997, 'The Conservative Stewardship of Northern Ireland 1979–97: Sound-Bottomed Contradictions or Slow Learning?', *Political Studies*, Vol. 45, No. 4, September

Oliver, D., 1992, *Government in the United Kingdom* (Milton Keynes: Open University Press)

Oliver, J., 1968, *The Church and Social Order: Social Thought in the Church of England, 1918–1939* (London: Mowbray)

Panitch, L. and Leys, C., 1997, *The End of Parliamentary Socialism: from New Left to New Labour* (London: Verso)

Parker, N., 1997, 'From Lion to Sheepdog: the Ex-Imperial State in the European State System', Paper presented to the 13th Lothian Conference, December

Perrigo, S., 1996, 'Women and Change in the Labour Party 1979–1995', in J. Luvenduski and P. Norris (eds), *Women in Politics* (Oxford: Oxford University Press)

Peters, A. R., 1993, 'Germany' in J. A. Chandler (ed.), *Local Government in Liberal Democracies: an Introductory Survey* (London: Routledge)

Pimlott, B., 1997, 'New Labour, New Era', *Political Quarterly*, Vol. 68, No. 4

Pratchett, L. and D. Wilson, 1997, 'The Rebirth of Local Democracy', *Local Government Studies*, Vol. 23, No. 1

Pratt, J. and T. Burgess, 1974, *Polytechnics: a Report* (London: Pitman)

Prison Service, 1997, *Prison Service Review* (London: HM Prison Service)

Public Service Committee, 1996, *Ministerial Accountability and Responsibility* (London: HC 313, 1995–96)

Radice, G., 1989, *Labour's Path to Power: the New Revisionism* (London: Macmillan)

Randall, V., 1979, *Women and Politics* (London: Macmillan)

Reeves, F., 1995, *The Modernity of Further Education* (Wolverhampton: Education Now)

Regional Policy Commission, The, 1996, *Renewing the Regions: Strategies for Regional Economic Development* (Sheffield: Sheffield Hallam)

Reich, R., 1992, *The Work of Nations* (New York: Vintage)

Rhodes, R A. W., 1994, 'The Hollowing-Out of the State: the Changing Nature of the Public Service in Britain', *Political Ouarterly*, Vol. 65, No. 2, pp. 138–51

Robinson, P., 1997, *Literacy, Numeracy and Economic Performance* (London: London School of Economics)

Rose, P., 1996, 'Labour, Northern Ireland and the Decision to Send in the Troops', in P. Catterall and S. McDougall, (eds), *The Northern Ireland Question in British Politics* (London: Macmillan)

Rosenbaum, M., 1997, *From Soapbox to Soundbite: Party Political Campaigning in Britain since 1945* (London: Macmillan)

Routledge, P., 1998, *Gordon Brown: the Biography* (Hemel Hempstead: Pocket Books)

Ruggie, J. R., 1982, 'International Regimes, Transactions and Change: Embedded Liberalism in the Postwar Economic Order', *International Organization*, Vol. 36, No. 3

Russell, B., 1995, *Power* (London: Routledge)

Sabatier, P., 1986, 'Top-Down and Bottom-Up Approaches to Implementation Research?' *Journal of Public Policy*, No. 6, pp. 21–48

Sachs, J. and Warner, A., 1995, 'Economic Reform and the Process of Global Integration', *Brookings Papers on Economic Activity*, Vol. 1

Sassoon, D., 1997, *One Hundred Years of Socialism* (London: Fontana)

Scammell, M., 1995, *Designer Politics: How Elections are Won* (London: Macmillan)

Scott, P., 1995, *The Meanings of Mass Higher Education* (Buckingham: Open University Press)

Select Committee on Public Administration, 1997a, *Role and Responsibilities of the Chancellor of the Duchy of Lancaster* (London: HC 221, 1997–98)

Select Committee on Public Administration, 1997b, *Your Right To Know: the Government's Proposals for a Freedom of Information Act* (London: HC 398-ii, 1997–98)

Semetko, H., *et al.*, 1991, *The Formation of Campaign Agendas: a Comparative Analysis of Party and Media Roles in Recent American and British Elections* (New Jersey: LEA)

Syed, P., 1987, *The Rise and Fall of the Labour Left* (London: Macmillan)

Syed, P., 'Tony Blair and New Labour' in A. King *et al.*, *New Labour Triumphs: Britain at the Polls* (Chatham: Chatham House)

Seyd, P. and P. Whiteley, 1992, *Labour's Grass Roots: the Politics of Party Membership* (Oxford: Clarendon)

Shadow Communications Agency (SCA), 1997, *Shadow Communications Agency Report* (London: Labour Party)

Sharpe, L. J., 1982, 'The Puzzle' in D. Kavanagh (ed.), *The Politics of the Labour Party* (London: Allen and Unwin)

Shaw, E., 1988, *Discipline and Discord in the Labour Party* (Manchester: Manchester University Press)

Shaw, E., 1994a, *The Labour Party since 1979: Crisis and Transformation* (London: Routledge)

Shaw, E., 1994b, 'Conflict and Cohesion in the British Labour Party', in D. S. Bell and E. Shaw (ed.), *Conflict and Cohesion in Western European Social Democratic Parties* (London: Pinter)

Shaw, E., 1996, *The Labour Party since 1945* (Oxford: Basil Blackwell)

Shaw, M., 1994, 'Towards a Global Policy for Labour', *Renewal*, Vol. 2, No. 1, January

Sheppard, D., 1983, *Bias to the Poor* (London: Hodder and Stoughton)

Smith, M. J., 1994, 'Neil Kinnock and the Modernisation of the Labour Party', *Contemporary Record*, Vol. 8, No. 3

Smith, M. J. and J. Spear (eds), 1992, *The Changing Labour Party* (London: Routledge)

Smith, M. and M. Kenny, 1996, 'Reforming Clause IV: Tony Blair and the Modernisation of the Labour Party', Paper delivered to the Political Studies Association Conference, Glasgow

Smith, M. and M. Kenny, 1997 '(Mis)understanding Blair', *Political Quarterly* Vol. 68, No. 3

Smyth, G., 1995, 'Northern Ireland: Is Labour in a Cul-de-sac Too?', *New Statesman and Society*, 29 September

Sopel, J., 1995, *Tony Blair: the Moderniser* (London: Michael Joseph)

Spours, K., 'The Best and Worst of GNVQs: an Analysis of a Curriculum Model and Principles of Redesign', *Briefing Paper No. 2*, Learning for the Future Project (London: London University)

Standing, G., 1997, 'Globalization, Labour Flexibility and Insecurity: the Era of Market Regulation', *European Journal of Industrial Relations*, Vol. 3, No. 1

Stanford, P., 1994, *Lord Longford* (London: Heinemann)

Stedman Jones, G., 1980, *Languages of Class* (Cambridge: Cambridge University Press)

Stoker, G., 1991, *The Politics of Local Government* (London: Macmillan)

Streeter, M., 1996, 'Modeo Man Puts Low-Rev Chancellor in Slow Lane', *The Independent*, 27 November 1996

Stoker, G., 1991, *The Politics of Local Government* (London: Macmillan)

Streeter, M., 1996, 'Modeo Man Puts Low-Rev Chancellor in Slow Lane', *The Independent*, 27 November 1996

Suggate, A., 1987, *William Temple and Christian Social Ethics Today* (Edinburgh: T. & T. Clark)

Tant, A., 1988, 'Constitutional Aspects of Official Secrecy and Freedom of Information: an Overview', Paper presented to the Political Studies Association Annual Conference, April

Tawney, R. H., 1921, *The Acquisitive Society* (London: G. Bell and Son)

Tawney, R. H., 1926, *Religion and the Rise of Capitalism* (London: John Murray)

Tawney, R. H., 1972, *The Commonplace Book* (Cambridge: Cambridge University Press)

Taylor, G., 1997, *Labour's Renewal? The Policy Review and Beyond* (London: Macmillan)

Temple, W., 1942, *Christianity and the Social Order* (Harmondsworth: Penguin)

Terrill, R., 1974, *R. H. Tawney and His Times: Socialism as Fellowship* (London: Andre Deutsch)

Thain, C. and Wright, M., 1995, *The Treasury and Whitehall* (Oxford: Oxford University Press)

Theakston, K., 1992, *The Labour Party and Whitehall* (London: Routledge)

Thompson, N., 1996, 'Supply-side Socialism: the Political Economy of New Labour', *New Left Review* 216, March–April

Thompson, P., 1995, 'Clause and Causes', *Renewal*, Vol. 3, no. 1, January

Thorpe, A., 1997, *A History of the British Labour Party* (London: Macmillan)

Tiratsoo, N. and Tomlinson, J., 1994, *Industrial Efficiency and State Intervention: Labour 1939–51* (London: Routledge)

Walsh, T. and S. Tindale, 1992, 'Time for Divorce', *Fabian Review*, Vol. 104, No. 4

Waterman, A. M. C., 1991, *Revolution, Economics and Religion: Christian Political Economy, 1798–1833* (Cambridge: Cambridge University Press)

Watson, M., 1998, 'The New Malthusian Economics: Globalisation, Inward Investment and the Discursive Construction of the Competitive Imperative' in C. Hay and D. Marsh (eds), *Globalisation, Welfare Retrenchment and the State* (London: Macmillan)

Watson, M., 1999a, 'Rethinking Capital Mobility, Re-Regulating Financial Markets', *New Political Economy*, Vol. 4, No. 2

Watson, M., 1999b, 'Globalisation and the Development of the British Political Economy', in D. Marsh *et al.*, *Post-War British Politics in Perspective* (Cambridge: Polity)

Watson, M. and Hay, C., 1998, 'In the Dedicated Pursuit of Dedicated Capital: Restoring an Indigenous Investment Ethic to British Capitalism', *New Political Economy*, forthcoming

Watson, S., 1994, 'Producing the Right Sort of Chap: the Senior Civil Service as Exclusionary Culture', *Policy and Politics*, Vol. 22, No. 3

Webb, P., 1992, 'Election Campaigning, Organisational Transformation and the Professionalism of the British Labour Party', *European Journal of Political Research*, Vol. 21

Westcott, B. F., 1890, *Socialism* (London: Guild of St Matthew)

Whiteley, P., P. Seyd and J. Richardson, 1994, *True Blues: the Politics of Conservative Party Membership* (Oxford: Clarendon)

Wickham-Jones, M., 1996a, 'Anticipating Social Democracy, Preempting Anticipations: Economic Policy-Making in the British Labour Party, 1987–92', *Politics and Society*, Vol. 23, No. 4

Wickham-Jones, M., 1996b, *Economic Strategy and the Labour Party: Politics and Policy-Making 1970–83* (London: Macmillan)

Wilkinson, A., 1986, *Dissent or Conform? War, Peace and the English Churches, 1900–1945* (London: SCM Press)

Wilkinson, A., 1992, '*The Community of the Resurrection: a Centenary History* (London: SCM Press)

Wilkinson, A., 1996, *The Church of England and the First World War*, 2nd edn (London: SCM Press)

Wilkinson, A., 1998, *Christian Socialism: Scott Holland to Tony Blair* (London: SCM Press)

Wilson, D. and C. Game, 1998, *Local Government in the United Kingdom* (London: Macmillan)

Wintour, P., 1997, 'Downing Street Opens Doors to Trade Unions', *The Guardian*, 31 August

Wright, A., 1990, 'British Socialists and the British Constitution', *Parliamentary Affairs*, No. 43, pp. 323–45

Wright, A., 1994, *Citizens and Subjects: an Essay on British Politics* (London: Routledge)

Wring, D., 1996, 'From Mass Propaganda to Political Marketing: the Transformation of the Labour Party's Election Campaigning', in Colin Rallings, *et al.*, (ed.), *British Parties and Elections Yearbook 1996* (London: Frank Cass)

Young, H., 1997, 'Amazingly Good so Far', *The Guardian*, 30 December

Index

240